HARVARD THEOLOGICAL STUDIES

HARVARD THEOLOGICAL STUDIES

XIX

AN ESSAY ON THE DEVELOPMENT OF LUTHER'S THOUGHT ON JUSTICE, LAW, AND SOCIETY

BY

F. EDWARD CRANZ

ISSUED AS AN EXTRA NUMBER OF THE
HARVARD THEOLOGICAL REVIEW

CAMBRIDGE
HARVARD UNIVERSITY PRESS
LONDON: OXFORD UNIVERSITY PRESS

1964

To

Charles Howard McIlwain

PREFACE

THE PRESENT STUDY arose out of an examination of the relation between Luther's social thought and the ancient-medieval tradition. It soon proved necessary as a preliminary task to distinguish between the various stages in Luther's social thought and also to relate the development of his ideas on society to his thinking on the fundamental theological problems of justification and the Law. Hence what is here offered is an essay on the general development of Luther's thought on justice, law, and society.

It is a pleasure to thank those who have helped me. President Rosemary Park and the Trustees of Connecticut College relieved me of half my teaching load during the academic year 1955–56, and it was during this time that the bulk of the essay was written. Among my colleagues at Connecticut College, Miss Marion Monaco, Mr. Richard Birdsall, and Mr. George Haines IV have read all or part of the manuscript, and I am grateful for their suggestions. And to conclude with a more general debt, I have for many years profited by the never-failing encouragement and understanding of Arthur Darby Nock.

CONNECTICUT COLLEGE   *October 4, 1957*
NEW LONDON, CONNECTICUT

CONTENTS

signs of emerging tensions, but no break with earlier ideas. Human justice still of little significance.

Changes in Luther's doctrine of law, 1515–18; development but here too no decisive re-orientation. Emphasis now on the unity of all law, and on the contrast between law and grace. The letter as the law without grace; the spirit as grace without the law. Virtual disappearance of earlier concept of the spiritual law which saves; all law condemning, particularly when spiritually interpreted. Double office of the Gospel; the spiritual, condemning interpretation of the law, and the giving of grace. New terminology on law not a fundamental change in theology.

The nature of the problem. Luther's contemporary writings our primary evidence. This evidence compatible but not identical with evidence of Luther's later autobiographical statements. Luther's recognition of two realms of Christian existence the basic change. Illustration of change in Luther's thought about grace and gift, about flesh and spirit, and about good works as sins, just men as sinners. Consequences of change for doctrine of justification seen in Kirchenpostille of 1522. The Christian already completely justified in Christ. Hence order of thinking about justification reversed; justice in Christ is antecedent, and sanctification in the world consequent. The "world" therefore of increased importance in the life of the Christian.

Luther's achievement of a more general statement of his new theology in the 1530's. New clarity on his relation to Augustine. A new set of contrasts as framework of new theology, e.g. contrast between passive, Christian justice and active, civil justice. Contrasts related to two realms of Christian existence, not to two parts of universe. Statement of theology in Lectures on Galatians (1531) and in Disputations (1535 f.). Relation of individual Christian to two realms. New statement of doctrine of justification.

General consequences of Luther's re-orientation for his doctrine of justice. Changes from 1518 through 1522 illustrated by Sermo de triplici iustitia (1518), Sermo de duplici iustitia (1519), Galatians Commentary (1519), Operationes in Psalmos (1519–21), Sermo of 1520 on John XVI, 5 f., and Rationis Latomianae confutatio (1521). Codification in Kirchenpostille (1522). New general statement in Lectures on Galatians (1531) with basic contrast between Christian, passive justice and active, civil justice.

Development of doctrine of law comparable to that of doctrine of justice. After 1518–19 continued and even increased emphasis on law as leading only to condemnation and death; at same time awareness of use of law in restraining "hand." New clarity in Sermones of 1520: double use of the law, first to reveal sin, and second, to maintain discipline.

General statement of 1530's in Lectures on Galatians (1531) and in Disputations. Christ not a legislator. The two uses of the law as civil and theological. Luther's doctrine of natural law.

IV. THE CHURCH AND SOCIETY.

Luther's need, after 1518–19, to construct a new doctrine of the church and of human society in general. The main outlines of his new solutions.

Doctrine of the church in the Dictata super Psalterium in harmony with Luther's early ideas on justice and law. Little emphasis on sacraments, much on the Word. Insistence on obedience to prelates. Indulgence controversy and the problem of the church. Luther attacked in terms of divine right of the hierarchic church; his eventual reply a denial of such divine right. Results of the controversy largely negative. Luther's positive reconstruction of the theology of the church a development from his distinction between the two realms of Christian existence. The communion of saints, and the church in Christ. The problem of the relation between the spiritual and external communions in the Sermo de virtute excommunicationis (1518) and in the Sermones of 1520. Fuller statements in Von dem Papsttum zu Rom (1520) and in the Ad librum Ambrosii Catharini responsio (1521). Distinction between the spiritual church and the external church. The spiritual church based on Christian, passive justice; the external church governed on the basis of reason and human ordinance. The unity of German society as the church in An den christlichen Adel (1520).

The new general statement of the 1530's. Its close connection with the basic dualisms of Luther's mature thought. The church, like the individual Christian, both just and sinful.

Polity in Luther's thought important as a general term for human existence in the world apart from Christ. The revision of older ideas in the development of a new concept of polity, a sphere which is subject to reason and where God appears only behind masks. Difficult problem of the relation between the church in the world and polity. The Christian person not the political person, but each individual Christian seen as bearing both persons. Luther not systematic on the relation between church and polity; nevertheless church's government in the world described like polity in terms of reason and of masks. Luther's doctrine of the "signs" of the church. His persistence in calling the actual society of his time Christendom.

Luther's starting point the traditional view that some estates in society are specifically Christian, some not. His revision in terms of the distinction between the two realms of a Christian's existence. Spiritual estate in strict sense, the Christian's heavenly existence in Christ. All estates in actual human society, even the priestly estate, worldly and to be analyzed as callings. Luther's terminology not systematic here.

Luther's early position as the traditional contrast between ecclesiastical and secular government. Re-orientation of 1518–19 and denial of any earthly and human spiritual rule. Luther's movement to a new theology slow in this area. Contrast between kingdoms of Christ and of Herod in 1521. New contrasts in Sermones of 1522. The spiritual kingdom and the worldly kingdom. Fuller statement in Von weltlicher Obrigkeit (1523) but still some ambiguities. Clarification of various aspects of kingdom in De servo arbitrio (1525). Luther's final position in Ob Kriegsleute (1526). Christians subject to both of God's governments, and the two governments parallel to Christian and civil justice. In Sermons on Matthew, V–VII two governments also related to two persons, world-person and Christian-person, borne by each Christian. Once again, Luther's terminology not systematized.

Luther's doctrine of the hierarchies connected both with doctrine of God's two governments and with that of the estates. Traditional doctrine of the three estates with its basic contrast between the spiritual and the secular estates in the world. Luther's reasons for modifying it. His solution that the three hierarchies (of the church, the household, and the polity) all equally holy. This a denial of the traditional exaltation of the "spiritual estate" as well as of the traditional degradation of the "secular estates." Luther's secularization. This secularization never in Luther to be removed from a Christian context.

INTRODUCTION

IN 1545 Luther reëxamined his early writings as he prepared the Preface to the first volume of his Opera Latina. What most impressed him was the extent of his development since these first publications; like Augustine, he had made gradual progress through writing and teaching.[1] The present essay endeavors to analyze this development and progress as it appears in Luther's thinking about justice, law, and society.[2]

[1] LIV, 186, 25: "Haec ideo narro, optime lector, ut, si lecturus es opuscula mea, memor sis, me unum fuisse (ut supra dixi) ex illis, qui (ut Augustinus de se scribit) scribendo et docendo profecerint, non ex illis, qui de nihilo repente fiunt summi." Luther makes the same reference to Augustine in the Preface to the Catalogue of his works published in 1533: XXXVIII, 134,18. He says the same even in his early Dictata super Psalterium (1513–15), IV, 330,28: "Sane ut et nos gratiam Dei agnoscentes fateamur, nos proficere scribendo et docendo. . . ." See also TR §352 (1532), I,146,12.

When no other reference is given, the writings of Luther are cited from the Kritische Gesamtausgabe (Weimar, 1883-). The Schriften are cited simply by volume, page, and line. (The abbreviation f. has rarely been used except when the citation extends to another page.) The other divisions of the Gesamtausgabe are cited by the usual abbreviations: TR (= Tischreden), Briefe (= Briefwechsel), and Bibel (= Deutsche Bibel). The dates given are regularly those of the Gesamtausgabe, except for the early Sermons, where I have followed E. Vogelsang, "Zur Datierung der frühesten Lutherpredigten," Zeitschrift für Kirchengeschichte 50 (1931), 112-45. For a useful concordance of the Weimar edition with other editions, see K. Aland, Hilfsbuch zum Lutherstudium (Gütersloh, 1957?).

[2] There appears to be no work dealing with this exact topic, though there are a number of studies of special aspects of the development, and these will be noted in their proper place later.

For a general history of Luther scholarship, see Otto Wolff, Die Haupttypen der neueren Lutherdeutung (Stuttgart, 1938); Horst Stephan, Luther in den Wandlungen seiner Kirche, 2nd. ed. (Berlin, 1951). For a survey of more recent work, see W. von Loewenich, "Zehn Jahre Lutherforschung," in Theologie und Liturgie. Eine Gesamtschau der gegenwärtigen Forschung in Einzeldarstellungen (Kassel, 1952), 119–70; E. Wolf, "Darstellungen und Forschungen zur Geschichte der Reformation," Verkündigung und Forschung 3 (1954), 150–72; H. Liebing, Reformationsgeschichtliche Literatur 1945–54," Deutsche Vierteljahrschrift 28 (1954), 516–37; J. Dillenberger, "Survey: Literature in Luther Studies 1950–55," Church History 25 (1956), 160–77. Valuable summaries on present Luther scholarship should also be found in the announced volume, Dokumentarischer Sammelband über den internationalen Kongress für Lutherforschung in Aarhus, 1956, hgg. von V. Vajta (Lutherisches Verlagshaus, Berlin, 1956?).

For a very useful survey of the history of Lutheran ideas on society, see Ernst Wolf, "Politia Christi. Das Problem der Sozialethik im Luthertum," Evangelische Theologie 8 (1948–49), 49–69 (reprinted in Ernst Wolf, Peregrinatio (München, 1954), 214–42). The most recent bibliography on Luther's ideas on society will be found in the notes of J. Heckel "Lex charitatis. Eine juristische Untersuchung über das Recht in der Theologie Martin Luthers," Bayerische Akad. der Wiss., Abh.,

We shall use a developmental approach, though in recent years weighty voices have been raised against it,[3] because in Luther's thinking on these topics the differences between the early and the mature works are so great that only confusion results from the assumption that we are dealing with a single, unified position. For example, in the Dictata super Psalterium (1513–15) the most important law is the spiritual law which saves through its grace; such a law is completely alien to the thought of the Lectures on Galatians (1531). On the other hand, Luther in the Lectures on Galatians centers his discussion of justice, or righteousness, on the distinction between passive Christian justice and all other justices; such a distinction is completely alien to the thought of the Dictata super Psalterium.[4]

Luther in the Preface of 1545 [5] not only emphasized how much he had developed, he also picked out one phase of the development as particularly important. This was his new insight into the meaning of the "justice of God" in Romans I,17, an insight which Luther dated in the neighborhood of 1518–19. We shall use the dating 1518–19 for a general chronological division of the material, not simply on Luther's authority but primarily because this is the point at which the material naturally divides. It should be remembered, however, that most Luther scholars reject 1518–19 as the date of Luther's crucial new insight; it may also be noted that they have not reached general agreement on any other date.[6]

Phil.-hist. Kl., NF XXXVI (1953). For a representative selection see Chapter IV, note 1, below.

[3] Compare the remark of Ernst Wolf, Peregrinatio (München, 1954), p. 53: " . . . es gehört mit zu den methodologischen Erkenntnissen der neueren Luther-forschung, dass man dem Versuch, scheinbare oder wirkliche Widersprüche in den Aussagen Luthers 'entwicklungsgeschichtlich' aufzulösen, mit wachsender Ablehnung zu begegnen hat, und dass an Stelle der hier beliebten Scheidung des 'jungen' und des 'alten' Luther das Wiederfinden des 'jungen' im 'alten' sich durchsetzt." Wolf's position is noted with approval by R. Prenter, Spiritus Creator (München, 1954), p. 13 and by J.-N. Walty, Revue des Sciences Philosophiques et Théologiques 39 (1955), p. 496.

[4] For details, see below in Chapters I and III.

[5] Vorrede zu Band I der Opera Latina (1545), LIV, 179–87. For further discussion of the problem, see Chapter II, pp. 41 f. below.

[6] Compare, for example, the survey of the various attempts to solve the problem in W. Link, Das Ringen Luthers um die Freiheit der Theologie von der Philosophie (Forschungen zur Geschichte und Lehre des Protestantismus, IX, 3), München, 1940, pp. 6–77.

We have accordingly grouped together the early writings through about 1518. There is, to be sure, development within this period, but it merely carries further tendencies already present in the Dictata super Psalterium (1513–15); we do not find the forms of thought characteristic of the mature Luther. We have placed in a second grouping all the later writings from about 1518 on. Here again there is development, and it is important. However, after a brief transitional period, the development moves steadily in a different direction from that of the early period of 1513–18, and Luther never thereafter made any fundamental change in his orientation.

The material has been further divided topically into the following chapters:

    I. Justice and Law, 1513–18.
   II. The General Re-orientation of 1518–19 and Luther's Mature Position.
  III. Justice and Law, 1518 and Later.
  IV. The Church and Society.

The nature of Luther's thought justifies certain limitations of our problem, and it also compels certain extensions. In the first place, Luther was primarily a theologian, and only his theology concerns us directly. He often, for example, made interesting excursions into German law and politics, but he regarded these areas as outside his competence,[7] and we shall notice such excursions only when they impinge directly on his theology. In the second place, Luther's theology is so constituted that one cannot treat parts of it in isolation. In his mature period, he regularly works with a pair of contrasting concepts, such as "heaven" and "earth," neither of which can be defined except in terms of the contrast with the other. Hence we cannot, for example, understand Luther's analysis of "earthly" society, unless we also take note of its heavenly counterpart.

No discussion of Luther's "sources" has been attempted. The first problem is to see the development in Luther's own thinking; here his own writings are the first evidence.[8]

[7] Compare Briefe (Jan., 1531), VI,16,14; TR § 1715 (1532), II,191,24.
[8] Only incidental use has been made of the Marginalia of 1509 and of the Genesis Commentary (1535-45). The Marginalia contain little that is relevant to Luther's

The crucial turning-point in Luther's general development occurs when he begins toward 1518–19 to recognize two "realms" of Christian existence, two realms which are in the Christian's experience simultaneous and yet distinct. There is the Christian's existence in Christ, and there is the Christian's existence in the world; there is only one Christian individual who exists in both realms. The two realms of existence are simultaneously real, but they must be precisely distinguished, for to confuse them is to destroy all Christian theology.

The most familiar illustration of the two realms is found in Luther's two basic theses on justification: first, that the Christian is already totally just in Christ, and second, that the same Christian is only partially just in the world, where he is in a process of gradual sanctification. In this positive statement of the Christian experience, total justification is always primary and antecedent; gradual sanctification is always secondary and consequent. On the other side, there is the negative statement of the Christian experience in temptation or *Anfechtung*; here one starts from a threatened mixture of the two realms or a reversal of their order as antecedent and consequent. The Christian may be partly just in the world, but if any such Christian is placed in the realm of existence before God and without Christ, he is seen to be totally a sinner. In both positive and negative statements, the basic category of thought is the distinction between two simultaneous realms of Christian existence. In the total realm of existence before God, the Christian is totally just in Christ or totally sinful apart from Christ; in the partial realm of existence in the world, the Christian is partly just and partly sinful.

Luther's thought during his early period of 1513–18 does not provide for the simultaneity of the two realms nor for their proper order as antecedent and consequent. As against simultaneity, Luther in 1513–18 thinks about justification in terms of a contrast between present and future. The Christian is now through

---

ideas on society, and they are not usefully discussed except in terms of detailed comparison with late scholastic thinkers. The Genesis Commentary appears to contain minor but possibly significant differences of emphasis as against other writings of Luther's mature period, but these differences can be properly evaluated only along with a treatment of the redactional history of the Commentary.

God's grace partially just, and God will in the future justify him totally. As against the proper order of the two realms where total justice is antecedent and gradual sanctification consequent, Luther in 1513–18 sees man's partial justice as the antecedent of his future total justification.

Luther's recognition of the two realms of existence first appears explicitly in his analysis of salvation and damnation. It gradually spreads throughout all his thinking, and in consequence he must, for example, rethink his old ideas of justice, law, and society. Here the development of his thinking about justice is typical, and it may serve to suggest what happens in the case of law and of society in general. (It should be noted that the English "justice" is often an inadequate translation for Luther's "iustitia" or "Gerechtigkeit" and that "righteousness" often comes closer to Luther's main meaning. But "righteousness" too is often inadequate, and in the present study "justice" has been retained as the single term through which we can best analyze Luther's wrestling with the various levels of meaning involved in the single Latin and German terms that he himself used.)

During the period 1513–18, Luther's thinking about justice turns on the Christian's gradual movement, through grace, toward the complete justice which he will achieve only after death. Most commonly this movement is away from a fleshly, visible justice toward a spiritual and invisible justice. Sometimes it appears as a "Platonist" passage from image to exemplar; more often it takes the form of a "theology of the cross," where one believes in a spiritual reality hidden under its sensible opposite. In either case, the Christian is partly just through God's grace now, and because of this, God in his mercy will in the future restore him to complete justice. Luther during this early period gives little attention to human justice; the Christian centers his efforts as far as possible on a higher, spiritual justice.

All this changes with Luther's assertion of two simultaneous realms of Christian existence, and Luther must accordingly work out a new doctrine of justice. He now maintains that in Christ and in heaven, the Christian is already totally just, and to explain how this can be so, Luther develops the new concept of a "passive" justice, apprehended only in faith. On the other hand, the Christian's life in the world now gains in positive significance, and Luther moves to explain this through a new doctrine of "active" or "civil" justice, a justice which is not a stage on the way to salvation but which is to the Christian an ordinance and creature of God. What passive justice does for the new realm of "heaven," active or civil justice does for the new realm of "earth." And to ensure that earthly justice makes no claim to be heavenly, Luther maintains the extreme thesis that however just the Christian may be on earth in active and civil justice, before God and without Christ, he is nothing but the most wretched sinner.

Luther's development of a new theology of justice is paralleled by other developments in his theology of society, and in each case the distinction of the two realms provides the fundamental categories of his mature thought. Thus, in the theory of law, we find a new contrast between the civil and the theological use of the law. God uses the law "civilly" to keep order and restrain crime on earth; God uses the law "theologically" to show men that without Christ they are all damned in His sight. Similarly in the theory of society we find such new contrasts as between church and polity or between God's spiritual government and His world-government (Weltregiment).

Our problem now is to study this development in its details, and we shall begin with the analysis of Luther's thought during his early period of 1513–18.

CHAPTER I

JUSTICE AND LAW, 1513-18.

1. *The Dictata super Psalterium (1513-15).*

THE DICTATA SUPER PSALTERIUM [9] constitute a unique source
for our knowledge of Luther's early thought. In their triple form
of interlinear glosses, marginal glosses, and scholia, they fill more
than a thousand pages in the Weimar edition of Luther's Werke,
and while they lack systematic order, they were written with
a systematic purpose. In them Luther reveals not only the general
outline of his first theology but also the place of justice and law
within it.[10] We shall therefore discuss the Dictata separately
and reserve for future treatment the additions and modifications
found in the later works of the early period, notably the Lectures
on Romans (1515-16), on Galatians (1516-17) and on Hebrews
(1517-18).

[9] The Dictata super Psalterium (henceforth cited as Dictata) and the associated
Adnotationes Quincuplici Fabri Stapulensis Psalterio manu adscriptae (henceforth
cited as Adnotationes) are found in Vols. III-IV of the Weimar edition. Additional
fragments may be found in IX,116–21 and in G. Kawerau, "Ein wiederaufgefundenes
Blatt aus dem Dresdener Luther-Psalter," Theologische Studien und Kritiken 90
(1917), 521–26. Volumes III-IV of the Weimar edition are very faulty, and a
reëdition has been announced to appear shortly. Meanwhile see the corrections,
IX,793–95 and in K. A. Meissinger, Luthers Exegese in der Frühzeit (Leipzig,
1911), pp. 6–14. Selections from the Dictata and from the Adnotationes may be
found in a better text by E. Vogelsang in Luthers Werke in Auswahl, ed. O. Clemen
et al., 8 vols. (Berlin, 1950–55), Vol. V, 2nd ed. by K. Aland (Berlin, 1955),
pp. 38–221.
  The present text of the Dictata is not a unity, and parts of it belong to Luther's
reworking of the lectures for publication in 1516. The parts generally recognized as
belonging to this reworking (III,15,13–26,18 and 39,21–60,7) have been cited with
1516 added in parentheses. Possibly to be connected with this reworking are some
fragments found in XXXI, 1, pp. 464-80.
[10] For a general summary of modern scholarship on Luther's early period, see H.
Boehmer, Der junge Luther, 4th ed., with an appendix by H. Bornkamm (Stuttgart,
1951). See also H. Strohl, L'évolution religieuse de Luther jusqu'en 1515 (Strasbourg-Paris, 1922) and L'épanouissement de la pensée religieuse de Luther de 1515
à 1520 (Etudes d'histoire et de philosophie religieuses publiées par la Faculté de
Théologie Protestante de l'Université de Strasbourg. Fasc. 9), Strasbourg-Paris,
1924; Gordon Rupp, Luther's Progress to the Diet of Worms (London, 1951).
Heinrich Denifle, Luther und das Luthertum in der ersten Entwicklung, 2nd ed.,

The form of Luther's thought in the Dictata [11] is transitional from a philosophical theology (or a theological philosophy) to a new theology of the cross which is contrasted with a philosophy of appearances. The philosophical theology [12] may with qualifications be described as Platonist, and it centers on such concepts as image and exemplar, visible and invisible.[13] While Luther never

2 vols. with two vols. of Ergänzungen (Mainz, 1904-09) is so filled with hatred and ridicule that it is of little value for our general understanding of Luther; it is so full of learning and penetration on points of detail that no one interested in the early Luther can ignore it. K. A. Meissinger, Der katholische Luther (München, 1952) is very useful for Luther's biography and for his milieu but weak on his thought and theology. For the literary history of Meissinger's Luther studies, see L. von Muralt, "Zur Luther-Forschung und zum Luther-Verständnis," Zwingliana IX (1953), 576–96.

The writings of Karl Holl are of particular importance for the early thought of Luther; see his Gesammelte Aufsätze zur Kirchengeschichte, Vol. I, 6th ed. (Tübingen, 1932), and especially I. "Was Verstand Luther unter Religion?"; II. "Die Rechtfertigungslehre in Luthers Vorlesung über den Römerbrief mit besonderer Rücksicht auf die Frage der Heilsgewissheit"; III. "Der Neubau der Sittlichkeit" and IV. "Die Entstehung von Luthers Kirchenbegriff." The present essay, in contrast to Holl, will conclude that there is a fundamental contrast between the early writings and Luther's mature position, but what Holl says of the early Luther must always be taken seriously. For a general evaluation of Holl's contribution to Luther studies, see W. Pauck, "The Historiography of the German Reformation during the Past Twenty Years," Church History 9 (1940), 305–40.

A useful index to the biblical quotations in Luther's early writings is L. Pinomaa, Register der Bibelzitate in Luthers Schriften in den Jahren 1509-19 (Helsinki?, 1953?).

A discussion of Luther's social thought during this period may be found in J. Heckel, "Recht und Gesetz, Kirche und Obrigkeit in Luthers Lehre vor dem Thesenanschlag von 1517," Zeitschrift für Rechtsgeschichte, kan. Abt. 26 (1937), 285–375. For a general criticism of Heckel's position, see Appendix.

[11] The best introduction to Luther's thought in the Dictata is G. Ebeling, "Die Anfänge von Luthers Hermeneutik," Zeitschrift für Theologie und Kirche, 48 (1951), 172–230. See also A. W. Hunzinger, Luthers Neuplatonismus in der Psalmenvorlesung von 1513-16 (Leipzig, 1906); E. Vogelsang, Die Anfänge von Luthers Christologie nach der ersten Psalmenvorlesung (Arbeiten zur Kirchengeschichte XV), Berlin, 1929; A. Hamel, Der junge Luther und Augustin, 2 vols. (Gütersloh, 1934-35), Vol. I; G. Ebeling, "Luthers Auslegung des 14(15) Psalms in der ersten Psalmenvorlesung im Vergleich mit der exegetischen Tradition," Zeitschrift für Theologie und Kirche, 50 (1953), 280–339; and further, the bibliography in E. Vogelsang, op. cit. (note 9, above), Vol. V.41).

[12] For the unity of "philosophy" and "theology" in the Dictata, see III, 192, 9: "In hac igitur remotiore et intimiore philosophia et theologia. . .."; III, 560, 33: "Plus philosophie et sapientie est in isto versu: 'Aperiam in parabolis os meum,' quam si mille metaphysicas scripsisset Aristoteles. Quia hinc discitur, quod omnis creatura visibilis est parabola et plena mystica eruditione . . . / . . ." 561, 4: "Ex operibus enim istis invisibilia dei intellecta conspiciuntur. Ro. 1." (Note the different treatment of Romans I, 20 here from what it will receive in the theology of the cross, e.g. Heidelberg Disputation (1518), I,361,32 f.). See also Sermon (1514), I,28,19; 29,27.

[13] For a careful analysis of the "Platonist" ideas of the Dictata, see Hunzinger,

in the Dictata denies this philosophical theology, he comes more and more to find it irrelevant to the salvation of the sinner. Man is saved not as he sees the exemplar in the image but when God paradoxically reveals to him the exemplar under its opposite image, pre-eminently in the cross of Christ, where strength lies hidden under weakness, triumph under defeat, and life under death. As Luther emphasizes this new theology of the cross,[14] which is not philosophical, we find signs of the emergence of a new view of philosophy as not theological. "Philosophy always speaks of things visible and of appearances, or at any rate of what is deduced from appearances. Faith, however, is neither of appearances, nor of what can be deduced from them; indeed, it is from heaven, since from appearances it is rather the opposite of faith which is always deduced." [15] Luther has little to say in the Dictata of the place of such a philosophy in the life of the Christian; it is obviously of little importance when compared with the theology of the cross.

Such a transitional form of thought is typical of all of Luther's thinking in the Dictata and in the following years, though he does not move with equal speed in all areas. One can usually recognize an original statement in the form of a Platonist philosophical theology. This is gradually overshadowed by a theology of the cross, which soon becomes dominant. Finally there are hints of a new human or worldly philosophy.

The world-view of Luther's early theology is that of a dualism finally reconciled and transcended in Christ. Many different terms are used to point to this dualism. Some of these suggest an ultimate philosophic origin, such as visible against invisible or sensible against intelligible. Others suggest a biblical origin, such as flesh and spirit, creature and creator. However, the various terms are all used to explain one another, and we must be very careful not to introduce tensions between the two terminologies where none exist.

---

op. cit. (note 11, above). Hunzinger has been attacked for overemphasizing these Platonist elements, but there is no doubt that they are present and his description of them is most useful.

[14] On the theology of the cross, see W. von Loewenich, Luthers Theologia Crucis, 4th ed. (München, 1954); for its appearance in the Dictata, see G. Ebeling, "Die Anfänge. . . ," (note 11, above).

[15] Dictata III,508,1. Compare III,176,3; 419,37 f.; IV,188,12; 324,2.

Luther suggests two main ways in which man was originally meant to relate the two members of this fundamental dualism. In the first place, as we have already seen, the members stand to one another as image and exemplar. All sensible and visible things are merely the images and shadows of things intelligible and invisible. The thing seen is merely the sign, but the thing signified is reality. In the second place, the members are related as inferior and superior. The flesh should always be subordinate to the spirit, and the creature should always be as nothing in the presence of the creator.

But sin destroyed man's understanding of figure and exemplar, of inferior and superior, and it split and falsified his universe. Man attached himself to the figure as if it were the reality. He exalted the flesh to the place of the spirit, and he asserted his own creaturely justice and wisdom even against God.

Christ came to free man from the disorder of sin and to show him once more his proper place in the universe. In terms of a philosophical theology, He exhibited in Himself the proper relationship between the members of the original dualism. More important, in terms of a theology of the cross, He illustrated in His life and death the paradoxical ways in which God frees man from the worship of vain images and restores him to true reality.

Christ in His own person is both figure and exemplar, flesh and spirit, man and God; in Him the two members of the dualism are properly related and finally unified. Thus in the scheme of figure and exemplar, Christ's humanity is the figure, His divinity is the reality. His humanity is "the sign in which all things were signified," [16] but as He is glorified, He is "the thing signified by all things." [17] "Therefore Christ is the goal of all things and their center, toward whom all look and toward whom all point, as if they said: Behold, He is the one who IS, while we ARE NOT, but simply signify." [18] In the scheme of flesh and spirit, Christ again exemplifies the proper order. "The wills of Christ are the mortification and crucifixion of the flesh and the contempt of all

---

[16] Ibid., III,314,6. Compare IV,13,4.

[17] Ibid., III,375,32. Compare IV,173,23: ". . . ita ipse (Christus) nostrum abstractum, nos ipsius concretum"; 172,28; 242,10.

[18] Ibid., III,368,22.

things visible, similarly the sanctification of the spirit and the love of things invisible." [19] Finally Christ through His lack of worldly strength revealed the nothingness of the world that men might have faith in God. Men ordinarily trust in the "substance" of the world to support them, but Christ on earth had only a "not-substance." "The substance . . . of the ambitious is glory, of the rich riches, of the gluttonous food and the stomach, of the luxurious pleasure. But Christ through His not-substance (*non substantiam*) destroyed all these substances so that the faithful should not subsist in them nor trust in them but should be without substance. The faithful should have in place of such substances faith, which is a different substance, to wit, the substance of God." [20]

In Luther's Christology, as can be seen from these passages, the theology of the cross gradually transforms the original relationship of image and exemplar, of inferior and superior, into a more paradoxical form. What was once a question of analogy and proportion tends to become a question of opposites. We who merely signify "are not"; the flesh is to be "mortified and crucified"; and the substance of the world is a "not-substance." Similarly the final solution appears as a coincidence of opposites. Christ, says Luther, "is both God and man, dead and living, mortal and immortal; almost every contradiction is here resolved." [21]

The viewpoint of the theology of the cross is even more dominant in Luther's discussion of the ways in which God leads man to salvation. Sinful man had falsely valued the sign and figure as if they were true reality; God gives His eternal goods "under their (temporal) opposites, and He makes the sign contradict the thing signified." [22] "Thus through the present time, all those things in the world which are beautiful, pure, strong, and good are the ones which most fitly signify things spiritual. But nevertheless Christ ordered that they all be spurned and their opposites

[19] Ibid., III,104,27.

[20] Ibid., III,440,34 f.; compare III,419,25 f.

[21] Ibid., III,52,25(1516); III,515,31. For other passages, see Ebeling, "Die Anfänge. . . ," pp. 197 ff. (note 11, above).

[22] Ibid., IV,82,17: "Nunc autem, quia dat sub contrariis, et discordat signum a signato: ideo non tantum profunde sed 'nimis profunde' facte sunt." Compare IV,77,37; 81,28; 449,35 f.

chosen." [23] All of this is finally summed up in the Cross. "The judgment of God is contrary to the judgment of men. It condemns the things which men choose; it chooses the things which men condemn. And this judgment is shown us in the cross of Christ." [24]

The cross of Christ is thus the center of the theology of the Dictata, and everything else radiates from it. Luther's theory of biblical interpretation makes it possible for him to develop such a theology in the form of a commentary on the Psalms, for he holds that the Psalms are prophetic and that as prophecies their literal meaning refers first of all to Christ.[25] Further, whatever is true of Christ literally is true of each individual Christian tropologically or morally and of the Christian church allegorically.[26] Among these various meanings Luther regularly gives primacy to the tropological sense of his text.[27] Hence his first purpose is to find out what the Psalms say about Christ, but his final aim is to discover how the individual Christian escapes sin and participates salvation through Christ's cross.

When Luther discusses the existence of the individual Christian, he looks at the problem under the two main rubrics of intellect (or faith) and justice. In the Dictata, "intellect" is an important technical term for man's apprehension of the things that are invisible, spiritual, and eternal; in this sense intellect and faith are synonymous.[28] Man in his sin had become attached to the merely sensible things; he had become blind to the things of the spirit imaged by these sensible things. By grace man is restored in his intellect or spirit, and he comes to see, under the limitations of the present life, true reality. In particular, he comes through God's grace to see this reality as it is revealed

[23] Ibid., IV,45,4. Compare III,64,5.

[24] Ibid., III,463,16. Compare III,31,11; 330,26.

[25] See G. Ebeling, "Die Anfänge . . ." (note 11, above).

[26] Dictata, III,13,6: "Omnis prophetia et omnis propheta de Christo domino debet intelligi, nisi ubi manifestis verbis appareat de alio loqui. . . . Quicquid de domino Ihesu Christo in persona sua ad literam dicitur, hoc ipsum allegorice de adiutorio sibi simili et ecclesia sibi in omnibus conformi debet intelligi. Idemque simul tropologice debet intelligi de quolibet spirituali et interiore homine . . ."; compare also III,46,17 f. (1516).

[27] Ibid., III,335,21. See Vogelsang, Die Anfänge . . . , p.27 (note 11, above).

[28] On *intellectus* in the Dictata, see Hunzinger, op. cit. (note 11, above), pp. 45 ff.; Hamel, op. cit. (note 11, above), I,215 ff.

under its opposite. "Intellect in the sacred scriptures has its name from its object rather than from a power (of the mind), contrary to the usage of philosophy. . . . And it is, briefly, nothing but the wisdom of the cross of Christ." [29]

Justice, which we shall presently consider in more detail, is man's comparable restoration in his will and in his actions. Man in sin loves what is carnal and sensible; he asserts against God "his own" justice. Through grace, however, man comes to recognize the higher justice which is intelligible and spiritual. More important, he comes to recognize and accept this even when it is hidden under evil and suffering, even when it involves the denial of his own justice. And he thus achieves a true "justice of the cross." [30]

When Luther discusses the church, as against the individual Christian, he simply moves from the tropological to the allegorical meaning of the Psalms. "And therefore let us see how tropology leads to allegory and anagogy. The work of God and His strength is faith, for this makes men just and works all the virtues; it chastises and crucifies and weakens the flesh . . . and thus it saves and strengthens the spirit. Moreover, as it does this, all who do these things become God's allegorical work and strength. And thus the church is the work and strength of God." [31]

Within this general theology of the Dictata, Luther has a great deal to say in detail about justice.[32] Indeed the concept of justice is so central that it involves the whole of Luther's theology, though from one particular aspect.

Occasionally, Luther in the Dictata makes use of his original dualism to contrast two different justices as figure and exemplar. They can also be described with the other contrasts of his theology, such as sensible against intelligible, visible against invisible,

[29] Dictata, III,176,3.
[30] Ibid, III,201,37.
[31] Ibid., III,532,11; compare III,369,7.
[32] For a discussion of the general problem of justice and justification in the Dictata, see E. Hirsch, "Initium theologiae Lutheri," in: Festschrift Julius Kaftan (Tübingen, 1920), 150–69 (reprinted with some slight modifications in his Luther-Studien (Gütersloh, 1954), Vol. II, 9–35); E. Vogelsang, Die Anfänge (note 11, above), Chapter II; A. Hamel, op. cit. (note 11, above), I, 131 ff.

or earthly against heavenly.[33] Sometimes Luther states the contrast abstractly. "Every human law and every human justice is a shadow and a figure of that justice which is in the spirit before God; without the latter, the former is necessarily hypocrisy."[34] Similarly the true justice of faith is "signified by the justice of the law and of nature."[35] More often, however, Luther works out the contrast between the two justices historically in terms of the Jews and the Christians. The good and simple people of the Old Law, who did not understand the grace of Christ, "lived only in the schoolmaster (*in pedagogo*) and in the shadow of faith and in the figure of the justice of Christ."[36]

Though Luther continues to make use of his original dualism in discussing justice, his interest comes to center more and more on the new situations where justice is destroyed by sin or restored by Christ. Injustice, as Luther analyzes it, is not merely attachment to the figure in ignorance of the exemplar; it is primarily the assertion that the figure is the exemplar and in consequence the denial that the true exemplar exists. Similarly the new justice of the Christian is not merely the recognition of the original figure-exemplar relationship; it is the recognition of this relationship in its new paradoxical form where justice lies hidden under sin. Man's injustice was to assert his own justice and deny God's; his Christian justice will be to accept God's justice by denying his own.

Throughout the Dictata Luther constantly attacks those who assert "their own justice." It is the fault of the Jews, for example, "that they establish their own justice and are not subject to the justice of Christ."[37] "Whoever establishes his own justice, denies the justice of God and makes Him a liar."[38] Luther asserts again and again that the recognition and confession of one's injustice

[33] E.g. Dictata, III,107,29; 323,3; 455,29; IV,1,24.

[34] Ibid., III,129,20. Compare III,204,1: "Unde iudicium publicum in officialibus est litera et figura istorum iudiciorum dei supradictorum"; IV,16,24: "Quia lex civitatis punit iniustos. Et tamen hec est vix figura iustitie et pacis, que est in civitate dei."

[35] Ibid., III,369,4: "Opus dei tropologice est iustitia fidei, non iustitia proprie legis, per legis et nature iustitiam significata."

[36] Ibid., III,200,36.

[37] Ibid., III,152,38. A few other typical examples may be cited: III,26,22; 29,26; 76,9; 107,26; 117,17; 225,1; 285,5; 326,13; IV,64,10; 79,26; 94,6; 204,26; 372,20.

[38] Ibid., III,170,33.

is the first stage of justice.[39] "The justice of God will not be in us nor does it arise in us, unless first our own justice shall fall and perish." [40] "The just man is in the first place the accuser of himself, the condemner of himself, and the judge of himself." [41]

Luther develops this thesis with some care as a commentary on the words of the Psalmist in Psalm L(LI),4: ". . . that Thou (God) might be justified in Thy words." [42] God has declared all men to be sinners; hence when a man claims justice for himself he is calling God a liar and denying His justice. Contrariwise, the man who admits his sin accepts God's statement as true and "justifies Him in His words." "Thus he is like God (*conformis Deo*), and he is true and just, as is God, with whom he agrees." [43]

When Luther in the Dictata discusses how man attains to this justice, he usually explains it as the tropological aspect of God's "judgment and justice." [44] God's judgment condemns the flesh, while God's justice gives life to the spirit.[45] And Luther argues that in the Psalms God's "judgment and justice" is most often used in its tropological sense; the phrase refers not to God's action in Himself but to His action as it is seen in the individual Christian.

Thus in the important scholia on Psalm LXXI (LXXII) he comments on the tropological judgment of God. "This is a most frequent meaning in the scriptures. It is the judgment by which God condemns and by which He makes us condemn whatever we have of ourselves, the whole old man with his acts, and even our justices. . . . This is called the judgment of God in the same

[39] E.g. ibid., III,26,24; 185,6; 289,31 f.; 29,16 f. (1516).

[40] Ibid., III,31,9 (1516).

[41] Ibid., III, 288,31.

[42] Ibid., III,287,20 ff. In a series of articles Fr. Loofs analyzed Luther's argument that man is justified when he declares himself a sinner and "justifies God in His words." Loofs maintained that here was the origin of Luther's idea of the "iustitia Dei passiva," but while this thesis of Loofs is to be rejected, his articles remain valuable for their analysis of the Dictata and of the Lectures on Romans (1515–16). Fr. Loofs, " 'Justitia Dei passiva' in Luthers Anfängen," Theologische Studien und Kritiken, 84 (1911), 461–73; idem, "Der articulus stantis et cadentis ecclesiae," ibid., 90 (1917), 323–420; idem, "Zur Frage nach dem Zeitpunkt des Durchbruchs evangelischer Erkenntnis bei Luther," ibid., 92 (1919), 370–71.

[43] Dictata, III,289,34. Compare III,409,33: "Ergo confiteri peccatum et esse iustum idem sunt."

[44] On this general problem, see Hamel, op. cit. (note 11, above), I,143 ff. See also the interesting parallel discussion in Adnotationes, IV,468,27 f.

[45] Dictata, III,349,5; IV,38,19; 114,3; 116,10; 204,35 f.

sense as the justice, strength, or wisdom of God, that is to say, as that by which we are wise, strong, just, and humble or judged." [46] Man accordingly participates the judgment of God by recognizing and condemning his own injustice.

Luther argues that not only God's judgment but also His justice regularly bears a tropological sense in the Psalms. "Tropologically the justice of God is the faith of Christ. . . . And this is the most common use in the Scriptures." [47] "Hence whoever wishes fully to understand the Apostle and the other Scriptures must take all these words in their tropological sense. The truth, the wisdom, the strength, the salvation, and the justice of God are to be understood as the truth and so on by which He makes us strong, saved, just, wise, and so on. Similarly the works of God, the ways of God, all of which Christ is literally, and all of which the faith of Christ is morally." [48]

The justice of God, as seen tropologically in the individual Christian, can be called the justice of faith, and this is one of the most common phrases of the Dictata.[49] Luther does not discuss it at length; it is not so much the starting point of an argument as a summary of conclusions already reached. In the first place, it is contrasted with "one's own justice," for the justice of faith recognizes that only God is just and that all men are sinners.[50] In the second place, it is not a merely human justice, for it justifies "before God" and not only "before men." [51] Positively it is a justice of faith, or a spiritual justice, because only faith or the intellect or the spirit can see beyond the figure, particularly beyond the contradictory figure, to the exemplar. It is a justice of Christ and of His cross, because sinful man achieves justice only as the tropological work of Christ and because this work is summed up in the cross.[52]

----

[46] Ibid., III, 465,1.

[47] Ibid., III, 466,26. Compare III,369,4; 463,1; and Adnotationes, IV,469,29. In the last passage, it is noteworthy that at this time Luther can interpret II Corinthians, V,21 tropologically.

[48] Dictata, III,458,8.

[49] E.g. ibid., III,154,32. For a list of additional passages, see Fr. Loofs, "Der articulus. . ." (note 42, above), p.351, note 4 and p.352, note 1.

[50] Ibid., III,76,9; 510,24; IV,241,24; 443,9.

[51] Ibid., III,451,18; 269,21; 320,20; IV,443,13.

[52] Ibid., III,201,37: "Prophetat ruinam Iudeorum ex superbia eorum, quia per

In the Dictata, Luther regularly identifies the justice of faith with God's grace, and he denies that any man can fully merit it.[53] From this standpoint he attacks an "Aristotelian" interpretation of the justice of God, for Aristotle argues that justice is produced by just works. "This is human justice, which comes from and is imputed from works, but the justice of God is before any work. Just as original sin is before any of our bad works, so original justice would have preceded any of our good works, and in its place the justice of Christ is now given us before any meritorious work." [54]

Luther further argues that in this life the justice of the Christian is never more than partial; the justice of the spirit is counterbalanced by the sinfulness of the flesh. Luther here makes use of his basic division of man into spirit and flesh. "There are two things in man, the spirit and the flesh." [55] "The spirit is the higher (part) and the flesh is the lower (part) of man in this life." [56] "And since the flesh and the spirit are one man, without doubt it is the fault of that man, when his flesh is so bad and acts so badly." [57] Luther accordingly explains the present state of the Christian as a mixture of justice and injustice. Everyone still has something of the letter so that he is not all spirit, something of the old man so that he is not entirely of the new, and likewise for the flesh, the earth, the world and the devil.[58] The Christian's partial justice in this life would not in itself be enough to justify him before God, and he must continue to pray for God's mercy.

---

iustitiam crucis Christi contemnunt salvari." Compare III,152,23; 170,38 f.; 422,24.

[53] For a list of passages, see Vogelsang, Die Anfänge. . . (note 11, above), p.72, note 2. Contrary to Vogelsang, Luther continues to recognize a merit arising from grace; see Hamel, op. cit. (note 11, above), I,186 f. For a while Luther also recognizes a "congruent" preparation for grace; see Dictata, IV,262,4; 312,36, but see also IV,329,31. Luther denies this, Lectures on Romans (1515–16), LVI, 503,1; Quaestio de viribus et voluntate hominis sine gratia (1516), I,147,10.

[54] Dictata, IV,19,26 f.; compare IV,3,26; 113,14.

[55] Ibid., IV,109,13.

[56] Ibid., IV,175,14; compare III,49,2 (1516); XXXI,1 p.469,27 f.

[57] Ibid., IV,364,12. Compare III,203,18: "Sed quia caro et anima sunt unus homo, ideo tandem utrumque salvatur"; IV,252,28: "Nam licet iustificatus sit homo in spiritu, tamen quia pugnat in corpore mortis cum lege membrorum, semper indiget gratiis aliis secundum multitudinem tentationum."

[58] Ibid., IV,320,17. Compare IV,165,31. On the general topic see L. Pinomaa, "Die profectio bei Luther," Werner Elert Festschrift (Berlin, 1955), 119–27.

"Indeed, both the faith and the grace by which we are today justified would not justify us of themselves, unless a covenant (*pactum*) of God did this." [59]

Thus Luther in the Dictata can speak of the Christians as both just and unjust, but we must be careful not to read into such statements his mature doctrine of the two realms of Christian existence.[60] Luther in the Dictata does not mean that man is in any sense "totally" just or "totally" a sinner; he means simply that man is in this life, partly just, in the spirit, and partly unjust, in the flesh.

While the Christian's justice in this life is only partial, it is nevertheless a real justice, valid even before God. The justice of God or of faith is an actual restoration of the Christian's spirit, which God makes just. Further, while the justice of God depends on grace and while God himself originally "works" it, still the Christian himself also "works" it after God. Hence Luther paraphrases the Psalmist. "But though I have not yet achieved perfection, I am nevertheless at work on it. I have done this and I am doing it (*feci et facio*)." [61] Accordingly the justice of God in the Dictata may not be identified with either the "active" or the "passive" justice of Luther's mature period; it is not the "active" justice, for it is valid in the realm of salvation, and it is not the "passive" justice, for it is partial and active.[62]

Finally, Luther in the Dictata regularly looks forward from the Christian's partial justice to his complete justification in the final judgment of God, and his partial justice is in some way a causal antecedent of his complete justification. For the most part Luther says little of God's ultimate anagogic "judgment and justice," and

[59] Dictata, III,289,1. Compare, for a similar statement in the terminology of imputation III,282,40 f.

[60] Compare, for example, ibid. IV,336,12: "Nam cum nullus sit in hac vita perfectus, semper ad eam bonitatem, quam nondum habet, dicitur malus, licet ad eam quam habet, sit bonus. . . . Igitur semper medii sumus inter bonitatem, quam ex deo habemus et malitiam, quam ex nobis habemus, donec in futuro absorbeantur omnia mala. . ."; 251,10; 363,3; 364,10. For the development of these ideas during 1515–18, see pp. 26 f., below.

[61] Ibid., IV,362,32. Compare III,541,26 f. and from a slightly different standpoint, III,463,30: "Hoc est, ut nostro more loquar: Evangelium est realiter et formaliter Iudicium et Iustitia, quando sic opere vivitur, sicut ipsum nos docet. Est autem ostensive et doctrinaliter Iudicium et Iustitia, quando docet sic vivendum." III,258,6; IV,241,8.

[62] See below, Chapter III, pp. 91 f.

he explains that the Psalms deal primarily with God's tropological judgment and justice. "The reason for this is that the Old Testament specially (*proprie*) prophesies only the first advent of Christ, in which He rules with a benign and saving judgment. . . . However the New Testament specially prophesies the future judgment and justice, for it prophesies the second advent of Christ, which shall be in the judgment of severity and of eternal punishment." [63] In this final judgment the Christian must hope that a merciful God will save those who possess the justice of faith. "Therefore to announce that God is judge is to announce a universal judgment. It will not suffice for anyone to have the justice which he can have before men, but the justice of God will be required, so that he may be just before God." [64] Luther does not emphasize the point nor elaborate upon it; there was no reason for him to do so, since it was entirely traditional.

In the Dictata, Luther gives little importance to human justice or to "justice before men" in the life of the Christian. He has of course no intention of attacking such justice, and it remains in theory a figure of the true spiritual justice of faith and of Christ. But the theory has not much relevance to the religious existence of the Christian, or of the sinner either. The sinner perverts the figure by making an idol of it as "his own justice" and by turning it against God. The Christian, on the other hand, starts by recognizing "his own justice" as injustice, and he goes on to magnify God and to condemn himself. He mortifies his "flesh"; he welcomes tribulation and persecution, for he knows that true justice lies hidden under the cross of injustice. Thus Luther in the Dictata seems to suggest that as a person becomes more Christian and spiritual, he will more and more withdraw from the world of human justice.

Hence what the Dictata have to say about such human justice is unproblematic and incidental. And this is quite consistent with the general viewpoint of the Dictata. "We must forget all the things outside us, which are visible and temporal, and be mindful only of the things which are within and invisible." [65]

[63] Dictata, III,462,1.
[64] Ibid., III,283,36.
[65] Ibid., IV,11,4.

The doctrine of law [66] in the Dictata is second only to that of justice in importance, and here again Luther's discussion involves the whole of his theology. We find the original dualism of figure and exemplar, the disordering of their proper relationship by sin, and the reconstruction of a new relationship of salvation through Christ. In general, however, the original dualism shows more vitality in Luther's thinking about law than about justice, and the theology of the cross does not become so dominant.

The problem of law in the Dictata is essentially the problem of the relationship between the two laws of the Old and the New Testaments, between the legislation of Moses and the legislation of Christ.

Luther first relates the two laws in the familiar pattern of image and exemplar. "The Law did not have the works of salvation but only the words and signs of future works. . . . Therefore all the sayings of the Law are, as it were, only words and signs; the sayings and deeds of the Gospel, however, are the works and the reality itself (res ipsa) which had been signified." [67] The law of Moses contained figures of the future law, but these figures did not themselves possess justice, "for they simply signified the justice of the Gospel." [68]

From a slightly different aspect, the two laws are related as letter and spirit. Luther declares that the important Psalm CXVIII (CXIX) deals with "the difference between the Old Law and the New Law, or between the letter and the spirit." [69] "The letter is all that which extends only as far as the body and the senses, not as far as the spirit. Hence, since everything which was done in the Law was done only carnally and sensibly (sensualiter), it is therefore called carnal and literal and vain, for it did not help the spirit at all. But in the New Law spiritual things are given and grace, by which what is carnal and literal is taken away." [70] In part, the relation between letter and spirit is

---

[66] For a discussion of Luther's ideas on law in the Dictata, see J. Heckel, "Recht und Gesetz. . ." (note 2, above), pp.315 f.; Hamel, op. cit. (note 11, above), I,129 f.; Ebeling, "Die Anfänge. . ." (note 11, above), pp.208 f.

[67] Dictata, III,258,4; compare III,295,33; IV,6,25.

[68] Ibid., III,129,2 and 20. Compare III,258,8; 515,39 f.; IV,9,28 f.; Adnotationes, IV,482,8.

[69] Dictata, IV,325,18. Compare IV,305,19–25.

[70] Ibid., III,37,34.

equivalent to that between image and exemplar, "for the Law does not become spiritual, except by transmutation and exposition of the figures." [71]

Thus in Luther's doctrine of law the most important concept is that of the New Law. He can call it the evangelical or Gospel law, the law of Christ or of the Lord or of God, or the law of faith, but his favorite name for it is the spiritual law (*lex spiritualis*).[72] Two characteristics of the law receive special emphasis. In the first place, as we have already seen, it is a law which deals in reality, not in figures, a law concerned with the things that are spiritual, invisible, and eternal, not with those that are merely sensible and temporal.[73] In the second place, it is a law with grace. Moses, like any legislator, could obligate his subjects, but he could not give them the grace to obey; Christ, in contrast, not only obligates but also gives the grace to meet the obligation.[74] From this second standpoint, the spiritual law becomes synonymous with other terms which refer generally to the process of Christian salvation, such as grace, justice, faith, and notably charity.[75]

In contrast the Old Law, the law of Moses, is carnal, literal,

---

[71] Ibid., IV,135,14.

[72] The following citations may serve as examples of the various titles of this law in the Dictata.

lex evangelica: III,611,38; IV,128,3; 285,34; 328,17.
lex evangelii: III,277,30; 550,7; IV, 90, 2; 285,10; 312,12.
lex Christi: III,107,29; 430,29; IV,42,4; 317,28; 353,5.
lex domini: III,17,1(1516); 28,30 f.; IV,281,3; 315,22.
lex dei: III,27,13 (1516) 155,31; 174,35; IV,366,2.
lex fidei: III,86,7; 551,4; IV,305,20; 322,7.
lex spiritualis (or *lex spiritus*); III,143,5; 150,3; 457,30; IV,134,20; 135,14; 160,12; 209,24; 215,10; 285,37; 322,36 f.; 334,30; 353,5; 354,6; 355,8; 365,33; 370,25; 379,3; Sermon (1514), I,35,23.

[73] Dictata, III,244,21; IV,9,29; 285,10; 323,27; III,37,37(1516); Theologische Studien und Kritiken, 90 (1917), 525 (= Dictata).

[74] Ibid., III,641,28; Adnotationes, IV,509,2

[75] E.g. Dictata, III,462,15: "Lex Christi, lex pacis, lex gratie, Evangelium, vocatur multis nominibus aliis, ut 'via domini' . . . . Nunc igitur mirum, quomodo gratia seu lex gratie (quod idem est) sit Iudicium et Iustitia"; III,454,17: ". . . quod contra legem agunt, scilicet nolentes ex peccatoribus iusti fieri per fidem Christi, que est lex vera et lux vera"; III,29,1: "Fides autem est lex domini immaculata, purificans corda eorum." For the identification with charity, compare IV,355,9: "Quia illam (legem mortis) docentes docent et homines sunt et hominem veterem docent in iustitia carnali, sed illam (legem spiritus) tu solus et unus Magister, qui es in coelis, non homo sed deus, doces intus per spiritum diffundens ipsam charitatem, que est lex tua"; IV,328,13; 354,31; 361,4.

and valid only before men. "The Law covered only the sins which
were against the justices of the flesh, but grace covers those too
which are against the justices of God and of the spirit . . . ." [76]
"Hence the Gospel is said to restrain not only the hand but also
the mind (*animum*), while the law of Moses restrained only the
hand." [77] "We are all, as it were, on the road, that is to say on
the road of Moses, of the letter and of human justice, and in this
road we appear without fault before men. Meanwhile we are
within ourselves full of all fault, because we do not have the justice of faith and the law of the spirit." [78]

How are these two laws related in God's plan of salvation?
Luther's simplest answer, and one which harmonizes well with his
original dualism, is that the two laws are related as imperfect and
perfect. "Imperfection is related to perfection as is the Old Law
to the New Law." [79] "The synagogue was the beginning of the
church, and the Law was the beginning of the Gospel, which
made perfect the Law and its people." [80] Christ perfected the
Law by revealing the spirit beyond the letter and the exemplar
beyond the image. "The Lord shaped and formed the law of the
spirit out of the letter of the Law, as from an unwrought mass.
He led the letter back to the spirit." [81]

On other occasions Luther uses the relation of spirit and letter
to argue that the Old Law and the New Law are not so much two
different laws as two different interpretations of the same law.
"The Gospel of Christ is a pure and holy speech, but the Law
of Moses is not: which is to be understood as follows — the Law,
if understood and followed only literally, is neither pure nor holy,
for it does not sanctify the soul but only the hand or body. However, the Law when spiritually understood is the same as the
Gospel." [82] "The Law of Moses had both, that is to say, the

---

[76] Ibid., IV,1,24.

[77] Ibid., III,28,30(1516); compare III,128,17–129,3; IV,250,27.

[78] Ibid., IV,306,1.

[79] Ibid., III,200,40; 281,38 f.

[80] Ibid., III,605,20.

[81] Ibid., IV,97,35. Compare III,249,13: "Sic vetus lex est quasi rude quid: hoc
rude evangelium, rude baptisma, et omnia ruda, sed per Evangelium ex illa ruditate
in politiorem modum ducta. Ideo erudire est secundum novam legem docere,
quasi extra ruditatem litere in spiritus intelligentiam ducere"; III,33,10; 93,30;
571,14; IV,135,14; 457,8.

[82] Dictata, IV,96,23.

signifying letter and the spirit which was signified by the letter." [83]
"On the other hand, even the Gospel, if it is treated carnally, is
a dead reed, and all that which is said of the Law of Moses." [84]

So far we have noticed Luther's discussion of the two laws as
it appears in the context of his original dualism of image and
exemplar, of letter and spirit. But we also find in the Dictata,
particularly in the later sections, a more complicated and paradoxical approach to the problem of the two laws. Here the theology of the cross is the dynamic factor, and the emphasis is no
longer on the proportion between image and exemplar, between
letter and spirit. The exemplar lies hidden under its opposite
image, and the spirit is the death of the letter.

Thus Luther argues that Christ passed from this transitory life
to eternal life through death, and "so he wished that the law and
the synagogue should pass from the life of the transitory and
visible letter into the invisible spirit and the eternal church
through the killing and death of the letter and the shadows and
the figures." [85] "And all the things which were in glory in the
law, Christ changed into ignominy. They were figures of things
internal and spiritual, and the figures were meant to cease and to
be polluted and profaned when that which they figured had come
to pass." [86] Luther continues with his general thesis that while
the strong and good things of the world are the best symbols for
things spiritual, it was these very strong and good things which
Christ spurned; this is how God saves men through the foolish-
ness of the cross.

Similarly Luther maintains that as the old law was literally a
law of the flesh, so its spiritual meaning is the denial of the flesh.
"The Old Law spiritually understood is nothing but the crucifixion of the flesh. . . . Therefore it prophesies nothing but Jesus
crucified. The New Law, however, is the salvation of the spirit.
And thus all those things agree with the Old Law which pertain
to the destruction of the old man; all those things agree with the

[83] Ibid., IV,306,11.
[84] Ibid., III,457,8; 451,22.
[85] Ibid., IV,47,30. On this, see Ebeling "Die Anfänge. . ." (note 11, above),
pp.213 f.
[86] Ibid., IV,45,2.

New Law which pertain to the construction of the new man." [87]

In such passages the doctrine of the spiritual law becomes another way of stating the general theology of the cross or of explaining God's "judgment and justice." "The law of the Lord is spiritual, and it works justifications in the spirit but judgments in the flesh." [88] The testimonies of the New Law are marvellous, "because they offer such great goods and joys, and because they promise much greater ones, under evils and sufferings." [89] "The marvellous things of the law of Christ are that the Gospel decrees good to be evil, and evil to be good, light to be darkness, and darkness light, bitter to be sweet, and sweet bitter, namely that what is good according to the flesh is bad according to the spirit, and *vice versa*." [90]

Luther has little to say in the Dictata of human law or of natural law. When he mentions them, he regularly connects both with the Mosaic law, and his position seems to be that for the Christian, the Mosaic, human, and natural laws fall into one broad category as against the new or spiritual law of Christ. In a typical passage Luther states that the judgments of the Gospel are true and not shadowy (*umbratica*); these judgments are not, like the law of Moses, simply figures of a future law. He then glosses "shadowy": "Since every human law and every human justice is a shadow and figure of the justice which is in the spirit before God." [91] There are very few references to natural law or natural right, and these few link it with the Mosaic law. Luther speaks, for example, of the wickedness "which all have who are under the law, whether it be the law of nature or the written law." [92]

[87] Ibid., IV,174,17. Somewhat later in the same discussion, Luther remarks, IV,176,27: "quia vetus lex et nova lex conveniunt, sicut homo vetus occisus et homo novus suscitatus. Vetus lex hominem veterem monstrat mortuum, nova vivum novum exhibet." Compare Adnotationes, IV,498,25.

[88] Dictata, IV,379,3; compare III,108,9.

[89] Ibid., IV,298,35. Luther here contrasts the paradoxical marvellousness of the New Law with that of the Old Law which says one thing literally and means another spiritually.

[90] Ibid., IV,314,34.

[91] Ibid., III,129,1 and 20; IV,16,25. Compare III,369,5: ". . . iustitia fidei . . . per legis et nature iustitiam significata." Luther regularly emphasizes the mutability of all human law, III,91,9; IV,285,9; 323,22.

[92] Ibid., III,65,8; compare IV,52,16 and III,429,17: ". . . an per singulas dies et horas in tota vita tua deum laudaveris et gratias egeris, ad hoc enim teneris stricto precepto et iure naturali."

Accordingly, human and natural law, like human and natural justice, play only a very subordinate rôle in the Dictata. In the original dualism, they fall among the images, and the Christian should rise as far as possible to their spiritual exemplars. In the theology of the cross, they are even further depressed, for the spiritual law now appears as the direct opposite of ordinary law.

Such then in summary form are the ideas of Luther in the Dictata. Despite the attempts of some scholars to classify this theology as "Neoplatonist" or "Augustinian," [93] we do well to recognize Luther's position in the Dictata as a Christian theology in its own right, though we may at the same time note its special connection with various ancient and medieval traditions.

There are changes in emphasis between the early and the late portions of the Dictata; for example, Luther makes more frequent mention in the later sections of the unmerited quality of God's grace, and the theology of the cross gradually gains in importance. But the changes in emphasis do not lead to any fundamental reorientation, and Luther's theology of 1515 is essentially the same as it had been in 1513. Similarly there appears to be no fundamental change in the ideas of justice and of law.[94]

[93] The most important assertion that Luther's position is Neoplatonist comes from Hunzinger (notes 11 and 13 above). It is doubtful if such a description serves to clarify Luther's general theology, since his dualism denies the fundamental Neoplatonist notion of stages and hierarchy and since the paradox of the theology of the cross is alien to the Greek Platonist tradition. Hamel, op. cit. (note 11, above), emphasizes the "Augustinian" character of the Dictata. While it is doubtless true that Luther makes considerable use of Augustine's Enarrationes in Psalmos, it does not appear that he draws from this source the particular form either of his philosophical theology or of his theology of the cross. Among thinkers closer to Luther in time, one might find some parallels to his thought in Nicolaus Cusanus and even more in Faber Stapulensis. However, as noted above, the problem of Luther's sources has been excluded from the present essay.

[94] While most of the writers on the so-called "initium theologiae Lutheri" have made some use of the Dictata, there have been only two significant attempts to locate the emergence of Luther's new understanding of Romans I,17 within the Dictata, by E. Hirsch, "Initium. . ." (note 32, above) and E. Vogelsang, Die Anfänge. . . (note 11, above). E. Hirsch sees the new position of Luther for the first time clearly at Dictata, III,199,18, where Luther glosses: "*Iustitia* fidei *tua* qua coram te iusti sumus," and he finds the scholia on Psalm XXXI (XXXII) the first attempt to expound the new position doctrinally. E. Vogelsang follows much the same method as Hirsch, but he finds the decisive break in the scholia on Psalm LXXI (LXXII).

It is not possible to criticize Hirsch's and Vogelsang's argument in detail here, but two general points may be made. In the first place, it is difficult to believe that Luther ever in the Dictata held a position substantially different from what

On the other hand, Luther's general theology and his ideas on justice and law in the Dictata do differ fundamentally from his mature thought. Justice, in the Dictata, means primarily the justice of God; it is a real, though partial, justice of the Christian which is valid before God and in relation to salvation. The Christian hopes that in the future God will in His mercy accept him partly because of this justice. Law, in the Dictata, is analyzed primarily in terms of the contrast between Moses and Christ. The spiritual law of the Gospel is a law with grace and a law that saves. Luther does not question either that the Gospel is a law or that Christ is a legislator.[95]

2. *The Biblical Commentaries and Other Writings, 1515–18.*

In the Dictata super Psalterium (1513–15) Luther expounded a theology of the cross against the background of a philosophical theology of image and exemplar; within this context he worked out his ideas of justice and of law. We have now to notice the modifications and additions to be found in his writings from 1515 through the first part of 1518. Of these, the Lectures on Romans (1515–16) is the longest and most important; we shall also have to take account of the Lectures on Galatians (1516–17), the Lectures on Hebrews (1517–18), the Heidelberg Disputation (1518), together with some significant Sermons and a number of minor works.[96]

Hirsch and Vogelsang describe as his new position. Both admit "ambiguous" glosses earlier than the point at which they would locate the break, and it would appear that the justice of God or of faith is clearly present in the early commentary on Psalm I (which they do not discuss at all, though only parts of it belong to the 1516 reworking); compare Dictata, III,11,28; 13,6 f.; 31,9. In the second place, as will be argued in greater detail in the body of the present essay, what Hirsch and Vogelsang describe as Luther's new position is typical of Luther's early theology, and it is clearly prior to the fundamental re-orientation of 1518–19.

[95] E.g., Dictata, III,86,7; 641,19; IV,53,14; Adnotationes, IV,509,1; Theologische Studien und Kritiken, 90 (1917), 525–6.

[96] The Lectures (henceforth cited as Romans, Galatians and Hebrews) are superbly edited in LVI and LVII of the Weimar edition. The glosses on Galatians may be supplemented in a few instances by H. Volz, "Eine neue studentische Nachschrift von Luthers erster Galaterbriefvorlesung von 1516–17," Zeitschrift für Kirchengeschichte, 66 (1954–5), 72–96. For bibliography on the lectures, see E. Vogelsang, in Luthers Werke (note 9, above), Vol. V, 222; 327; and 344–5. On Romans, see also J. Hilburg, Luthers Frömmigkeit in seiner Vorlesung über den Römerbrief, microfilm (Göttingen, 1951).

A preliminary question concerns the relation of the writings of 1515–18 to the Dictata super Psalterium. No simple and unqualified answer can be given, but two general points may be made here. In the first place, two of the movements of thought already under way in the Dictata are continued and accelerated. The original dualism of figure and exemplar, of visible and invisible, becomes steadily less important, though it does not disappear. The theology of the cross becomes more and more central, receiving its programmatic statement in the Heidelberg Disputation.[97] In the second place, none of the developments of 1515–18, though they may lead to new emphases and new tensions, result in any fundamental changes. To a first approximation, Luther in early 1518 has not abandoned the general theology of the Dictata.

A second preliminary question concerns the relation of the writings of 1515–18 to the general re-orientation of 1518–19. Here again no simple answer is possible, though two guiding hypotheses may be suggested. In the first place, the re-orientation of 1518–19 does not come entirely unprepared; looking backward, we can see that it makes use of certain of the new emphases of 1515–18 and resolves some of its new tensions. But in the second place, the re-orientation of 1518–19 also represents radical newness in relation to the preceding period. Looking forward from the writings of 1515–18, we see it as an unpredictable mutation and not as an inevitable development. And all this is to say again that Luther's writings of the early period from 1513 through the first part of 1518 represent a general unity in themselves and as contrasted with his mature theology.

Erich Vogelsang has published some fragments of a Lutheran commentary on Psalms IV–V, as Unbekannte Fragmente aus Luthers zweiter Psalmenvorlesung, 1518 (Arbeiten zur Kirchengeschichte XXVII), Berlin, 1940 (henceforth cited as Unbekannte Fragmente (1518?)). Vogelsang's dating has been questioned by H. Bornkamm in his review, Theologische Literaturzeitung 67 (1942), 321–3, and by H. Beintker, "Zur Datierung und Einordnung eines neuen Lutherfragmentes," Wissenschaftliche Zeitschrift der Universität Greifswald, I (1951–2), sprachwiss. Reihe, Nrs. 2–3, pp.70–8. The Praelectio in librum Iudicum (1516 f.) printed in the Weimar edition IV 529–86 is not by Luther; see C. Stange "Luthers angebliche Vorlesung zum Richter-Buch," Zeitschrift zur systematischen Theologie, 23 (1954), 303–33.

[97] For a general account of the theology of the cross, see W. von Loewenich, op. cit. (note 14, above), and E. Ellwein, "Die Entfaltung der theologia crucis in Luthers Hebräerbriefvorlesung," Festschrift Karl Barth (München, 1936), 382–404.

Luther in the Lectures on Romans has little to say of the original dualism of image and exemplar, though he continues to make use of it on occasion here and in the Lectures on Hebrews.[98] Similarly Luther gradually drops the technique of tropology and allegory which was earlier so important.[99]

The theology of the cross now dominates his thought, and, as earlier, Luther emphasizes the paradox that our goods are hidden under their opposites. "Our good is hidden, and so profoundly that it is hidden under its opposite. Thus our life is under death, love of ourselves under hate of ourselves, glory under ignominy, salvation under perdition, . . . justice under sin, strength under infirmity, and universally every one of our affirmations under its negation, so that faith may have its place in God." [100] Luther now contrasts such a "theology of the cross" with scholasticism and its false "theology of glory." [101] In his own thinking, the theology of the cross with its paradox appears as complementary to a "philosophy" of appearances and comprehensibility.[102]

The problem of justice [103] is of course central in the Lectures on Romans, and Luther's Preface points out his general approach. "The summary of this Epistle is to destroy and to pluck out and

[98] Compare Romans, LVI,291,1; 406,24 f.; 447,21. Galatians, LVII,2,p.69,4; 98,12; Hebrews, LVII,3 p. 124,9; 222,17.

[99] See, e.g., the general discussion in Galatians, LVII,2 pp.95,23 f.; Decem praecepta Wittenbergensi praedicata populo (henceforth cited as Decem praecepta) 1518, I,507,25 f.

[100] Romans, LVI,392,28. Compare LVI,376,32 f.; 380,31; 446,31; Sermon (1516), I,97,18: "Sic, sic Christus in signum contradictionis ponitur, ut revelentur cordium cogitationes."

[101] Compare Heidelberg Disputation (1518), I,362,21 f.

[102] Compare Romans, LVI,447,17: "Ita enim in omnibus sanctis agit Deus, Ut faciat eos summa voluntate facere, que summe nolunt. Et contrarietatem mirantur philosophi et non intelligunt homines." Luther several times in Romans contrasts a theology of paradox with a philosophy which deals with appearances and with what can be comprehended; see LVI,371,2; 380,31; Unbekannte Fragmente (1518?), 77,12.

[103] For a general treatment of the problem of justification in Romans, see Hamel, op. cit. (note 11, above), Vol. II, 52 ff.; K. Holl, "Die Rechtfertigungslehre in Luthers Vorlesung über den Römerbrief," in Gesammelte Aufsätze zur Kirchengeschichte, Vol. I, 6th ed. (Tübingen, 1923), 111–154. On many aspects, the most penetrating study is H. J. Iwand, Rechtfertigungslehre und Christusglaube. Eine Untersuchung zur Systematik der Rechtfertigungslehre Luthers in ihren Anfängen (Leipzig, 1930). For our purposes, it is not always possible to follow Iwand since he places Luther's ideas in Romans in the context of later statements from 1519 and the following years; see, for example, the works of Luther cited in the general section, Chapter I, §1,pp.10 f.

to ruin all wisdom and justice of the flesh, that is howsoever great they may be in the sight of men, even in our own sight, . . . and to plant and to establish and to magnify sin, however much this may not exist or shall be thought not to exist." [104] Luther explains that Paul is not attacking human justice as such, but the Christian must learn to have no regard for this justice.

On the positive side, Luther argues that God wishes to save and to justify us not by any domestic justice of our own but by an alien justice which comes from without. We should not glory before men even in this alien justice of Christ. The Christian should be as one having nothing who awaits the mercy of God, who may reckon (*reputantis*) him just and wise. "Which God will then do, if the Christian shall have been humble and shall not have preceded God in justifying himself and in reckoning himself to be something." [105]

In general, Luther here remains within the position of the Dictata, that our justice begins with the assertion of our own injustice, but the phrasing is more extreme and new tensions are present. The Christian must deny himself any justice and any claim to God's favor, and yet this denial is itself in some way a justice and a claim. Some of the difficulties which this involves for the religious life may be suggested by Luther's statement that God is marvellous in His saints, "for He has so hidden them, that while they are holy (*sancti*), they seem to themselves to be nothing but profane." [106]

In Luther's more detailed analysis, the primary concept is the justice of God, which is regularly contrasted with another, merely human justice. There are a few scattered references which relate the two justices, after the manner of the Dictata, as exemplar and image, but Luther now gives little weight to this explanation.[107] There are also a very few passages where Luther develops a tropological interpretation of the justice of God.[108] For the most part, however, Luther simply describes the justice of God as the

---

[104] Romans, LVI,157,2.
[105] Ibid., LVI,159,14.
[106] Ibid., LVI,290,21.
[107] E.g., Romans, LVI,291,1; 408,1 f.; 447,22; Galatians, LVII,2 p. 14,19; 98,12; Die sieben Busspsalmen (1517), I,188,24.
[108] E.g., Galatians, LVII,2 p.96,23; Romans, LVI,224,22.

justice which He gives us or by which He makes us just.[109]

The most careful discussion, in the Lectures on Romans, of the justice of God as it appears in man makes use of the same ideas which Luther had developed in the Dictata as a commentary on Psalm L (LI), 4.[110] The Psalmist says that God is justified in His words, and Luther had explained that God is so justified when man accepts God's condemnation of him and of all men as sinners. In the Lectures on Romans, Luther again starts from the "justification of God in His words," and he finds three meanings for the phrase. The third, and most important, describes what happens "when He justifies the impious and infuses grace, or when He is believed to be just in His words. By such belief He justifies, that is, reckons (*reputat*) just. Hence this is called the justice of faith and of God." [111] In another draft of the argument, Luther makes essentially the same point when he speaks of the "effective" [112] meaning of God's being justified in His words. This takes place "when we cannot justify ourselves by ourselves, and when we approach Him, so that He may make us just who confess that we cannot conquer sin. God does this when we believe His words. Through such belief He justifies us, that is, He reckons us just. Hence it is called the justice of faith and the justice of God in its effective sense (*effective*)." [113]

Somewhat later Luther develops the same argument more schematically and systematically. "Moreover by God's being justified, we are justified. The passive justification of God, in which He is justified by us, is our active justification by Him, for He reckons just the faith which justifies His words." [114] In this way God makes us like His word, just, true and wise. "Thus He trans-

[109] E.g., Romans, LVI,36,11; 159,2; 172,4; 215,16; 262,19: "Patet similiter ex isto textu, Quod Deus Iustus dicitur Apud Apostolum a Iustificando seu Iustos faciendo. . ."; Sermon (1516), I,84,17; Galatians, LVII,2 p.69,25; Die sieben Busspsalmen (1517), I,192,33; 219,30; Hebrews, LVII,3 pp. 187,5 f.; Auslegung des 109 (110) Psalms (1518), I,703,33; Unbekannte Fragmente (1518?), p. 74,12.

[110] Dictata, III,287,20 f. See above p. 9 and the articles by Loofs cited in note 42. See also Decem praecepta (1518), I,427,31 f.

[111] Romans, LVI,220,9.

[112] For Luther's earlier use of the term, compare Dictata IV,19,37: "Quocirca Christus non dicitur iustitia, pax, misericordia, salus nostra in persona sua nisi effective. Sed fides Christi, qua iustificamur, pacificamur, per quam in nobis regnat." III,114,26; 126,10; 247,35; IV,289,21.

[113] Romans, LVI,221,15.

[114] Ibid., LVI,226,23.

forms us into His word and not His word into us. He makes us such, when we believe His word to be such, that is, just and true. Then there is a like form in the word and in the believer, that is, truth and justice. Hence, as He is justified, He justifies, and as He justifies, He is justified." [115] Finally, the whole process rests on God's grace and gift. "The passive justification of God and the active justification of God and faith or belief (*fides seu credulitas*) in Him are the same, for it is His gift when we justify His words, and because of this same gift He holds us just (*iustos habet*), that is, He justifies us." [116]

Luther can reach similar results from other starting points. He maintains, for example, that "the saints are intrinsically always sinners, and in consequence they are extrinsically always justified." [117] Here "intrinsically" means how we are in ourselves, in our own eyes and estimation; "extrinsically" means how we are before God and in His reckoning (*reputatione*). Or he can explain that "God is marvellous in His saints" (Psalm LXVII (LXVIII), 36), for they are to him at the same time just and unjust. "Since while the saints always have their sin in their sight and beg justice from God in accord with His mercy, by this very fact (*eoipso*), they are also always reckoned just by God." [118]

Luther thus describes the Christian's experience of the justice of God as a phase of his theology of the cross. Our justice is always hidden under its opposite, and we are justified only through the recognition of our sinfulness. Both our justice and our sin are hidden, spiritual realities, and we cannot see or comprehend them. "Just as the justice of God lives in us through faith, so sin lives in us through the same faith, that is, by faith alone are we to believe that we are sinners. . . ." [119]

If the justice of God is experienced primarily as the Christian's recognition of his own sinfulness, what is the justice of God in itself? It is hard to be sure of Luther's final opinion during the 1515–18 period, and he gives his most technical statement of the

[115] Romans, LVI,227,4.
[116] Ibid., LVI,227,18.
[117] Ibid., LVI,268,27.
[118] Ibid., LVI,269,25. Compare Unbekannte Fragmente (1518?), p.44,11 and 85,8; Quaestio de viribus et voluntate hominis sine gratia (1516), I,149,8.
[119] Ibid., LVI,231,8.

problem in the Lectures on Romans in his difficult doctrine of
God's non-imputing of sin and His reckoning (*reputatio, imputatio*) of justice to the Christian. To summarize the doctrine
inadequately, Luther holds that original sin remains in the Christian, but through God's mercy it is not imputed to those who
acknowledge it and resist it.[120] These "justify God in His words,"
and they accordingly have the first form of justice, the confession
of their own sin. Luther describes the justice of God more positively in this context as "that very inclination to good and turning
away from evil, which is given us inwardly by grace."[121] The
Christian with such justice fights against the remnants of sin
within him, and he believes that God will finally free him from all
sin. Such a man God reckons just, and Luther uses "reckoning"
(*imputatio*) to include both the granting of this real, though partial, justice and the acceptance of those who have it as just.[122]
God does not impute to such a man his failure to conquer sin completely in this life, and He will finally justify him completely.

In Luther's more general statements on the justice of God during the years 1515–18, he regularly restates the position which we
have already seen in the Dictata super Psalterium (1513–15),[123]
and he does not advance to the fundamentally different position,
based on the distinction between two realms of Christian existence,
of his mature period.

First of all, in the writings of 1515–18 the justice of God in the
Christian is still a partial justice of the spirit as against a partial
sin of the flesh. "Because of the flesh he is carnal and bad . . .
because of the spirit he is spiritual and good. . . . But since the
same one whole man is constituted by flesh and spirit, therefore

---

[120] On this difficult problem, compare Iwand, op. cit. (note 103, above), Chapter
III.

[121] Romans, LVI,271,11.

[122] Compare, for example, Sermon (1516), I,84,17: ". . . iustitia enim Dei est,
quando iusti sumus ex Deo iustificante et imputante, quae iustitia non consistit
in operibus, sed in fide, spe, charitate"; Disputatio contra scholasticam theologiam
(1517), I,227,4 §57: "Non potest deus acceptare hominem sine gratia dei iustificante. Contra Occam." For a fuller statement, see the Galatians Commentary
(1519), II,511,15: "Quod et verum est, et ideo refertur, ne divina reputatio extra
deum nihil esse putetur. . . ." This passage has no parallel in the Nachschrift of
the Lectures on Galatians (1516–17), but the entire verse is skipped (LVII,2
pp.78–9); it does not appear that the statement of the Commentary of 1519
represents a new idea for Luther.

[123] See pp. 11 f. above.

the whole man receives the contrary (attributes) which come from his contrary parts. Hence we have the sharing of characteristics (*communio ideomatum*), so that the same man is spiritual and carnal, good and bad, just as the one person of Christ was at the same time dead and alive, at the same time suffering and blessed, at the same time working and at rest, etc. . . ." [124]

Hence, while Luther in the Lectures on Romans can say that the Christian is both just and a sinner, he does not intend this as the "total" contrast of his mature period. He means simply that the Christian is partly just and partly a sinner now or that the Christan will be just in the future though a sinner now. Hence he makes frequent use of the story of the good Samaritan, where the wounded man can be described as both ill and well. Similarly the Christian is not completely just "but he is at the same time a sinner and a just man, a sinner in truth (*re vera*) but a just man by the reckoning and certain promise of God. . . . And thus he is entirely healed (*sanus*) in hope, but in fact (*in re*) a sinner, though having the beginning of justice, so that he will always seek it more, since he always knows that he is unjust." [125]

---

[124] Romans, LVI,343,11. Compare 342,33 f.: "Quia eadem persona est spiritus et caro; ideo quod facit carne, totus facere /343 dicitur. Et tamen quia resistit, totus non facere, Sed pars eius etiam recte dicitur. Utrunque ergo verum, Quod ipse et non ipse operatur," 344,31 f. "Et ita secum ipse pugnat, Sed quia spiritus et caro coniunctissime sunt /345 unum, licet diverse sentiant, ideo utriusque opus sibi toti tribuit, quasi simul sit totus caro et totus spiritus." In Romans, LVI, 350,22 f. Luther uses a somewhat different approach, but he reaches the same kind of solution, one which involves a substantive unity which is partially just and partially unjust. He argues here that flesh and spirit are one as the wound and the flesh are one. "Ubi etsi aliud sit proprium vulneris, aliud proprium carnis, tamen quia vulnus et caro unum sunt, et non est aliud quam ipsa vulnerata caro seu infirma, ideo carni tribuitur, quod est vulneris. Sic idem homo simul est spiritus et caro. Sed Caro est eius infirmitas seu vulnus, Et inquantum diligit legem Dei, spiritus est; inquantum autem /351 concupiscit, est infirmitas et vulnus peccati, quod sanari incipit." Compare also Romans, LVI,260,23; 442,15; Galatians, LVII,2 p. 102,14 (Luther here summarizes Augustine with approval); Heidelberg Disputation (1518), Explicatio conclusionis sextae I,369,9.

[125] Romans, LVI,272,16. Luther made some slight use of the analogy of the Samaritan in the Dictata, e.g., III,231,38; IV,398,1. See also Romans, LVI,258,21; 347,12; 351,18 f.; 441,14; 513,12; and Sermon (1517–18?), I,42,29. In part Luther uses the analogy of the Samaritan to say what he can also say in terms of man's division into flesh and spirit; in part he uses the Samaritan for the different contrast between present and future. In neither case does he say that the Christian is totally just now or totally a sinner now, which is what he will say in his mature period in the thesis that the Christian is at the same time just and a sinner. The main secondary accounts of this thesis do not adequately separate Luther's context in Romans from that of his mature period, e.g., R. Hermann,

In the second place, the partial justice or the "beginning of justice" in the present Christian is a real justice, valid even before God. It depends on God's reckoning, but this means that it comes only from grace and that the Christian who has it still needs mercy and forgiveness.[126] It is not a "metaphysical" justice, but this means simply that it is not found on the level of things visible and appearances; it lies hidden under its opposite, and it is known only through the theology of the cross.[127]

In the third place, Luther speaks of human action and work in relation to this justice, and man may be said to be a "co-worker" in it. Thus in a careful statement on grace in the Lectures on Romans, Luther declares that God first gives "operating grace, which he allows to be used and to coöperate, until He begins to infuse another grace, which when it has been infused, he again allows to be coöperating." [128]

Lastly, Luther regularly assumes that the Christian's justice of God is a condition of his future acceptance by God. He remarks in a typical passage, "Therefore if we destroy and persecute ourselves truly (*vero corde*), if we offer ourselves to hell because of God and His justice, then we have satisfied His justice, and He will have mercy and liberate us." [129]

Luthers These 'Gerecht und Sünder zugleich' (Gütersloh, 1930); W. Joest, Gesetz und Freiheit (Göttingen, 1951); Hans Iwand, Glaubensgerechtigkeit nach Luthers Lehre, 2nd ed. (München, 1951).

[126] Compare Romans, LVI,271,20 f.; 268,26 f.; 287,20.

[127] Compare, for example, Romans, LVI,380,31 f. For the meaning of "metaphysics" in such statements where it is contrasted with the apprehension of spiritual reality by intellect or faith, especially in a theology of the cross, see Romans, LVI,334,14; 335,11; Galatians, LVII,2 pp.72,28 f.; Hebrews, LVII,3 p.215,8–14; Unbekannte Fragmente (1518?), p.86,4. Luther seems to intend the same point when in Romans he denies that justice in the scriptures is a "quality"; compare LVI,287,16 with 312,2 f.

For a late statement on the "real" character of an "informing" justice of God, see Hebrews, LVII,3 pp.187,5 f. and spec. 18 f.: ". . . ac sic ipsa /188 divina iustitia sit cordis iustitia quodammodo, ut illi dicunt 'informans,' sicut in Christo humanitas per unionem cum divina natura una et eadem facta est persona."

[128] Romans, LVI,379,13; compare 170,7; 205,29 f.; 249,10; Disputatio contra scholasticam theologiam (1517), §80, I,228,4; Dictata (?1516?), XXXI,1 p. 473,18; Auslegung des 109 (110) Psalms (1518), I,710,5. See also Unbekannte Fragmente (1518?), p. 57,8; Luther is here summarizing Augustine's De spiritu et litera, as in Romans, LVI,256,29 f.; 264,5.

[129] Romans, LVI,393,29. See also 172,3: "Iustitia enim Dei causa est salutis." Compare 227,18 f.; 259,18; 350,9; 419,11; Disputatio contra scholasticam theologiam (1517), §56, I,227,4.

While Luther's general doctrine of the Christian's justice thus remains substantially that of the Dictata super Psalterium, there are also a few passages which point to emerging tensions within this doctrine. As Luther gradually drops his older tropological explanation of the Christian's justice, he can relate the Christian more immediately to Christ and in a few instances this leads to a description of the Christian's justice rather as total than as partial.

Thus in a strong section of the Lectures on Romans, Luther says that the accused sinner turns to Christ and exclaims: "This one did satisfaction, He is just, He is my defense, He died for me. He made His justice mine, and my sin His. And if He made my sin His, then I no longer have it and am free. And if He made His justice mine, then I am now just with the same justice by which He is just. My sin cannot absorb Him, but it is instead absorbed itself into the infinite abyss of Christ's justice." [130] Similarly in Die sieben Busspsalmen (1517), we read: "Christ is God's grace, mercy, justice, truth, strength, comfort and holiness, given to us by God quite apart from any merit. I do not say, as some speak with blind words, that Christ is this causally (causaliter), as if He were to give us justice but to remain Himself outside us. Such justice is dead, and indeed, it is never given except when Christ Himself is there, just as the brightness of the sun or the heat of the fire are never (found) where the sun and the fire are not." [131] Finally, in the Lectures on Galatians (1516–17) Luther connects the concept of justice with the union of the Christian with Christ. Justice, he declares, is usually defined as giving to each his own, but Paul presents the new definition that justice is faith. Luther

[130] Romans, LVI,204,17. In the immediately following scholia on Romans, II,21 Luther presents a typical analysis of the spiritual law which perfects the heart and will, e.g., LVI,205,1: "Sed Apostolus ex hoc aperte indicat se de spirituali doctrina et eruditione legis loqui, qua seipsos non erudiunt, qui alios literaliter docent. Non docent, inquam, seipsos, nedum alios, quod voluntate et puritate cordis sint opera legis facienda, ac per hoc, cum iam nobilior, maior et Deo gratior portio hominis (i.e., cor et voluntas) non assit operi, certe coram Deo nequaquam legem implent, quantumlibet viliorem portionem, i.e., corpus invita et non spontanea voluntate in lege exerceant." For a later passage in which Luther relates "infinite justice" to a justice of the heart, see LVI,234,15–21.

[131] Die sieben Busspsalmen (1517), I,219,30. The position which Luther criticizes closely resembles his own earlier "effective" interpretation; compare the passages cited in notes 112–3, above.

then reconciles the two definitions: "He who is just by faith does not give any one his own through himself but through another, to wit, Christ, who alone is so just that he gives to all what should be given, nay, all things are in debt to him. Therefore, whoever believes in Christ not only satisfies all, but brings it to pass that all are indebted to him, since through faith he is made one with Christ." [132]

Such passages on Christ's infinite justice, on His presence in the Christian, or on the Christian's union with him may seem to threaten the theology of justice which we have so far studied in the Dictata super Psalterium and in the writings of 1515–18. In Luther's own thinking and writings, however, they do not lead to any immediate re-orientation of his thought. To some extent they may be analyzed as a transitional phase connected with the disappearance of Luther's tropological approach, and it is perhaps significant that such passages are more frequent in the Lectures on Romans (1515–16) or on Galatians (1516–17) than in the Lectures on Hebrews (1517–18).[133] More important, it seems that Luther intended even these passages to be placed in the context of the division of man into just spirit and sinful flesh; Christ's infinite justice or the union of the Christian with Christ justifies the Christian's spirit, not the whole Christian, in Luther's thought of 1515–18.[134] Luther's thinking about salvation still assumes the

---

[132] Galatians, LVII,2 p. 69,15. In the following discussion Luther shows that he has no intention of abandoning his general theology of 1515–18. He dwells at some length on faith as universal justice (the section was not incorporated at all in the Galatians Commentary of 1519). Faith is the death of the old man and the life of the new: "Inde propriissimo vocabulo frequenter vocantur anime fidelium absconditae in obscuro, recte corde, in occultis immaculate," p.70,20. Secondly faith is never as great as it should be: "Ideo pro augmento eius operanda sunt bona et cavenda mala," p.70,27. Compare Hebrews, LVII,3 p. 114,2: "Tota itaque substancia nove legis et iusticia eius est unica illa fides Christi. . ." and the analysis of faith pp.151,20 f., where Luther contrasts the substance of this world with that of the future life, 152,10: "Et hanc incipit fides, seu fides est inicium eius, quia per fidem incipimus possidere quod in visione perfecte possidebimus."

For two other passages from 1516–17 illustrating possibly new tensions, see Sermon (1516), I,104,4–25 and Sermon (1517), I,139,34 f.

[133] One may explain the less frequent discussion of the justice of God partly by the different emphasis of the biblical text being commented, but there remains an evident contrast between the discussion of justice, e.g., in Romans, LVI,204,17 and that in Hebrews, LVII,3 pp.110,15–27 or 187,4 f.

[134] It is difficult to prove such a negative thesis. It will be noted that the problem of the historian is not whether the statements in Romans, for example,

substantive unity of man, despite his division into flesh and spirit; he does not yet make use of the approach of his mature theology, according to which the Christian as a whole lives simultaneously in two distinct realms of existence, in Christ and in the world.

In contrast to the "justice of God," "human justice" receives comparatively little attention in the writings of 1515–18. Nevertheless one may detect a tendency to evaluate it more positively than in the Dictata super Psalterium. It is no longer so exclusively connected with the assertion of "one's own justice," and it begins to appear as a true justice, though of course immeasurably inferior to the justice of God.

Luther's systematic starting point is the contrast between the justice of God and the justice of men. "In human doctrine there is revealed and taught the justice of men, that is to say, who, and in what way, is and becomes just before himself and men. Only in the Gospel is there revealed the justice of God, that is to say, who, and in what way, is and becomes just before God, through faith alone, by which God's word is believed." [135] As we have seen,[136] Luther in the Lectures on Romans rarely explains justice in terms of the contrast of image and exemplar, and he usually speaks of human justice simply as a justice of the law or of works in contrast to God's justice of faith or grace.[137]

Luther is then prepared to describe the human justice of works much as Aristotle had done. He speaks, for example, of the "jus-

---

are understandable in the context of Luther's mature theology; most of them are. The question is whether we have any right to read back this mature theology into a period where there is no evidence for it and when all the positive evidence points to the persistence of the general theology which we saw first in the Dictata super Psalterium, and which continues through the 1515–18 period. Isolated statements which seem to imply or affirm this mature theology turn out on closer inspection to be well integrated into Luther's early theology; see for one last example Romans, LVI,347,2: "Vide, ut unus et idem homo simul servit legi Dei et legi peccati, simul Iustus est et peccat. . . . Vide nunc quod supra dixi, Quod simul Sancti, dum sunt Iusti, sunt peccatores; Iusti, quia credunt in Christum, cuius iustitia eos tegit et eis imputatur, peccatores autem, quia non implent legem, non sunt sine concupiscentia, Sed sicut egrotantes sub cura medici, qui sunt re vera egroti, Sed inchoative et in spe sani sunt seu potius sanificati, i.e., sani fientes. . . ."

[135] Romans, LVI,171,27; compare 419,2; Hebrews, LVII,3 p.110,14.
[136] See above, p. 23.
[137] Romans, LVI,414,21; compare 100,22; Galatians, LVII,2 p.98,12; Hebrews, LVII,3 pp.113,21 f. Sometimes Luther contrasts internal and external justice, e.g., Romans, LVI,208,27 f.; Galatians, LVII,2 p. 68,25; Decem praecepta (1518), I,416,28.

tice of men, which comes from works. Just as Aristotle clearly concludes in Book III of the Ethics, for according to him justice follows and comes from acts. But justice according to God precedes works and works come from it." [138] Elsewhere Luther speaks of the acquisition of the justice of faith as "against, or above, Aristotle, since (according to Aristotle) justice is produced from acts, and particularly from external acts frequently repeated. But this is political justice, that is to say, a justice which is spurious before God (*coram Deo*)." [139]

Luther in the Lectures on Romans takes the first steps toward adopting a philosophical classification of the types of justice, but he never develops this very far. He notes, for example, that "the justice of the philosopher is divided into distributive and commutative, and further into general (and particular) justice." [140] It is illustrative of Luther's ambivalent attitude toward human justice during this period that he first attacks such a theory as coming from the blindness of man's mind but that he then suggests as an alternative explanation "or from human wisdom concerned only with the discussion of temporal things according to reason." [141]

During the years 1515–18 Luther still has little to say on the place of human justice in the life of the Christian. In a careful statement in the Lectures on Romans, he explains that we are of course not to avoid just works but simply to destroy our false valuation of them. We should do them zealously "so that through them as preparatory, we may become suited for and capable of the justice of God." [142] Luther's general attitude during these years is well reflected in an argument of the Lectures on Galatians (1516–17). The works of the law are good, and they are to be rejected only because men falsely put their trust in them for salvation. "No man is justified by them, but they are nevertheless so

[138] Romans, LVI,172,8. Compare Romans, LVI,3,13 f.; 273,6; 395,4; Hebrews, LVII,3 p. 188,6; Sermon (1516), I,84,15; Dictata (? 1516 ?), XXXI,1 pp. 465,36 f.; Sermon (1517), I,119,30; Disputatio contra scholasticam theologiam (1517), §40, I,226,8.

[139] Romans, LVI,418,27.

[140] Ibid., LVI,419,2. The Nachschrift of the lectures indicates that Luther intended to contrast general and particular justice, LVII,1, p. 209,9. Compare Romans, LVI,234,15; 448,1; Hebrews, LVII,3 p. 110,15.

[141] Romans, LVI,419,4.

[142] Ibid., LVI,233,27.

necessary that justice cannot stand firm inwardly, unless the works are done outwardly, particularly in the age of youth and in the state of those who are only beginners." [143] Luther goes on to make explicit the suggestion that works of human justice become less important as a person advances in maturity and in Christianity. "Therefore salvation and justice can be had neither without works nor from works, but only along with works, with the qualification, however, that by so much as interior justice grows and makes progress, by so much are external works lessened." [144]

To turn now to the doctrine of law in the period 1515–18, here even more than in the case of justice there are changes of phrasing and emphasis in contrast to the Dictata super Psalterium. But these changes do not, any more than in the case of justice, deny the basic theology of the Dictata nor do they introduce any fundamental re-orientation of Luther's thinking. The factors making for change were both present in the Dictata: on the one hand, the feeling that the Old Law and the New Law are ultimately only one law differently interpreted, and on the other hand, the strong sense of the contrast between any law and grace. But while in the Dictata these factors remained within the context of the theory of the two laws, the literal law and the spiritual law, in the Lectures on Romans and in the following years they supplant this context almost entirely. We shall first notice Luther's treatment of the unity of all law and then consider his development of the sharp contrast between any law and the Gospel or grace.

Luther presents his position on the unity of all law in the Lectures on Romans in the commentary on Romans II,12 f. He here maintains the essential unity of the whole Mosaic law with the natural law and with the Gospel law. Luther first argues that Paul by "the law" refers not merely to the ceremonial law but to the whole Mosaic law, including the Ten Commandments with their love of God and of neighbor. He goes on to assert that the Gentiles, though they lacked the law of Moses itself, possessed the spiritual law signified by the law of Moses. Finally, he identifies the spiritual law with the natural law of the Golden Rule as proclaimed by Christ. "However the Gentiles received the

[143] Galatians, LVII,2 p. 68,21.
[144] Ibid., LVII,2 p. 68,28.

spiritual law, which the Mosaic rites and ceremonies signified morally, and the spiritual law is impressed on all . . . and all are obligated by it. Hence the Lord, Matthew VII: 'All those things which you wish men to do to you, do you also unto them. This is the Law and the Prophets.' See how the whole traditional law (*lex tradita*) is nothing else than this natural law, which is known to everyone, and with respect to which, therefore, no one is excusable." [145] Similarly, in the Lectures on Galatians, Luther warns, "We should be no less cautious in using that most common distinction between the law of nature, the law of scripture, and the law of grace, since Paul here (Galatians V,14) says that they are all fulfilled in one statement. . . . If the laws differ, it is rather by the vice of those interpreting them than by their own functions." [146]

But if one tendency in Luther's thought during 1515–18 thus leads to a virtual identification of what had once been contrasted as the Old Law against the New Law, another tendency so emphasizes the contrast between law and grace that the New Law of the Gospel almost ceases to be a law at all.

Thus in the continuation of the commentary on Romans II,12 f. Luther attempts to explain the difference between the "work of the law written in their hearts" (Romans, II,15) and the "law written in their hearts." He concludes that the first refers to the merely literal law which lacks the grace for its performance. The second, however, means "that charity itself is diffused in their hearts by the Holy Spirit, and this law is properly the law of Christ and the fullness of the law of Moses. Indeed it is a law

---

[145] Romans, LVI,197,19; compare Luther's gloss ibid., 23,8: "Naturaliter enim impressa est menti lex nature. . . ." In the Nachschrift of another gloss, we read, LVII,1 p.25,19: ". . . (gentiles) peccaverunt tamen in lege interiori, viva, et naturali." Compare Romans, LVI,199,21: "quia 'sine lege peribunt' (gentes), sicut sine lege quoque salvabuntur. Si suam legem servassent, que est nata et concreata, non data, Inventa, non tradita, viva, non scripta." For another general discussion of Romans II,14, see Quaestio de viribus et voluntate hominis sine gratia (1516) I,146,29 f.

In other roughly contemporary passages, as throughout his life, Luther identifies the content of natural law with the Golden Rule; compare Quaestio de viribus et voluntate hominis sine gratia (1516), I,149,28; Eine kürze Erklärung der zehn Gebote (1518), I,251,25; I,259,14; Decem Praecepta (1518), I,480,1; 502,20; 503,37.

[146] Galatians, LVII,2 p. 101,3. Luther can also state this as a unity of the Old Law and the New Law; Romans, LVI,408,18; see above pp. 16 f. for parallels in the Dictata.

without law (*lex sine lege*), without mode, without limit, but extended above all those things which the law commands, or can command." [147] Similarly, later in the Lectures on Romans, Luther starts from his familiar contrast between the Old Law and the New Law, but in his conclusion he again comes close to denying that the New Law is a law at all. "This is the proper distinction between the Old Law and the New Law. The Old Law says to those who are proud in their own justice: You ought to have Christ and His spirit. The New Law says to the humble, who seek Christ in their poverty: Behold, here *is* Christ and His spirit. Therefore, whoever takes the Gospel in any other way than as the Good News does not understand the Gospel, as those fail to understand it who have made it into a law rather than grace and who have made Christ into a Moses toward us." [148]

Luther's most careful systematic statements on the relation between the Law and the Gospel turn on the contrast between the letter and the spirit. In the Dictata super Psalterium, as we have seen,[149] Luther had frequently interpreted this contrast by the scheme of figure and reality, whether in terms of an original analogy or in terms of a paradoxical theology of the cross. In the period 1515–18, however, he comes more and more to emphasize the contrast, after Augustine, between the letter as the law without grace and the spirit as grace without the law.

Luther so compares the two laws in the Lectures on Galatians. "Therefore the law of the spirit is that which is not written with any letters, nor set forth in any words, nor thought with any concepts, but it is the true living will itself and the experienced life 'written by the finger of God' that is, by the Holy Spirit, 'in our hearts,' Romans V, that is to say, the whole of justice at once, both within and without. . . . But the law of the letter is that

---

[147] Romans, LVI,203,9. During this period, Luther regularly identifies the *lex Christi* or the *lex spiritus* with *charitas*. Compare his glosses in Romans, LVI,72,10: ". . . *legi mentis meae*, i.e., charitati, que est lex spiritualis, immo spiritus," 72,29 f. "(charitas et concupiscentia) sunt leges vive ambe." 74,9: "*lex enim spiritus* . . . i.e., charitas diffusa in cordibus per spiritum sanctum." Hebrews, LVII,3 p. 39,17: "Haec autem est lex Christi, i.e., charitas, non scripta in libris, sed 'diffusa in cordibus per spiritum sanctum'." Resolutiones disputationum de indulgentiarum virtute (1518), I,580,31; Disputatio contra scholasticam theologiam (1517), §84, I,228,11.

[148] Romans, LVI,336,27 f. Compare Sermon (1518) I,333,30.

[149] See above, p. 14.

which is written with letters, or said with words, or thought with concepts, without the will delighting in it. Hence it is the law of sin and death, for it neither justifies nor gives life, but kills and unjustifies." [150]

As a consequence of this approach, much that in the Dictata super Psalterium has been regularly assumed to be the spiritual law, now becomes the law of the letter. Luther argues in the Lectures on Romans, for example: "The 'letter' in Paul is not merely a figurative passage in Scripture or the doctrine of the Law, but any doctrine whatsoever which commands those things which are of the good life, whether the doctrine be evangelical or Mosaic." [151] Hence, maintains Luther, the spiritual interpretation of the Bible deals only with charity and with man's basic disposition (*affectus*), with man's love of justice and hate of iniquity.[152] A law is not spiritual because it deals with things spiritual as against things fleshly; what is spiritual is simply man's willing and cheerful acceptance of a law in his heart and spirit. Consequently, says Luther, when Paul in I Corinthians XIII speaks of knowing all mysteries and of having all knowledge and faith, but without charity, "it follows clearly that the mysteries and the whole Gospel and all spiritual understanding is 'the letter.' Since if they are dead, they are without the spirit. 'For the spirit gives life, and the letter kills.' But they are killed, and therefore are in the letter." [153]

While Luther does not explicitly discuss the law of nature as a law of the letter, he comes to feel that it by itself can no more lead men to salvation than can the law of Moses. Thus in the Lectures on Romans, in the course of an attack on man's power of free choice, he observes: "Hence our breath reeks of philosophy, as if reason always urged the best; and we do a great deal of idle talking (*fabulamur*) about the law of nature. It is indeed true that the law of nature is known to all and that reason urges the best. But what best? Not according to God, but according

---

[150] Galatians, LVII,2 p.73,15. Compare the passages cited in note 145, above, and Decem Praecepta (1518), I,461,24 f.

[151] Romans, LVI,336,25.

[152] Ibid., LVI,337,10.

[153] Ibid., LVI,337,28; compare Galatians, LVII,2 p.96,13; Decem Praecepta (1518), I,461,3–467,18.

to us, that is, it urges the best badly, since it seeks itself and its own in all things and not God, who is sought only by faith in charity." [154]

Ultimately, Luther's new position on the letter and the spirit dissolves the concept of a separate spiritual law as presented in the Dictata super Psalterium. We have seen that the law of the spirit, when identified with charity, is hardly a law at all or only in a metaphorical sense as a "law without law." [155] On the other hand, when Luther speaks of law in the strict sense, he can no longer set up a contrast between a law which is spiritual and one which is not. We have seen him argue that no law as such is spiritual because all lack grace. From another standpoint, however, Luther can maintain that every law is spiritual because all demand grace. He remarks in the Lectures on Galatians: "Therefore every law is at the same time letter and also spiritual, since it is without grace and yet it signifies grace." [156] "The law of the spirit is that which the law of the letter demands, to wit, the will, that is, charity. . . ." [157]

Luther in the period 1515–18 is mainly interested, among the various possibilities of his theory of law, in working out the doctrine that all law condemns and that the law of the spirit, or the spiritual law, condemns most totally. At times he states this as a paraphrase of Paul and in terms not too different from those of the Dictata super Psalterium: "The law does nothing but to show sin and to make men guilty and to make anxious the conscience; the Gospel tells the longed for remedy to those who are thus anxious. Hence the Law announces evils, the Gospel goods, the Law wrath and the Gospel peace." [158] At other times Luther develops these ideas in the specific terminology of the spiritual law. Thus in the Lectures on Hebrews he points out that while it is quite true that the ceremonial law was the "force of sin" (I Corinthians XV,56), he adds: "Thus by much more the true spiritual law of the Decalogue itself was 'the force of sin.' " [159]

---

[154] Romans, LVI,355,13; compare Decem Praecepta (1518), I,426,25.

[155] See above, pp. 34 f.

[156] Galatians, LVII,2 p.96,17.

[157] Ibid., LVII,2 p.73,25. Compare Sermon (1516), I,106,6.

[158] Romans, LVI,424,8; compare 426,6; Galatians, LVII,2 p.80,22; Heidelberg Disputation (1518), I,355,30 f.

[159] Hebrews LVII,3 p.211,8; compare Sermon (1516), I,114,33–8.

But if the spiritual law kills and condemns, then Luther must rethink his older ideas on the relation of the spiritual law to the Gospel. In the Dictata, Luther had worked with a simple contrast; there was a Mosaic law of the letter without grace, and there was a spiritual law of the Gospel with grace.[160] But now he has developed the idea of a law which is the more condemning as it becomes more spiritual. How is this related to the old Law and how is it related to Gospel grace?

We find a preliminary statement in the Lectures on Galatians where Luther faces the obvious question: why should a Gospel of grace contain so much of what appears to be moral and legal exhortation? In his reply, Luther begins with his contrast of 1515–18 between the Law and the Gospel; the Law preaches things to be done and omitted, while the Gospel preaches the remission of sins and the accomplished fulfilment of the Law.[161] But Christ in the Gospel also exercised another, though less important, office. He did and taught many things "for the sake of a clearer knowledge of the law and, in consequence, of a greater knowledge of sin, so that grace might be sought more ardently and be given more generously and be preserved more diligently, by so much more as sin was more profoundly known." [162]

In some Sermons on the Decalogue, roughly contemporary with the Lectures on Galatians (1516–17), Luther develops an explicit theory of a double office of the Gospel. He begins by explaining that we must not understand the Gospel, as many do, to consist of commands for living in the New Law.[163] It is true that the Gospel has a double office or function, and that in the first place it includes the spiritual interpretation of the Old Law in contrast to its merely literal meaning. "Moreover this spiritual understanding of the Law kills all the more, for it makes the Law impossible of fulfilment, and in consequence it makes man desperate and humbled in his own forces." [164] But as against this alien office of

---

[160] See above, pp. 20 f.

[161] Galatians, LVII,2 p.59,18 f.

[162] Ibid., LVII,2 p. 60,10.

[163] Sermon (1516), I,105,3.

[164] Ibid., I,105,14. Compare a later Sermon of the same series, I,108,13: "Haec autem sunt mysteria, quia spiritualis intelligentia legis, quae est Evangelium, erudit homines ad perfectissimam cognitionem peccati. . . ."

An interesting letter of M. Bucer, in which he describes the Heidelberg Disputa-

the Gospel, its proper and essential office is that it offers grace; it announces to the desperate conscience the Good News of help and comfort.

Thus in the period 1515–18, Luther introduces extensive changes in his terminology of law, notably in connection with the spiritual law. In the Dictata super Psalterium, despite some other emphases, Luther remains generally faithful to the scheme of the two laws as a framework for thinking about the Old Testament and the New Testament, and for all the contrasts between them, they are comparable as laws. But in the period 1515–18 Luther tends more and more to take the Law and the Gospel as opposites, on the one hand, the law without grace, and on the other, grace without the law. Hence the crucial early concept of the spiritual law of the Gospel virtually disappears. As identical with the Gospel, it ceases to be a law in any precise sense; as a law, it kills and damns all the more as it becomes more spiritual.

These changes are significant, but they must not be over-emphasized; it will be remembered that the dynamic factor, the sharp contrast between the Law and the Gospel, is an inheritance from the Dictata. Luther in his doctrine of law, as in his doctrine of justice, develops and expands the basic theology of the Dictata super Psalterium, but he does not during the period 1515–18 break through to the fundamentally different theology of his mature period. God through His law, as through His justice, makes demands upon man which the sinner cannot meet. God through the law of the spirit, which is charity, as through the justice of God or of faith, enables man to meet these demands at least partially; as a God of mercy, He will not impute to the believer his failure to meet them completely.

Thus the "law of the spirit" remains within the same context as the "justice of God." It is a law which demands and contains a real grace, which may be identified with charity or justice or faith.[165] In the Lectures on Romans Luther characterizes the

---

tion of 1518, suggests that by this time Luther was very cautious in speaking of a "new law." Bucer is summarizing what Luther had to say of the "lex spiritus," and he describes it as an entelechy divinely flowing into the human mind; he continues, "eam ipsam appellari quoque subinde gratiam, nonnumquam fidem, legem vitae, legem spiritus, ac etiam novam legem." IX,163,4.

[165] See the passages cited in note 147, above, and Hebrews, LVII,3 p. 114,2.

spiritual law as that which "requires the heart and the will," [166] and similarly in the Lectures on Hebrews, he declares, "It is not enough for the law to be said 'objectively' in the mind (that is, as an object of knowledge) but it must also be there 'formally' (that is, as the form of the mind), that is to say, through love of the law, the law should be written in the heart." [167]

In summary, Luther during the period 1515–18 makes no fundamental break with the thought of the Dictata super Psalterium (1513–15) either in his general theology or in his ideas of justice and of law. Nevertheless one can see, particularly in the case of justice, some signs of emerging tensions. For example, Luther is convinced that in some way the Christian is the recipient of a justice of Christ which in its infinity can swallow up all sin; he is also convinced that the Christian in some way remains a very real sinner. It does not appear that his theology of 1513–18 can give a coherent and unified statement of these two cardinal convictions. But if we can observe the emergence of such tensions in Luther's thought, the writings of 1515–18 do not tell us in what way, if at all, the tensions will be finally resolved.

[166] Romans, LVI,264,31. Compare ibid., 205,1; 334,3; Decem Praecepta (1518), I,447,23; 499,32.
[167] Hebrews LVII,3 p. 196,17.

CHAPTER II

THE GENERAL RE-ORIENTATION OF 1518–19
AND LUTHER'S MATURE POSITION.

OUR PROBLEM now is to describe the new orientation of Luther's thought which begins to appear toward the end of 1518 and which finally leads both to a new general theology and also to new ideas of justice, law, and of society.

It must immediately be admitted that the problem is one of exceptional difficulty. As already noted, many scholars deny the validity of any basic distinction between the "young" and the "old" Luther; those who have asserted such a distinction have been unable to agree on the dividing line between the two periods.[1]

Our main difficulties result from the nature of the re-orientation itself. As we have seen in a preliminary summary, Luther toward 1518–19 begins to think in terms of the simultaneity of two distinct realms of Christian existence, but this development, for all its crucial importance, has a number of negative characteristics which complicate its historical analysis. In the first place, the re-orientation does not immediately produce a new set of propositions which deny or modify the older propositions of 1513–18. What happens in most cases is rather that the same propositions take on new meanings as they are related to one or the other of the new realms of existence. In the second place, the re-orienta-

---

[1] Compare the survey by Link, cited in note 6, Chapter I, above. See also the later survey in U. Saarnivaara, Luther Discovers the Gospel (St. Louis, 1951); the present essay accepts the general thesis of Saarnivaara on the date of Luther's new insight into Romans I,17 and his refutation of modern attempts to place it during the time of the Dictata super Psalterium (1513–15) or of the Lectures on Romans (1515–16). Of the various attempts to state the contrast between the "young" and the "old" Luther, perhaps the most significant is the special study of Hans Thimme, Christi Bedeutung für Luthers Glauben, unter Zugrundelegung des Römerbrief–, des Hebräerbrief–, des Galaterbriefkommentars von 1531 und der Disputationen (Gütersloh, 1933); see also the introductory remarks in Günter Jacob, Der Gewissensbegriff in der Theologie Luthers (Beiträge zur historischen Theologie IV), Tübingen, 1929. For the denial of the distinction between the "young" and the "old" Luther, see note 3, Chapter I, above.

tion does not make any sharp break within the writings of 1518–19. The signs of the change appear at different times in different areas of Luther's thinking, and it does not appear that the earlier signs are necessarily causally or logically antecedent to the later. To use inadequate language, the change appears as the breaking through at various points of the same "unconscious" dynamic into the conscious, propositional structure of Luther's thought. In the third place, Luther in 1518–19 and in the immediately following years does not have any terminology by which he can make the general change explicit. Once Luther, by about 1522, has worked out a new doctrine of justification, he evidently feels that this is enough for the time being, and not until about 1530 does he turn to the elaboration of an over-all statement of his position.

Scholars have perhaps increased the difficulties of our problem by trying to define and solve it too exclusively in terms of Luther's own autobiographical remarks, such as those of the Preface of 1545. Doubtless such remarks help to suggest what we should look for, and they should help to confirm our findings. But the comparable problem of Augustine's development offers an instructive parallel, and it warns us against using Luther's mature statements as a direct description of his early thought. Augustine in the Confessiones of 400 A.D. evaluates his early experiences of 386–87 A.D. in the light of a theology not fully realized until a decade after these experiences. Similarly Luther looks back to 1518–19 in the light of his more clearly developed position of 1530. As we cannot use Augustine's Confessiones directly to describe his thought of 386–87, so we cannot, for example, use Luther's Preface of 1545 to describe his thought of 1518–19. In each case the early writings are our primary source for the author's early thought.

How then are we to relate the evidence of Luther's early writings to that of his later autobiographical reminiscences? [2] Broadly speaking, the two bodies of evidence are compatible but not identical, and to combine them is a delicate task. First, Luther in his recollections from about 1530 on clearly felt that a new insight

---

[2] The following remarks can do no more than to suggest the hypotheses adopted for the present essay; despite the useful work of Saarnivaara, cited in the preceding note, it is still difficult to interpret the Preface of 1545 in detail.

into the meaning of the "justice of God" was the copestone of his theological development.[3] The writings of 1518–22 do not speak of this event (if indeed it was an "event"), and they show that in any case the new insight was not on the propositional level and did not immediately produce a new theology. Secondly, Luther in his later recollections regularly identifies his new insight with the concept of "passive" justice.[4] The phrase "passive justice" is not found in the writings of 1518–22, and the concept is not developed systematically until the Lectures on Galatians (1531). In the Lectures, however, the contrast between passive, Christian justice and active, civil justice is a paradigm for the general distinction between the two realms of Christian existence. On this point, therefore, Luther in the Preface of 1545, for example, is accurately describing his re-orientation of 1518–19 but he is doing so in terminology not accessible to him until considerably later. Lastly, Luther in the Preface of 1545 dates his new insight toward 1518–19, and it is at this time that we find the first clear signs of the distinction between the two realms of Christian existence.[5]

We have had occasion to mention the distinction between Luther's statement of his position in the writings of 1518–22 and the later, more general statement which is first found toward 1530. The two statements are significantly different in form and terminology, and we shall regularly treat them separately. It should be

[3] It is unfortunate that the discussion of Luther's new insight into the meaning of Romans I,17 has been placed under the rubric "initium theologiae Lutheri." Luther himself regularly presents this not as a beginning but as a culmination of his development. Thus in the Preface of 1545, for example, he clearly indicates an important earlier stage: LIV,183,25: "Ego, qui iam tunc sacras literas diligentissime privatim et publice legeram et docueram per septem annos, ita ut memoriter paene omnia tenerem, deinde primitias cognitionis et fidei Christi hauseram, scilicet, non operibus, sed fide Christi nos iustos et salvos fieri. . . ." Compare Commentary on Genesis (1535-45), XLIII,537,12; TR §335 (1532), I,136,14; §5518 (1542-43), V,210,7.

[4] See Commentary on Genesis, XLIV,485,25 f.; Preface to the Opera Latina (1545), LIV,186,6. As E. Hirsch has shown op. cit. (note 32, Chapter I), II,16, the technical phrase "iustitia passiva" is first found in De servo arbitrio (1525), XVIII,768,36. The first full theological development of the concept is found in the Lectures on Galatians (1531), on which, see below Chapter II, pp. 61 f. and Chapter III, pp. 91 f.

[5] This appears the most natural interpretation of Luther's Latin. For a detailed discussion, see E. Stracke, Luthers grosses Selbstzeugnis 1545 über seine Entwicklung (Schriften des Vereins für Reformationsgeschichte, Nr. 140), Leipzig, 1926.

noted, however, that the appearance of a more general statement
toward 1530 does not involve any fundamental re-orientation like
that of 1518–19. Roughly speaking, Luther by 1522 was in possession of the main "parts" of his theology. What he then lacked,
and what he began to gain toward 1530, was simply a coherent
conceptual framework within which these parts could be explicitly
related and harmonized.

Let us now turn to the details of Luther's development in 1518–
19 and later. We shall begin, in the present chapter, with the
changes in his general theology and in his theory of justification.
We shall then in the following chapters notice the more specific
changes in his ideas of justice, law, and society.

As we have already noted, Luther in the writings of 1518–22
does not work out an explicit statement of a new general theology
in terms of the distinction between the two realms of Christian
existence. What happens is rather that he begins to imply such
a distinction in various special phases of his thought and that he
eventually develops a theory of justification which depends on it.

Three examples may illustrate the way in which Luther in the
period 1518–22 modifies his ideas of 1513–18 because he now
assumes a new distinction between two realms of Christian existence. The first deals with the relation between "grace" and "gift"
in Romans V,15; the second has to do with the relation between
"flesh" and "spirit" in man; and the third, the most important,
involves the new sense in which good works are also sins, the just
man also a sinner.

Paul in Romans V,15 uses two phrases, "the grace of God" and
"the gift in grace"; he does not specially emphasize them, and
he does not explicitly identify or distinguish them. "For if through
the offence of one, many be dead, by much more the grace of God
and the gift in grace (*gratia Dei et donum in gratia*) of one man,
Jesus Christ, abounded to many." Luther comments on the passage with some care in the Lectures on Romans (1515–16); he
concludes that grace and gift are the same. He discusses the passage again in the Rationis Latomianae confutatio (1521); he
concludes that the two are separate and distinct. The separation
of 1521 reflects a new distinction between man's total justification

or condemnation on the one hand, and on the other the gradual sanctification of the Christian.

In the Lectures on Romans Luther admits that Paul appears to separate "grace" and "gift." He argues, however, that Paul does this simply so that he can clearly show that "while we are justified of God and accept grace, this grace we do not receive by our merit, but it is a gift which the Father gave to Christ to give to men." [6] After his analysis of the text Luther concludes: "Moreover, 'the grace of God' and 'the gift' are the same, that is to say, the very justice which is freely given through Christ." [7] The conclusion reflects Luther's general position in the 1513–18 period. The justice of God, by which He makes us just in this life, is not to be separated from the justice by which we are justified before Him.

Luther considers the relation between grace and gift again in 1521, in a subtle and powerful section of the Rationis Latomianae confutatio.[8] The context of the argument is the basic distinction between the Law and the Gospel as God's two ways of dealing with sin. The Law reveals sin and points out its two evils; the first is internal, the sin itself and the corruption of our nature, while the second is external, the wrath of God.[9] The Gospel, in contrast, frees us from the two evils of sin, and it grants us two corresponding goods, an internal good which is justice or faith and an external good which is the grace of God. Luther in the 1513–18 period would have identified justice or faith with the grace of God, but he now separates them as he had separated the two evils of sin. Justice, or faith, heals the corruption of our nature, while the grace of God, or His favor, frees us from His wrath.

Luther then applies these distinctions to Romans V,15 and to the relation between grace and gift. "Faith is an internal gift and a good opposed to sin, which it drives out (*expurgat*). . . . But the grace of God is an external good, the favor of God, which is opposed to His wrath. These two he (Paul) thus distinguished in

---

[6] Romans, LVI,318,13. It appears that Luther still maintains this interpretation in the Galatians Commentary (1519), II,511,15.

[7] Romans, LVI,318,28.

[8] Rationis Latomianae confutatio, VIII,103,35 ff. For a detailed analysis of the argument, see Hermann, op. cit. (note 129, Chapter I), pp.75 f.

[9] Ibid., VIII,103,35.

Romans V,15. . . ." [10] Luther makes the further important point
that while God's gifts are divisible and divided, His grace is necessarily total. "Hence it follows that these two, God's wrath and
His grace, have this characteristic that since they are external to
us, they are applied to one of us as a whole, so that whoever is
under wrath, is wholly under wrath, whoever is under grace is
wholly under grace, for wrath and grace look to the persons. . . .
God does not divide His grace as He divides His gifts. . . . The
just and faithful man without doubt possesses both God's grace
and His gift: the grace which makes him totally graced (*quae eum
totum gratificet*), so that the person is entirely accepted . . . and,
on the other hand, the gift, which heals him of sin and from the
total corruption of his soul and body." [11]

Thus by 1521 Luther has moved away from his earlier theology,
where grace and gift were discussed as equivalent, to a new approach where grace and faith still both apply to the Christian but
where grace is in a "realm" of totality, while gift, along with faith
and justice, is in a realm of the divisible and the partial.

A second illustration of the general change in Luther's thinking
may be found in his different treatment of the contrast between
flesh and spirit before and after 1518–19. To a first approximation, flesh and spirit in the period 1513–18 remain within a single
substantive context which, in modern language, can be charac-
terized as both anthropological and religious. After 1518–19 the
two aspects begin to be distinguished, and one can often separate
an anthropological from a religious statement. There are now two
contexts, and "flesh" and "spirit" have different meanings as they
are applied in the one or the other.

In the period 1513–18 Luther in the Dictata super Psalterium

---

[10] Ibid., VIII,106,20.

[11] Ibid., VIII,106,37. For a similar comparison see Preface to Romans (1522),
Bibel VII,8,10; while the distinction is not important in Luther's later thought,
he appears to have maintained the special exegesis of Romans V,15 which is here
involved; see Enarratio Psalmi LI (1532), XL,2 pp.421,1 f.

It is worth noting that the distinction between grace and gift as total and
partial appears to have emerged independently of Luther's new direction of thought
about justification (see below. pp. 54 f.). Thus in the Rationis Latomianae confutatio, where Luther discusses grace and gift, he remarks VIII,106,6: "Huic fidei
et iustitiae comes est gratia seu misericordia." Later, when he discusses the problem
from the explicit context of justification, he argues VIII,114,18 f. that grace is
always primary and gift secondary (see also below, Chapter III, pp. 89 f.).

regularly takes flesh and spirit as anthropological terms for the two parts of man. At the same time he uses the terms religiously, for sin has destroyed man's spirit and God justifies him by restoring it.[12] In the later years of the Pauline commentaries (1515–18), Luther of course continues to use the division into flesh and spirit, but he now prefers the tripartite division into flesh, soul (or reason), and spirit. If necessary, he can reconcile the two divisions by pointing out that the soul or reason in the triple division belongs on the side of the flesh in the double division.[13]

In the writings of 1518–19 Luther in his discussion of flesh and spirit begins, though not always clearly, to imply a new distinction between two realms of existence. Thus in the Galatians Commentary (1519) Luther notes the triple division which some have found in Paul, and he explains how this may be reduced to the simpler division into flesh and spirit. More important, he goes on to explain how the whole triple division constitutes a unity on the human or anthropological level. "I in my temerity do not at all separate flesh, soul (*animam*), and spirit, for the flesh does not lust except through the soul (*animam*) and spirit, by which it lives. On the other hand, I understand by spirit and flesh the whole man, especially the soul." [14] So far Luther has modified his ideas of the early period by reducing spirit and flesh to an anthropological unity. In the remainder of the argument he tries to relate this unity to the religious dualism between spirit and flesh.

[12] See above, Chapter I, pp. 11 f.

[13] For the triple division, see Sermon (1515), I,26,4; Marginalia to Tauler (1516), IX,103,39 f.; Romans LVI,480,18 with 476,5; Galatians LVII,2 pp.77,25 f.; Hebrews, LVII,3 pp. 158,18 f.; 163,3; 196,22 f.

On Luther's "psychology," valuable material will be found in H. Bornkamm, "Äusserer und innerer Mensch bei Luther und den Spiritualisten," in Festschrift G. Krüger (Giessen, 1932), 85–109; E. Schott, Fleisch und Geist nach Luthers Lehre (Leipzig, 1928); idem, "Luthers Anthropologie und seine Lehre von der manducatio oralis in wechselseitiger Beleuchtung," Zeitschrift für systematische Theologie 9 (1932), 585–602.

[14] Galatians Commentary (1519), II,585,31. When Luther in the Commentary of 1519 first comes to the place where he had discussed the problem in the Lectures of 1516–17, he postpones the question (II,510,2 = LVII,2 pp.77,25 f.); compare Operationes in Psalmos (1519–21), V,207,34 f. For Luther's new position compare also Resolutiones Lutherianae super propositionibus suis Lipsiae disputatis, 1519 (henceforth cited as Resolutiones (1519)), II,415,6: "Causa erroris est, quod subiectum gratiae dant solam animam eiusque nobiliorem partem, Deinde quod carnem et spiritum distinguunt metaphysice tanquam duas partes, cum totus homo sit spiritus et caro, tantum spiritus quantum diligit legem Dei, tantum caro quantum odit legem Dei."

He argues that the same man, the same soul, the same spirit of man (all of this is on the anthropological level) is spirit, so far as he loves the things of God, or flesh, so far as he is moved by the desires of the flesh (the contrast between spirit and flesh is now intended on the religious level). But when such a religious dualism of spirit and flesh is applied to an anthropological unity, man can no longer as in the early period be described as "partly" spirit and "partly" flesh. In a brief exclamation Luther foreshadows his later "total" contrast. "Thus there are two whole men and one whole man (*Sunt duo toti homines et unus totus homo*), and so it happens that a man fights with himself and is contrary to himself, wills and does not will." [15]

Luther presents a comparable argument in Das Magnificat ver-deutschet (1521). He comments on the statement of Mary: "My soul doth magnify the Lord" (Luke I,46). He mentions the Pauline triple division of man into spirit, soul, and body, and he adds: "Each of these, along with the whole man, is also divided in a different manner into two parts (*stück*), which are called spirit and flesh. This division is not in terms of nature, but in terms of property (*eygenschaff*), that is to say, the nature (of man) has three parts, spirit, soul, and body; all of these parts may be good or bad, which means to be flesh or spirit, but it is not now the time to speak of this." [16] Here one sees the same tendencies as in the Galatians Commentary (1519). Luther is separating an anthropological description of man (for which he uses the triple division) from a religious account of his justification or damnation (for which he uses the double division between spirit and flesh).

Luther reaches further clarity in the Rationis Latomianae confutatio (1521) where he concludes that one and the same man may be said to be both spiritual and fleshly, but from different aspects. Luther here wrestles once more with the interpretation of Romans VII: what can the holy Paul mean by calling himself carnal or fleshly? Luther first offers a solution in the manner of his early theology. Paul does not mean to say that he is wholly carnal; he is carnal by his flesh and he is spiritual by his mind.

[15] Galatians Commentry (1519), II,586,16. There are parallels to the first part of the argument in Romans LVI,350,22 f., cited in note 124, Chapter I, above.

[16] Das Magnificat verdeutschet (1521), VII,550,23. Compare W. Maurer, Von der Freiheit eines Christenmenschen (Göttingen, 1949), p.93.

He goes on, however, to rephrase this solution so as to place it within the context of his general re-orientation of 1518–19. The reader, says Luther, should not be confused by Latomus and suppose that Paul is simply speaking of his two wills. "There is one man, Paul, who confesses both of himself, but under two different aspects (*alio et alio respectu*). Under grace he is spiritual and under the Law he is carnal, but it is the one and the same Paul in each case." [17] Here we see more clearly than in any of the earlier passages that Luther is abandoning his earlier approach to man as a substantive unity, partly just and partly sinful, but not sinful where he is just nor just where he is sinful. God regards the whole man in two ways, through grace and through the Law. Under the first aspect man is spiritual, under the second carnal, but it is one and the same man in each case.

Thus Luther's new treatment of flesh and spirit, like his new treatment of grace and gift, illustrates the emergence within his thinking of a distinction between two "realms of existence," even though the distinction as such is not made explicit. What we see is simply that terms and propositions which had once been applied within the single context of man as a substantive unity are now given new meanings according as they are applied in one or the other of two new contexts. "Grace" refers now to the total context of God's favor or wrath; "gift" refers to the different, partial context of God's gradual healing of man's sin. Or, as in Das Magnificat verdeutschet, "spirit" means one thing when it points to a part of man's nature, something else when it says whether that nature is good or bad in God's sight. Or, perhaps most important of all, the proposition "Paul is carnal" is true, but in the context of the law; the proposition "Paul is spiritual" is also true about one and the same Paul, but in the context of grace.

The third illustration of the general change in Luther's thought is found in his new solution to the problem of the relation between good works and sin. Luther's first position here, as expressed in anti-scholastic polemic, is that good works are sins

---

[17] Rationis Latomianae confutatio, VIII,119,14; compare 91,37: "Nam idem prorsus est motus irae et libidinis in pio et impio, idem ante gratiam et post gratiam, sicut eadem caro ante gratiam et post gratiam."

apart from grace.[18] Toward the latter part of the period 1513–18
he begins to emphasize that even good works done in grace are
at least partially sins.[19] Finally in 1518–19 and the following
years, he moves to a fundamentally new positon: even the good
works done in grace are, from a different aspect, sins, and even the
just Christian is, from a different aspect, a sinner.

Luther struggles with the problem a number of times in 1518–
19 and moves gradually to greater clarity. In the so-called Explicatio conclusionis sextae, connected with the Heidelberg Disputation of 1518,[20] Luther argues that the just man sins even
while doing good (*inter bene operandum*). In the course of the
argument Luther tries to reconcile the biblical texts which assert
the sinfulness of all men with the other texts which assert that the
justified do no sin (e.g., I John III,9 as against I,8). Luther concludes that, contrary to human reason, the same act is both accepted by God and not accepted (*acceptatus — deacceptatus*). [21]
It is accepted, since God in His mercy ignored what was not acceptable; it is not accepted in sin, insofar as it is done from the
wickedness of the flesh. Meanwhile, until God shall perfect us,
we live in the protection and shade of His wings. "And thus God
accepts His mercy in our works, that is, the countenance of Job
(Job XLII,8), to wit, the justice of Christ on our behalf. Christ
is the atonement (*propitiatorium*) of God, who excuses our works
and makes them possible to overlook (*ignoscibilia*), so that what
is lacking in us, we supply by His fullness." [22]

[18] E.g., Quaestio de viribus et voluntate hominis sine gratia (1516), I,146,26 f.;
Disputatio contra scholasticam theologiam (1517), §76 I,227,35; Hebrews, LVII,3
p. 208,7.

[19] E.g., Romans, LVI,289,7.

[20] Heidelberg Disputation (1518), I,367,2 ff. For the literary history of this
"explicatio conclusionis sextae," see Vogelsang in Luthers Werke in Auswahl (note
9, Chapter I, above), Vol. V,375–6. There is a closely parallel argument in Resolutiones Lutherianae super propositionibus suis Lipsiae disputatis (1519), II,410,35 f.
Luther here is somewhat more explicit that the prophet when he condemns all our
justices is also condemning that of grace and faith, e.g. II,411,12: "Sed verba
prophetae sunt manifesta: loquitur enim in persona sua et totius fidelis populi, qui
non iustitia legis, sed gratiae iusti erant. . . ."

[21] Heidelberg Disputation (1518), I,370,14 f. Compare the Resolutiones of
1519, II,420,17.

[22] Ibid., I,370,27 f. The passage from Job, which occurs in several discussions
of the problem, reads in the Vulgate, XLII,8: ". . . Job autem, servus meus,
orabit pro vobis. Faciem ejus suscipiam, ut non vobis imputetur stultitia; neque
enim locuti estis ad me recta, sicut servus meus Job."

A comparable discussion is found in the important Sermo de triplici iustitia, from some time in 1518,[23] and Luther alludes to some of the same Old Testament passages. He here starts from the difficulty that the Christian is supposed both to flee God's judgment and yet also to have confidence that his works are pleasing to God. "What then should we do? How can we at the same time both pray to escape judgment and yet also seek glory? In reply: the Cherubim instruct us with their opposing faces. The Cherubim are opposed in their countenances, but they agree in their regard to the place of atonement (*propitiatorium*). And so these biblical authorities which are contrary in themselves agree in Christ. Hence our works, if looked at in themselves, are sins, and you should accordingly pray to escape judgment, that is you should pray that your works be not examined in themselves without Christ. On the other hand, you should be confident that in Christ those very works are pleasing to God which by themselves cannot please Him." [24] Here again Luther has reached a position which clearly implies two distinct realms of existence. He no longer emphasizes the fact that our works are partly good and partly sinful or that all our works are finally accepted only through God's mercy. His point is rather that the same good works, even the works of grace, are in themselves and apart from Christ sins, but in Christ they are acceptable and pleasing to God.

Luther develops his thought further in the Galatians Commentary (1519), and he now extends the two realms of existence to persons as well as acts. He starts from much the same biblical texts as in the De triplici iustitia: the apparent conflict between I John I,8 and III,9 or between Job's calling himself a sinner and God's calling him truthful and just. "It must be that Job spoke the truth, for if he lied before God, then God would not pronounce him just. Therefore he was at the same time a just man and at the same time a sinner. (*Simul ergo iustus, simul peccator*). Who will resolve these countenances which contradict one another, or in what do they agree? Namely in the place of atonement, where the faces of the Cherubim, otherwise opposite to one another, are

[23] The date of the Sermo de triplici iustitia cannot be fixed precisely; it was published in 1518 and was probably written toward the end of the year. See II,41 for a discussion of the problem.

[24] II,46,26. In his earlier works Luther links the two Cherubim with his earlier

in agreement." [25] And in a roughly contemporary passage of the Operationes in Psalmos (1519–21) Luther asserts: "The just man is a sinner, but on a different stage and from a different aspect (*diverso theatro et conspectu*)." [26]

Luther adds a few points of final precision in the Rationis Latomianae confutatio (1521). As early as the Dictata super Psalterium (1513–15) he had denied that man's justice, whether of nature or of grace, could save him without God's mercy; he

---

dualism. E.g., Dictata III,607, 15: ". . . duo autem Cherubin est gemella fides, seu potius duo populus Iudeus et gentilis respicientes se mutuo in propitiatorium, id est in unum Christum per fidem unam copulati"; IV,174,23 (the two wings of the Cherubim correspond to the two laws, the old and the new, and to justice as against judgment) ; 176,26; Hebrews, LVII,3 p.201,17: "Ideo et hic dicit 'Cherubin gloriae' subindicans, quod alia sit sapientia Christi gloriosi et alia Christi crucifixi."

[25] Galatians Commentary, II,497,12. Compare Operationes in Psalmos (1519–21), V,504,26. It should be noted that Luther in the Galatians Commentary (1519) presents certain features of a new solution without drawing all their implications and without always denying his old solution.

Thus it is sometimes difficult to determine whether the Christian's total justice is primary or whether it is a consequence of his partial justice; similarly Luther seems sometimes sharply to separate these two justices while sometimes he speaks, as in the Dictata, of a contrast between a just spirit and an unjust flesh. Luther's basic intent seems usually clear and this points to his mature position; he does not appear always to be certain how far this will necessitate a change in his older terminology. Compare II,494,37 f. where Luther asks how those who believe in Christ can be without sin, when no man is without sin. "Respondeo: /495 Omnis qui credit in Christum iustus est, nondum plene in re sed in spe. Caeptus est enim iustificari et sanari, sicut ille homo semivivus. Interim autem, dum iustificatur et sanatur, non imputatur ei, quod reliquum est in carne peccatum, propter Christum, qui, cum sine omni peccato sit, iam unum cum Christiano suo factus, interpellat pro eo ad patrem. . . . Quare omnes eiusmodi iustorum commendationes eodem modo intelligendae sunt, quod non omnino in seipsis perfecti sunt, sed in deo reputante et ignoscente propter fidem filii sui Iesu Christi, qui est propitiatorium nostrum." Compare the earlier version of this argument in Lectures on Galatians (1516–17), LVII,2 p. 74,5–18 where the crucial sentence is p.74,9: "Respondetur, quod omnes fideles sunt iusti propter Christum, in quem credunt et cui incipiunt fieri conformes per mortificationem veteris hominis." Compare also Galatians Commentary (1519), II,592,12, where Luther apparently refers back to the passage cited at the beginning of this note but where in his summary he speaks simply in terms of spirit and flesh, 592,19: "Omnes ergo sancti habent peccatum suntque peccatores, et nullus peccat: iusti sunt iusti iuxta illud quod gratia in eis sanavit, peccatores iuxta quod adhuc sanandi sunt"; 584,16 (in summary of Augustine).

[26] Operationes in Psalmos, V,197,11: "Iustus vero ex multis iam dictis ps. 1 in spiritu et abscondito dicitur, qui non in suis nec hominum, sed dei oculis iustus est. Hic est, qui credit et fidit in deo, de quo recte dixeris: Iustus est peccator, sed diverso theatro et conspectu, ut diximus." For the use of *theatrum*, compare the discussion V,252,31. For a general analysis of the Operationes, see Horst Beintker, Die Überwindung der Anfechtung bei Luther. Eine Studie zu seiner Theologie nach den Operationes in Psalmos 1519–21 (Theologische Arbeiten, hgg. von H. Urner, Band I), Berlin, 1954.

now denies that man's justice can ever count for anything at all in God's judgment of wrath. And while God's judgment in the Dictata had been primarily a judgment of the flesh, and the Christian's spirit had tropologically coöperated in this judgment, now the whole person of the sinner is swallowed up in the judgment. Thus in the Rationis Latomianae confutatio Luther declares: "Even just and pious men, whose justice might be found pure outside God's judgment in the realm of mercy, are in His judgment not at all helped by this justice but are equal (*similes*) to the last and most vile sinners." [27] As a corollary, Luther now explicitly declares that not even the Christians' faith, as such, can save them. Christ alone is the Christians' atonement "so that they are safe under His grace, not because they believe and have faith and (His) gift, but because they have these in Christ's grace." [28]

Luther in the Rationis Latomianae confutatio also restates his general Christological approach, and as always he finds the key to all problems in Christ. "Now if anyone wishes to reason in a Christian manner about sin and grace, or about the Law and the Gospel, or about Christ and man, he must with decision reason no otherwise than about God and man in Christ. Here one must take most particular care that each nature with all its properties is predicated of the whole person, and at the same time one must beware lest he attribute to the person what is appropriate to God as such (*simpliciter*) or man as such." [29] It is one thing, says Luther, to speak of God incarnate or of man deified; it is quite another thing to speak of God or of man as such. In like manner the existence of sin outside grace is one thing, and the existence of sin in grace is another; Luther concludes in untranslatable Latin "ut possis imaginari gratiam seu donum Dei esse impeccatificatum et peccatum gratificatum, quamdiu hic sumus. . . ." [30]

---

[27] Rationis Latomianae confutatio, VIII,67,8. Compare 81,3; 93,38 f.; Operationes in Psalmos (1519–21), V,169,14 f. For Luther's position in the Dictata, see p. 9 f., Chapter I, above.

[28] Rationis Latomianae confutatio, VIII, 114,19. For a fuller discussion, see below pp. 89 f., Chapter III.

[29] Ibid., VIII,126,23.

[30] Ibid., VIII,126,29. I have not seen the article by R. Frick, "Von der 'einge-

These statements of the Rationis Latomianae confutatio remind us of Luther's remark in the Dictata super Psalterium, "And thus every contradiction is reconciled in Christ." [31] In the early period as in the later period Christ is the ultimate paradigm for all thinking. But in the Dictata Luther sees in Christ primarily the original dualism of figure and exemplar or else the theology of the cross where God's strength lies hidden under its opposite. In the Rationis Latomianae confutatio Luther's interest centers rather on the fact that God in Himself has a different existence from that of God incarnate, that man in himself has a different existence from that in Christ. In both 1513 and in 1521 Christ is the mainspring and center of Luther's thought, but His meaning for the life of the Christian has changed profoundly in the intervening years.

Along with the emerging distinction between two realms of existence, Luther also during the period 1518–21 introduces fundamental changes into his doctrine of justification. We have seen something of this in the discussion of good acts as both good and at the same time sinful, and we shall notice other aspects when we come to consider the changes in Luther's ideas on justice.[32] Here we may simply summarize the essential newness of Luther's statement as we find it in the Kirchenpostille of 1522.

The statement differs from Luther's early position at two basic points. In the first place, it too illustrates and presupposes the distinction between the two realms of Christian existence. In the second place, the distinction between the two realms is accompanied by what may be described as a reversal of the direction of Luther's thinking on total and partial justice. In the period 1513–18 Luther regularly starts from the present condition of the Christian, partly justified by God's grace, and he looks forward from this to his complete justification in the future. In the Kirchenpostille (1522), however, Luther starts from the complete justification of the Christian, already accomplished in Christ, and he

---

sündeten Gnade' und der 'eingegnadeten' Sünde," Jahrbuch der theologischen Schule in Bethel, 1950.

[31] Dictata, III,52,25 (1516), and see note 21, Chapter I, above. Compare also Hebrews, LVII,3 p. 202,5; Operationes in Psalmos (1519–21), V,602, 13 f. and spec. 32 f.

[32] Below, Chapter III, pp. 73 f.

only then goes on to consider in its light man's gradual sanctification in this life. From one standpoint, the new doctrine of justification is the culmination of the long attack of 1513–18 on the claims of human nature and merit; from another standpoint it reverses the position of 1513–18, for Luther had then regarded God's gifts or grace as the antecedents of final justification, while he now argues that these are always the consequence of the Christian's already complete justification in Christ.

Thus in the Kirchenpostille (1522) Luther distinguishes two works of Christ; he calls the one "example" and the other "gift." [33] Christ is an example for us when we take Him as a model to imitate in our life and works, but this, says Luther, is the least part of the Gospel. "The principal point and basis of the Gospel is that before you take Christ as example, you accept and recognize Him as a gift and present, which is given to you by God and which is your own. . . ." [34] Only when the Christian has done this can he go ahead to take Christ as example. Gift and example are to be as completely distinguished as faith and works, "for faith has nothing of your own but only Christ's life and work, while works have something of you, though they should not be yours but your neighbor's." [35]

Later in the Kirchenpostille Luther uses the same approach in the discussion of justice. He begins with the basic distinction between human justice and divine justice.[36] For our purposes the important point is that divine justice is already possessed by the Christian totally, though only in faith. Christ made him holy "all at once" and not "piecemeal." [37] "You must already possess heaven and be holy, before you do good works. Works do not merit heaven, but in contrast heaven through pure giving of grace, does the good works. . . . Therefore all the life of a good, be-

---

[33] Kirchenpostille (1522), X,1,1 pp.11,1 f. For a comparable statement from Luther's early period, see Sermon (1516), I,77,4.

[34] Kirchenpostille (1522), X,1,1 p.11,12.

[35] Ibid., X,1,1 pp.12,21 f. For a fuller discussion of faith in relation to justification, see below, pp. 89 f., Chapter III.

[36] Ibid., X,1,1 pp.106,1 f. See also X,1,2 pp.35,24 f.

[37] Ibid., X,1,1 p. 107,12: "Christus hatt unſſ auff eyn mal selig gemacht ynn tzweyerley weyſſe. . ."; 112,9: "alſſo auch die tawff macht den menschen gantz auff eyn mal reyn und selig"; 344,2: ". . . denn das testament hatts allis ynn sich, rechtfertigung, selickeytt, erbe und hewbtgutt. Es wirtt auch gantz auff eynn mal, nit stucklich besessen durch den glauben."

lieving Christian after baptism is nothing more than an awaiting the revelation of a holiness which he already has. He surely has it whole, though it is still hidden in faith." [38]

From the vantage point of 1522, certain of the characteristics of Luther's general re-orientation may now be seen more clearly. The development is deeply coherent and changes which are apparently disparate reflect the same shifting of the basic categories of thought. The coherence of Luther's development is, however, not the result of conscious derivation of conclusions from any first principle early arrived at. Throughout, his thought is always centered on Christ, but Luther's understanding of Christ developed as did the other aspects of his thought, and it does not seem directly to determine them. Finally, Luther shows little interest during the period 1518–22 in working out any systematic statement of his new position. The changes which we have studied are all limited in nature; they are coherent implicitly not explicitly. By the time of the Kirchenpostille (1522) Luther nevertheless seems to feel that the essential work has been accomplished. He has solved some difficult special problems, and he has achieved the goal of all his thought, an adequate statement on justification. To a first approximation, then, Luther's re-orientation is complete by 1522, and the direction of his thought is set for the rest of his life. He has not yet a general statement of his whole position, but this does not seem to trouble him in the years following 1522 and he will not take up the problem until toward 1530.

From the vantage point of 1522 it is also possible to discern something of the "reasons" for Luther's re-orientation of 1518–19 and something more of its implications. Luther's main concern in his religious thought had always been justification, and he early became clear on two main prerequisites of a successful solution. First, the solution must involve the real justice of the Christian and cannot be met by any simple decision on God's part; second, the solution must take account of the continued sinfulness of the Christian in this life. During the period 1513–18 Luther's solutions met these demands by explaining in one way or another that the saved Christian was partly just and partly a sinner. But as Luther read the promises and threats of the Bible, he came

[38] Ibid., X,1,1 p. 108,2.

more and more to feel that the Christian was also in some way to be regarded as "totally" just and "totally" a sinner. Luther could not express all these convictions in his theology of 1513–18 without self-contradiction.

With the change of 1518–19 the difficulties disappear. The Christian now exists within two realms, before God and in the world. Before God, he is already totally just in Christ, but totally condemned and a sinner outside of Christ and under the Law. In the world and in the area of works, however, the Christian is gradually being healed and sanctified by God's grace, and here one can properly speak of him as partly just and partly a sinner.

More important for our purposes and for the theology of society, Luther is by this re-orientation led to a new, positive evaluation of the world and of human justice, law, and society. We saw the typical attitude of the early period in the Lectures on Galatians (1516–17) where Luther argued that the more a person advanced in Christianity, the less he was concerned with external works and with human justice; the only real concern of the Christian was with the spiritual and invisible sphere.[39] But after the re-orientation of 1518–19, the direction of Luther's thought is reversed much as it had been in the case of justification. The complete justification of the Christian in Christ, which corresponds to the old sphere of the spiritual and invisible, is already done and accomplished; it is no longer a goal but rather a starting point. The Christian already justified in Christ now faces toward the world; only here can he be active, and only here can be begin, with God's help, his gradual sanctification.

But if the re-orientation of 1518–19 makes Luther face the world, it also reveals that he has no theology of the world. In a sense the materials for such a theology were present in his early thought of 1513–18, but they cannot be used without a fundamental transformation. For example, much of what Luther had previously said of the Christian's "justice of God" now belongs to the world, but only on condition that it be re-interpreted as in no way an antecedent to salvation. All of the little Luther had previously said about human justice also belongs to the world, and it can to a large extent be fused with the re-interpreted justice of

[39] See above, pp.32 f., Chapter I.

God; human justice, however, must be given a new description to make clear its fundamental importance in the life of the Christian.

The essential features of this new theology of the world and of society appear in Luther's thought during the same period 1518–22 during which Luther re-oriented his general theology. In their final form, they will emerge as his new doctrines of civil justice, of the civil use of the law, of God's world-government (*Weltregiment*) and so on. We shall have occasion to analyze them in some detail later; here we are simply pointing out that while the question of society was largely incidental in Luther's thinking in the period 1513–18, after 1518–19 and because of 1518–19 it will constitute half his theology.

Toward 1530, as we have already noted in passing, Luther turns again to the problem of stating his general theology, and we shall notice two phases of this. In the first place, he reaches greater clarity on his relation to the previous Christian tradition, and notably to St. Augustine; this is particularly important in view of the question whether Luther's own thought in the period 1513–18 may not with some justification be called "Augustinian." In the second place, he begins for the first time to work out a terminology by which he can give a more explicit and coherent statement of his new distinction between the two realms of Christian existence and of his new doctrine of justification.

When Luther attempted to define his relation to the previous tradition, scholasticism presented no problem; from an early period he was firmly anti-scholastic.[40] On the other hand, his relation to Augustine was changing and problematic. In the period 1513–18, Augustine was Luther's main authority and support; he himself speaks of his theology as "Augustinian," and it is from this standpoint that he regularly attacks the scholastics.[41] With

[40] See, e.g., Disputatio contra scholasticam theologiam (1517), I,224 f.

[41] Compare Heidelberg Disputation (1518), I,353,11: ". . . haec Theologica paradoxa, ut vel sic appareat, bene an male elicita sint ex divo Paulo, vase et organo Christi electissimo, deinde et ex S. Augustino, interprete eiusdem fidelissimo"; Letter to Lang, May 18, 1517, Briefe, I,99,8: "Theologia nostra et S. Augustinus prospere procedunt et regnant in nostra universitate, Deo operante. Aristoteles descendit paulatim inclinatus ad ruinam prope futuram sempiternam."

For a detailed analysis of the Augustinian influence on Luther in his early period, see A. Hamel, op. cit. (note 11, Chapter I, above). For some recent attempts

the changes of 1518–19, however, the frequent laudatory references to Augustine diminish, and Luther can even emphasize the sharp contrast between his own theology and that of any of the Fathers.[42] It does not appear, however, that Luther during the early and middle 1520's was prepared to give any explicit statement of his relation to Augustine.

In the early 1530's Luther reaches greater clarity on some aspects of the question, and he will sometimes criticize Augustine directly. Thus he declares in a Table-Talk (1532): "Augustine did not rightly understand the article of justification." [43] And in the Lectures on Galatians (1531) Luther will credit Augustine only with a partial grasp of the central distinction between the Law and the Gospel. "This distinction is not in any of the universities, doctors, theologians, nor is it in any of the Fathers. Augustine has little of it and Jerome, none." [44] But despite such criticism, Luther always felt himself in fundamental agreement with Augustine, though with the Augustine of prayer and praise rather than the Augustine of theological disputation.[45]

For a careful comparison of the "Lutheran" and the "Augustinian" doctrine of justification, our best sources are the correspondence with Brenz, of 1531, and the famous Disputation between Luther and Melanchthon, of 1536.

In 1531, Melanchthon with Luther's support criticizes Brenz

---

to evaluate the general relationship between the two thinkers, see W. von Loewenich, "Zur Gnadenlehre bei Augustin und bei Luther," Archiv für Reformationsgeschichte, 44 (1953),52–63 ; M. Bendiscioli, "L'agostinismo dei riformtori protestanti," Revue des études augustiniennes, 1 (1955), 203–24; L. Cristiani, "Luther et saint Augustin," Augustinus Magister, 2 vols. (Paris, 1955), II,1029–38.

[42] Compare, for the early period, Kirchenpostille (1522), where Luther is speaking of the Law and the Gospel. "Denn ich sage dyr, dass auſſer der schrifft biſſher keyn buch yhe geschrieben ist, auch von keynem heyligen, das furhanden sey, darynn diſſe tzwo predigt recht unterschiedlich weren gehandellt, do doch grosse macht an ligt tzu wissen." X,1,2 p. 155,24. See also Rationis Latomianae confutatio (1521), VIII,89,23 where Luther denies that even Augustine may contradict Paul.

[43] TR, §1572 (1532), II,138,7.

[44] Lectures on Galatians (1531), XL,1 p. 486,3. Compare Sermon December 11, 1530: "Hanc praedicationem non invenis in Gregorio, Augustino, Hieronymo, multo minus in papae libris. Ideo Evangelii praedicatio solum in sacra scriptura." XXXII,245,1 ; Enarratio Psalmi LI (1532), XL,2 p. 331,11: "Augustinus, Ieronymus semper ista vocabula 'Iustus, verax Deus' haben hin gezogen: 'Ego sum zelotes'."

[45] Compare In XV Psalmos Graduum (1532–33), XL,3 p. 354,2.

for not advancing beyond an Augustinian theory of justice and justification. Augustine was indeed right when he concluded that the justice of reason (*rationis iustitia*) does not rank as justice before God. However, he was wrong when he supposed that God reckons us just (*iustos reputari*) because of the fulfilment of the Law which the Holy Spirit works in us. In truth, argues Melanchthon, we are just and accepted only because of Christ. "Hence love (*dilectio*), which is the fulfilment of the Law, does not justify, but faith alone, and faith justifies not because it is any perfection in us, but merely because it apprehends Christ. We are just, not because of our love, not because of the fulfilment of the Law, not because of our renovation (*novitatem*), even though these be the gifts of the Holy Spirit; we are just because of Christ, and Him we apprehend only through faith." [46] Augustine did not therefore adequately represent the opinion of St. Paul, even though he approached it more closely than did the scholastics. Luther's postscript to Melanchthon's letter speculates on the way in which Christ is our justice, and he concludes in agreement with Melanchthon that we have our justice in Christ, not in the love or in the gifts which follow that justice.[47]

In the Disputation of 1536 many of the same points are at issue. Melanchthon attempts to distinguish the Augustinian and Lutheran positions on justification. In Augustine, he argues, justification by faith means only that we are justified by our renewal through grace; Augustine really denies no merit except that of the impious man, and his "by faith alone" excludes only the works which precede faith.[48] Luther agrees that this is a false doctrine of justification; our own justice, even that which is effected by grace, is never in any sense a cause of our justification but only an inevitable consequence of it. Yet Luther hesitates to classify the false doctrine as Augustinian, and he quotes a sentence from Augustine to illustrate agreement with Luther's doctrine.[49] Simi-

---

[46] Briefe, VI,100,17. This is also found in TR §3131, III,181,32 in German.

[47] Briefe, VI,100,49 f.

[48] The Disputation is clearer in the Latin version as found in the Erlanger edition LVIII,347–54. For the German translation see TR, §6727, VI,148,29 f. For the passage here cited see LVIII,352; for Luther's early acceptance of the position here denied, see Romans, LVI,249,5; Galatians, LVII,2 p. 97,27.

[49] Erlanger edition LVIII,352. Compare TR, §2066 (1531), II,309,10 and Disputations (1537) XXXIX,1 pp.228,38 f.

larly, Luther in his last statement on the problem, in the Preface of 1545, suggests that his interpretation of the "justice of God" has Augustinian support, though he adds that in Augustine this is not yet completely worked out and that the details on imputation are not yet all clarified.[50]

In summary, then, Luther in the early 1530's can distinguish two theories of justification with a clarity he had not yet achieved in the early 1520's; the one which he rejects may in general be identified with his own position from 1513–18. He also sees (though not so willingly as Melanchthon) that it is possible to classify the rejected doctrine as Augustinian and thus by implication to call Luther's own position anti-Augustinian, or at least non-Augustinian. But Luther rejects this line of argument as a final answer; he is convinced that his own position is true to Augustine's basic intent, truer perhaps than some of Augustine's own theories.

During this same period of the early 1530's, Luther devoted renewed attention to a general statement of his theology. As evidence, we have the fragments of the uncompleted treatise on justification, the important Lectures on Galatians (1531), the Sermons on Matthew V–VII (published in 1532), and, from a somewhat later period, the Disputations (1535–45).[51] We shall notice Luther's new general statement primarily insofar as it can provide us with a background for Luther's ideas on justice, law, and society.[52]

From a "systematic" standpoint, Luther's most important

[50] LIV,186,16.

[51] The fragments of the projected treatise on justification were gathered together by Veit Dietrich under the title Rhapsodia seu concepta in librum de loco iustificationis cum aliis obiter additis (hereafter cited as De loco iustificationis) XXX,2 p. 657–76. We do not know who reported or who edited Luther's Sermons on Matthew V–VII, preached during the years 1530–32. However, Luther supplied the edition with a preface, so we may assume that the general argument is authentic even where the actual words or phrasings are not Luther's.

[52] On Luther's general theology, perhaps the most useful introduction is that of R. Seeberg in his Lehrbuch der Dogmengeschichte IV,1 5th ed. (Basel, 1953). See also J. T. Koestlin, Luthers Theologie, 2nd ed., 2 vols. (Stuttgart, 1901); E. Seeberg, Luthers Theologie, Vol. I (Göttingen, 1929), Vol. II (Stuttgart, 1937); idem, Luthers Theologie in ihren Grundzügen, 2nd ed. (Stuttgart, 1950); Philip Watson, Let God be God, An interpretation of the theology of Martin Luther (London, 1947); Gordon Rupp, The Righteousness of God (New York, 1953). For a valuable account of the important Swedish studies on Luther, see Edgar M. Carlson, The Reinterpretation of Luther (Philadelphia, 1948).

achievement in this general statement is to establish a new dualism, or set of dualisms, which will constitute the framework of his later thought in much the same way that such early dualisms as image and exemplar, sign and reality, had provided a framework for the Dictata super Psalterium (1513–15).

Thus in the introduction to the Lectures on Galatians (1531) Luther summarizes Paul's aim in terms of a fundamental contrast between two justices. "The argument is that he wishes to establish the doctrine of justice, faith, grace, forgiveness of sins, so that we may have perfect knowledge of the difference between Christian justice and all other justices." [53] In the other justices we act, whether on our own or through the help of God. "But Christian justice is clean contrary to these; it is a passive justice, one which we simply receive, one where we do not act ourselves but suffer another, namely God, to act in us." [54] Luther equates the distinction between the two justices with the basic biblical distinction between the Law and the Gospel. "Whoever knows these distinctions well, let him give thanks to God and know himself a theologian, as he puts the Gospel in heaven and understands it as a heavenly justice, and as he puts the Law on earth, so that one is the day, the other the night. Just as God carefully separated heaven and earth, so we should carefully separate these two justices." [55]

The question immediately arises: how are the dualisms of the 1530's, such as the two justices, related to the dualisms of Luther's early thought as seen in the Dictata super Psalterium, such as image and exemplar, or flesh and spirit? A preliminary answer is that at the point of Luther's ultimate concern, in their relation to the Christian's existence, the dualisms of the 1513–18 period refer to the two parts of man; he is partly carnal and partly spiritual, partly attached to things visible, and partly to things invisible. On the other hand, the dualisms of the 1530's apply to the "whole" man. The Christian, and not simply part of him,

---

[53] Lectures on Galatians (1531), henceforth cited as Galatians (1531), XL,1 p. 40,2. Unless otherwise noted, all citations are from Rörer's Nachschrift. For the relation of this to the printed edition of 1531, see G. Schulze, "Die Vorlesung Luthers über die Galaterbrief von 1531 und der gedruckte Kommentar von 1535," Theologische Studien und Kritiken 98/99 (1926), 18–82.

[54] Galatians (1531), XL,1 p.41,3.

[55] Ibid., XL,1 p. 207,3.

exists in the realm of reason; the Christian and not just part of him, exists in the realm of grace. But is the Christian then dichotomized into two separate and unrelated whole men? No, because Luther will finally say that these two "existences" are only two "persons" both borne by the single Christian individual. The relevant analogy is not that of parts and a whole but of Christ who is perfect God and perfect man, two natures in one person.

In other words, the dualisms of 1513–18 in no way involve two realms of Christian existence. The dualisms of 1530 and later presuppose such a distinction and without it would simply bifurcate the Christian's experience into two unrelated parts. The older dualisms, it may be noted, do not disappear completely with the emergence of the new, but they are transformed and appear in a new context. Man is partly just and partly a sinner, partly spiritual and partly carnal, not in the realm of justification but only in the realm of gradual sanctification.

It is perhaps convenient to distinguish, though we cannot always separate, three different contexts of meaning which are involved in the dualisms. In the first place, there is the one we have used in all our preliminary accounts of it, the contrast between two realms of Christian existence. The Christian is now already justified in heaven; the Christian is now still being sanctified on earth. On the question of terminology, "realm" (*regnum*) is one of the terms used by Luther along with many others; it never becomes technical for him.[56] We have added the qualification, realms "of existence," simply as a summary for Luther's regular practice of saying that the Christian "is" in heaven, for example, at the same time that he "is" on earth.

In the second place, there is a contrast which might more exactly be described as between two realms of discourse. Certain propositions apply only in heaven, in the realm of justification; certain propositions apply only within the realm of reason. Or certain propositions and concepts have different meanings as they are applied in one or the other realm. When we are discoursing

---

[56] Ibid., XL,1 p.18,9 (= part of Luther's preparation for the Lectures): "Haec vera sunt in politia et regno racionis. Sed sicut in regno non facit quod est in se, ita in regno gracie facit quod est supra se"; XL,1 p. 292,6. "Si sum in regno rationis, edifico domum. . . . Da ghorts hin dictum: quantum; debet facere, — in /293 politico et oeconomico, non sic in regno spirituali."

of heaven, justice has a different meaning than when we are discoursing of earth. Here again, Luther's terminology never becomes technical. He sometimes speaks of "realms" but slightly
more often of "places" (e.g., *in loco iustificationis*).[57] Luther has
no term which corresponds exactly to our qualification of the
realm as "of discourse." He illustrates the meaning of the qualification most frequently in his biblical commentaries as he asks
again and again to which realm or "place" a proposition of Paul
should be properly referred so that we may give it its right interpretation. He discusses the problem explicitly, though in different
terms, when he compares the two different languages of philosophy and theology, and when he develops the idea that theology
has a different "grammar." [58]

In the third place, Luther's language often seems to imply another context of meaning in which heaven and earth are two objects or two parts of the universe. Heaven is heaven, and earth
is earth. This rarely appears at the heart of Luther's argument,
and we should probably take such statements as merely echoes
of his early thought or of an older view deeply embedded in common language; in his mature theology they are little more than
metaphors, and we can never start from them and reach his basic
contrasts of the realms of existence and discourse.[59] This is the
meaning of a crucial passage in Luther's projected treatise on
justification. "Further, one must not admit a separation of the
justice of faith from that of works, as if there were two different
justices after the manner of the sophists. But there is one simple

---

[57] E.g., ibid., XL,1 p. 392,7: "quia Paulus versatur non in loco politico, sed
theologico et spirituali coram deo"; 397,11: "Ideo videndum in quo loco sit,
scilicet spirituali extra politiam, extra leges"; De loco iustificationis (1530), XXX,2
p. 664,24: "Iacobus versatur in loco Morali, non in theologico, sicut fere totus
est moralis . . . . Sed nos hic in loco Theologico sumus, ubi de iustificatione coram
Deo loquimur."

[58] E.g., Disputations (1540), XXXIX,2 p. 104,24: "Spiritus sanctus habet suam
grammaticam." For a fuller discussion see the analysis of the Promotion-disputation of Palladius and Tilemann, below pp.66 f. For the general problem of theology
and philosophy in Luther's thought, see Bengt Hägglund, Theologie und Philosophie bei Luther und in der occamistischen Tradition (Lunds Universitets
Årsskrift. N.F. Avd. 1, Bd. 51. Nr. 4), Lund, 1955.

[59] In illustration, one might compare Luther's discussion of Christ's presence
in the sacrament and his denial that Christ's being in heaven is to be understood
localiter; see the valuable analysis in E. Metzke, Sakrament und Metaphysik
(Lebendige Wissenschaft, Heft 9), Stuttgart, 1948.

justice of faith and works, just as God and man are one person, and the body and soul are one man." [60]

To study Luther's dualisms in greater detail, we shall first notice the way in which he establishes the two realms of existence and discourse, second the way in which he explains how one Christian exists in both realms, and finally the restatement of the theory of justification in terms of the two realms.

Luther gives his classic statement of the two realms in the Lectures on Galatians (1531). We have already noted the contrast between Christian, passive justice and all other justices, and we shall have to consider this in more detail later.[61] Luther also contrasts the civil use of the law with the theological use of the law,[62] and this too we shall consider more carefully later.

In addition he makes use of a large number of other contrasts. He urges, for example, that we clearly distinguish morals and faith, works and grace, and polity and religion.[63] We must keep the political and economic realm of reason distinct from the spiritual realm of grace.[64]

In other passages his attention is more directed to the distinction between two realms of discourse. In his own "preparation" for the Lectures, he observes that in polity and in the realm of reason, it is true that God does not require anything impossible for man; on the other hand, man in the realm of grace must do what is beyond his abilities.[65] In the Lectures themselves, he comments in similar fashion on the statement that God is no "respecter of persons." This is true in the realm (*in loco*) of religion, but "we speak differently of things in religion than in polity, for in polity God wishes these 'persons' to be honoured as His masks

---

[60] De loco iustificationis (1530), XXX,2 p. 659,4 (= TR, §1886–1887, II,247, 10 and 40 f.). Compare Galatians (1531), XL,1 p.22,13 (= Luther's preparation for the Lectures): "Summa, sicut supra dictum est de iustificatione operum: quod hic locus (Galatians V,6) et similes sunt intelligendi de toto composito seu de fide incarnata et concreta. . . . Hic autem complectitur totam vitam Christianam, qualis sit intus coram deo et foris coram hominibus"; 426,6 f.

[61] See above p. 62, and below Chapter III, pp. 91 f.

[62] See below, Chapter III, pp. 100 f.

[63] Galatians (1531), XL,1 pp.51,10 f.: "quod Paulus docet illam iusticiam Christianam, et, sicut dixi, diligenter est observanda ista distinctio, ne confundantur mores et fides, opera et gratia, politia et religio, et valde /52 multum conducit istas 2 iusticias disiungere. . . ."

[64] Galatians (1531), XL,1 p. 292,6 (cited note 56, above).

[65] Ibid., XL,1 p. 18,9 (cited note 56, above).

and instruments." [66] On another occasion, he points out that Paul is arguing in a higher realm than the political (*in superiori loco, non politico*).[67] Or he can insist that the justices of faith and of the flesh are to be most carefully distinguished, "for Paul is reasoning not in the political realm but in the theological and spiritual realm (*loco*) which is before God." [68]

As Luther emphasizes the distinction of the two realms, so the primary fault of his opponents is that they confuse them. "Thus Peter confused the distinction, for he made one product of the Law and the Gospel. Similarly the Pope made the Gospel into laws. He mixed the polity with the church, the Law with the Gospel, and out of it all made nothing but laws." [69] Luther maintains that his opponents confuse political propositions (*dicta politica*) with churchly propositions. "I do not urge this distinction without reason; few observe it, and it is very easy to confuse celestial justice with political justice." [70]

A careful statement of the distinction between philosophy and theology as the two realms of discourse is found in the Promotion-disputation of Palladius and Tilemann (1537). In argument §14 Luther considers whether our renewal is a formal cause of our justification. He points out that all theologians should avoid terms such as "formal" which come from natural philosophy (*physica*). Each art has its own limits and its own vocabulary, and if they are transferred from their own realm (*ex suo foro et loco*) to another, confusion always results. If theology must use the terms of natural philosophy, it should give them a good bath first.[71]

Luther goes on to attack the thesis of the Sorbonne that whatever is true in natural philosophy is also true in theology. This thesis, he argues, simply confuses the two realms, and he demonstrates this in terms of justice. "It does not immediately follow: I am not a thief, not an adulterer, not punished by the

---

[66] Ibid., XL,1 p. 176,13.

[67] Ibid. XL,1 p. 305,7: "Paulus versatur in superiori loco, non politico. Politia et oeconomia est subiecta rationi."

[68] Ibid., XL,1 p. 392,6.

[69] Ibid., XL,1 p. 208,8 f.

[70] Ibid., XL,1 p. 293,2: "Non debent politica dicta trahi in ecclesiam. . ."; p.293,11: "Ipsi confuderunt dicta politica cum ecclesiasticis."

[71] Disputations, XXXIX,1 pp.227,1 ff., and spec. 229,16.

magistrate; therefore I am pure and just before God, and He will not punish me. There are two realms, the political and the theological (*Duplex enim est forum, politicum et theologicum*), for God judges far otherwise than the world. Political right is contented with my justice of any civil or external kind, but the justice which justifies me before the political judge is not immediately justice before God, though it does pertain to the preservation of this life and to discipline." [72]

Luther makes a series of similar points in his reply to argument §15. "All terms become new, when they are transferred from their own realm (*ex suo foro*) to another. The natural philosopher, and the jurist say: Works are good, just, and necessary. They judge rightly and in accord with their aim. But the theologian on the contrary says: Our works, however good they may be, are evil and damned before God, and not necessary. Then you say that our works are simply prohibited and not necessary? I say this, but it is to be understood theologically, not as a statement of natural philosophy or of the jurist (*non physice aut iuridice*). When we ascend to heaven, we must speak before God in new languages (*novis linguis*). . . . When we are on earth, we must speak with our own languages. . . . Thus you hear that our works are good and not good, that they are justice and not justice. Both statements are true but in their own realms (*in suo foro*). There are two different justices, one of the law, which is achieved by our own power and works, the other imputed to us through faith by divine mercy. . . . All these (distinctions) are to be diligently observed by you, lest you so confuse everything that it becomes impossible to see what Christ or theology or natural philosophy is." [73]

When Luther has thus divided and distinguished the two realms, the next question is the relation of the individual Christian to them. Sometimes Luther simply explains that the Christian "is" in both realms but from different aspects. In the third Disputation against the Antinomians (1538), Luther argues that the Christian as such is a person who is buried with Christ in His death, dead to sin, the Law, and the world. The person is not

[72] Ibid., XXXIX,1 p. 230,4.
[73] Ibid., XXXIX,1 pp. 231,1 ff.

in the present world at all. On the other hand the same Christian
is also a soldier in Christ's militia, and as such he is under sin
and under the Law. "Thus the Christian is dead and alive, but
from different aspects (*diverso tamen respectu*). But (the distinction of) these two neither the world nor the pope can understand."[74] Elsewhere Luther explains that the same Christian is
both militant and triumphant;[75] he has his polity in heaven (Phi-
lippians III,20), but he is also in a different aspect a citizen of
the world.[76] In the Lectures on Galatians (1531) Luther characterizes the Christian's existence as in two times. As Christ in history came after the Law, so in each Christian there is both a time
of the Law and a time of grace. "Hence the Christian is divided
into two times: as far as he is flesh, he is under the Law; as far
as he is spirit he is under the Gospel."[77]

Luther explains the double existence of the Christian most un-
ambiguously in his doctrine of the two persons of the Christian.
The doctrine is found most completely in the Sermons on Matthew
V–VII (published 1532), and there are allusions to it in other
writings. In the Sermons on Matthew V–VII, Luther starts from
the question whether a Christian may be a magistrate, and he
concludes that he can and should. Everyone must live in the
world, and therefore even the Christian must in some way act as
a world-person.[78] One must, however, be able to distinguish the
two "persons" the individual Christian bears, between the "world-
man" and the Christian, or between the "world-person" and the
"Christian-person." The world-person involves the Christian's
relations to others and defines his place in the differentiated structure of estates and callings. The Christian-person involves only

[74] XXXIX,1 p. 521,3. Compare Luther's Vorlesung über Jesaia (1532–34),
XXV,330, 19 f.

[75] XXXIX,1 p. 504,6.

[76] Zirkulardisputation über Matth. 19,21 (1539), XXXIX,2 p.81,16: "Christianus
ut christianus est in prima tabula, solus extra regnum coelorum est civis huius
mundi." Compare Thesis §30 of the same Disputation, p. 40,36: "Extra causam
confessionis christianus est civis huius mundi, debens facere et ferre, quae sunt
suae civitatis secundum tabulam secundam." Compare Galatians (1531), XL,1
p.662,6: "Ut fecerunt ecclesiam militantem, triumphantem, Anagogice. 'Nostrum
ius et civitas est in coelestibus' non localiter, sed omnis Christianus, quantum
credit, tantum est in coelis."

[77] XL,1 p. 526,2. Compare for an early foreshadowing of the same statement
Hebrews, LVII,3 p. 98,27.

[78] XXXII,390, 19.

the believer and his God, and here there is neither male nor female, slave nor free, nor any differences of estates of callings.[79] Here again, as in the general doctrine of the two realms, Luther accuses his opponents of "mixing." [80]

Finally, Luther in the 1530's and notably in the Disputations (1535 f.) works out a more explicit and coherent doctrine of justification on the basis of the distinction between the two realms of existence and discourse and of the two persons which the believer bears.

Luther's basic insight is still the simultaneous justice and sinfulness of the Christian, and with his new general statement of his theology, he can develop the implications of the insight much more freely and boldly than in the period 1518–22. "Thus we are in truth and totally sinners, but with regard to ourselves and our first birth. Contrariwise, in so far as Christ has been given for us, we are holy and just totally. Hence from different aspects (*diverso respectu*) we are said to be just and sinners at one and the same time (*simul et semel*)." [81] "The Christian is free by faith, but in relation to the flesh, he is the slave of sin. These two things, though contraries, are nevertheless reconciled in Christ, so that the same Christian is holy and a sinner, dead and alive. There is no sin at all, and all is sin; there is hell, and there is heaven." [82]

In his analysis of the process of justification, Luther's cardinal distinction is between our total justification in Christ and our partial justification through the Holy Spirit in the world. In the first case he speaks of our justice as imputed or reputed, in the second as formal or purifying. The Christian escapes and fulfils the accusing Law, "first, by imputation (imputative), when sins against the Law are not imputed to me and are pardoned because of the precious blood of the pure lamb, Jesus Christ; and second, by purification (expurgative), when the Holy Spirit is given me and when, having received it, I begin heartily to hate whatever offends

---

[79] Ibid., XXXII,440,1; 393,23 f.
[80] Ibid., XXXII,391,32.
[81] Disputations (1538), XXXIX,1 p. 564,3. Some further material on Luther's mature doctrine of the Christian as both just and a sinner may be found in the works cited in note 125, Chapter I.
[82] Disputations (1538), XXXIX,1 p.523,19; compare 507,12 f.

Christ's name, and when I become one who practices good works." [83]

Luther had used the terms "imputation" and "reckoning" or "reputation" in his early thought and notably in the Lectures on Romans, and at this period he used them to explain the justice of God by which He makes us just.[84] Now in the 1530's he uses them to point to the Christian's existence in the heavenly realm of passive justice. In neither case should we reduce imputation or reputation to a mere divine decision which has no real effect on the Christian himself; in the Disputation on Justification, Luther emphasizes that imputation "is not a nothing (*res nihili*) but is greater than the whole world and all the holy angels." [85] Thus in a passage already noted, Luther asserts that the Christian is a person already buried with Christ.[86] He goes on to suppose an opponent demanding to be shown such a Christian. "I cannot because they are hidden, they have died, Here there is no male nor female, no freeman nor slave. This is how it is, the Christian here lives 'reputatively' (reputative) just, holy beneath the wings of his clucking hen (*sub alis gallinae suae*). . . . The man believing in Christ is already just and holy by divine 'reputation'; he already lives and is in heaven, encompassed by the heaven of mercy." [87]

Thus by the 1530's Luther has achieved an adequate general statement of his theology, though he still hesitates to "systematize" his thought. Despite its manifold terminology, the statement possesses a fundamental coherence resting on Luther's constant references to his central canon, that the believing Christian lives simultaneously in two distinct realms of existence. Before God

[83] Disputations (1538), XXXIX,1 p.434,7. For other similar statements, see 383,3 f.; 431,8 f.; 491,23 f.

[84] See above, Chapter I, pp.25 f.

[85] Disputations (1536), XXXIX,1 pp.97,26 f. Compare XXXIX,2 (1540), p.141,1; Galatians (1531), XL,1 p. 372,7: "Sophistae rident hec, quia non intelligunt Christianam iustitiam. Non est pura reputatio, sed involvit ipsam fidem et apprehensionem Christi passi pro nobis, quae non levis res."

[86] See above, pp. 67 f.

[87] Disputations (1538), XXXIX,1 pp.520,11 f. It is in this general context that "justification by faith" receives its precise meaning. Compare Disputations (1537), XXXIX,1 p. 225,3: "Novitas nostra est quidem necessaria, sed non ad salutem, non ad iustificationem nostram. Ad salutem seu iustificationem nostram necessaria est sola misericordia Dei, quae apprehenditur fide. Ideo dicimus, nos sola fide iustificari."

and in Christ, he is already totally holy and just; here in the world, he is merely in the process of justification, partially just and partially sinful. Total justification in Christ is always primary and antecedent; partial sanctification in the world is always secondary and consequent. And to preserve and defend the order and direction of his thought, Luther places continued emphasis on the negative thesis that any Christian in himself, however far he be advanced in sanctification, is before God and *not* in Christ, totally a sinner.

CHAPTER III

JUSTICE AND LAW, 1518 AND LATER.

WE HAVE NOTICED Luther's new theology as it first appeared following the fundamental re-orientation of 1518–19 and as it received a more general statement beginning about 1530. We have now to study the related changes in his doctrines of justice, law, and society. Some repetition will be inevitable, notably in the case of justice, but our attention will be concentrated on a different aspect, not on the emergence of the general distinction between the two realms of Christian existence but on the way in which the distinction appears specifically in the contrast between two justices, for example, or between two uses of the law.

1. *Justice.*

Toward the beginning of 1518 Luther's doctrine of justice appears to be still firmly established in the context of his early theology. He is mainly interested in the justice of faith or of God, the justice by which God makes us just and which is a stage on the way to salvation. In contrast, he gives human justice only the briefest treatment, and it has little importance in the life of the Christian.

How will this doctrine change as it develops along with the general re-orientation of 1518–19? In the first place, on the negative side, the justice of God which is a stage on the way to salvation will disappear. The Christian, after 1518–19, is felt to be already totally just in Christ; any partial justice he possesses must be the consequence, not the antecedent, of his justice in Christ. In the second place, on the positive side, Luther must now work out a doctrine of this new justice in Christ which the Christian already possesses totally. In part Luther can transform for this purpose his earlier ideas on the justice of God as a stage toward salvation. In the third place, also on the positive side, Luther must now work out a doctrine of the partial justice which appears in the Christian's gradual sanctification in the world. In part he can here again transform for a different purpose his earlier ideas on the justice of God; in part he can use what little he had said earlier about human justice.

To a first approximation, the new ideas on justice are contemporary with those on general theology which we have already studied. Neither group of ideas seems to be the cause of the other. Luther develops his general and his special doctrines concurrently and in a process of mutual interaction.

We shall first analyze the gradual emergence of the new ideas on justice in the works of 1518–21, and we shall then turn to Luther's mature statement of his position, primarily as it is found in the Lectures on Galatians (1531).[1]

Luther in the Sermo de triplici iustitia (1518) discusses justice largely in the manner of his early theology, but there are also signs of a new position. The scheme of the Sermo is a triple classification of sin and justice. First, there is criminal sin, the public evil which the secular power punishes; corresponding to this sin there is a "simian" justice, by which one is honest "before men" and cannot be accused. Such justice is not properly a Christian justice, and Christians are to be urged beyond it to a higher form. Second, there is the sin which is essential, natal, original and alien (as coming from Adam); corresponding to it, there is a justice which is likewise "natal, essential, original, and alien, which is the justice of Christ"[2] and which becomes ours by faith. In his description of this justice, Luther moves away from his early concept of the tropological justice of God or of faith and toward

---

[1] Luther's doctrine of Christian or passive justice is discussed in all the general works on his theology and on his doctrine of justification; for a special study of this problem, see H. Iwand, Glaubensgerechtigkeit (note 129, Chapter I, above). For a somewhat different approach with a greater emphasis on *iustitia civilis*, see R. Bring, Das Verhältnis von Glauben und Werken in der lutherischen Theologie (Forschungen zur Geschichte und Lehre des Protestantismus X,7), München, 1955; Bring's often penetrating analysis sometimes suffers from an unwise attempt to analyze Luther's mature thought through a contrast between *iustitia actualis* and *iustitia civilis*. The problem of the two justices is also discussed in all the main works on Luther's social theory; see notably G. Törnvall, Geistliches und weltliches Regiment bei Luther (Forschungen zur Geschichte und Lehre des Protestantismus X,2), München, 1947, Chapter IV,2 pp.136–59.

[2] II,44,32.

his mature doctrine of the total justice of the Christian in Christ. Third, there is actual sin, which is the fruit of original sin; corresponding to it is actual justice, which flows from faith and from essential justice. Luther goes on to attack the traditional ideas of merit, and he then, in a passage already noted,[3] maintains that our good works in themselves are always sins, even though in Christ they are pleasing and acceptable to God. To the question as to what works we should chiefly practice, he replies: prayers, charities, and fastings.[4]

Luther's thinking in De triplici iustitia is clearly transitional. On the one hand, the relation between "simian" and original justice corresponds to the older division between human justice and the justice of God; as in his early theology, merely human justice is of little importance.[5] On the other hand, when Luther speaks of original justice flowing out into actual justice, one sees the new direction of thought of his mature theory of justification. But his position is still far from clear. He has only begun his redefinition of the justice of God, and he has not told us how to relate "simian" and actual justice.

In the Sermo de duplici iustitia (1519)[6] Luther advances to greater precision, and he possibly intended the Sermo to correct the no longer satisfactory formulations of De triplici iustitia. The ambiguous distinction between "civil" or "simian" and actual justice disappears, and Luther moves toward his later dualism of the two justices.

Luther begins with a strong statement on the Christian's alien justice, and here the new definiton of the justice as "in Christ" supplants the older tropological or effective sense of the justice of God. The alien justice of the Christian is that "by which Christ is just and justifies through faith."[7] Luther uses the metaphor of bride and groom to explain how the Christian possesses all that is Christ's, and he argues that this is the justice of God. "There-

---

[3] See above, Chapter II,p.51.

[4] De triplici iustitia (1518), II,47,4

[5] Compare the passage from Galatians (1516–17) cited above, Chapter I, p. 33.

[6] It is difficult to date the Sermon precisely, but Luther refers to it in a letter to Lang of April 13, 1519; see Briefe, I,370,74, with the footnotes on the letter of Spalatin which also mentions the Sermon, though in a passage where the text is uncertain.

[7] De duplici iustitia, II,145,10.

fore, through faith in Christ, Christ's justice becomes our justice, and all that is His becomes ours; indeed He Himself becomes ours. Hence the Apostle calls this the justice of God in Romans I,17: The justice of God is revealed in the Gospel, as it is written, 'The just lives by faith.' Further such faith is called the justice of God, as Paul says in Romans III,28. We believe men to be justified by faith. This is an infinite justice and one which absorbs all sins in an instant, for it is impossible that sin should inhere in Christ. But whoever believes in Christ, he also inheres in Christ, and he has the same justice as Christ." [8]

In contrast to the alien justice of Christ, Luther sets up a second justice "which is ours and belongs to us (*propria*), not that we alone work it but that we cooperate with that other first and alien justice. And this justice is a good life in good works." [9] Luther goes on to say that the first justice gives rise to the voice of the bridegroom, who says to the soul, "I am yours." The second justice gives rise to the same voice of the soul to Christ. "Thus the soul no longer seeks to be just to herself, but she has Christ as her justice; therefore she seeks only the salvation of others." [10]

The Sermo de duplici iustitia illustrates how Luther's ideas on justice and his ideas on the two realms of Christian existence develop together. As the Christian's justification in Christ is being distinguished from his sanctification in the world, so the justice of Christ or in Christ is being distinguished from his actual justice in the world. Luther can accordingly give free rein to his convictions on the infinity and totality of the Christian's justice in Christ. Likewise, as the Christian's justification in Christ becomes antecedent to his sanctification in the world, so Luther begins to look with greater interest on the achievements of an actual or a civil justice in contrast to his early slighting approach

[8] Ibid., II,146,8. In 146,23 Luther relates the justice of God to the "work of the Lord" which had been important in the Dictata (see p. 10, Chapter I, above), but he no longer understands it "tropologically": ". . . in iusticia Christi dei mei, quae est per fidem, per gratiam, per misericordiam dei nostra facta, et haec vocatur in psalterio per multa loca opus domini, confessio, virtus dei, misericordia, veritas, iusticia. Omnia haec sunt nomina fidei in Christum, immo iusticiae quae est in Christo." In 146,29, however, he still speaks of it as a "iustitia infusa."

[9] Ibid., II, 146,36.

[10] Ibid., II,147,30.

to human justice. In this connection, Luther at the end of the
De duplici iustitia adds a discussion of the position of the Christian as magistrate, and here again we see the increased positive
importance of the worldly sphere.[11]

In the first part of 1519 Luther revised for publication his early
Lectures on Galatians (1516–17), and they appeared in print as
the Galatians Commentary. In general, the Galatians Commentary represents much the same view of justice which we have seen
in the Sermo de duplici iustitia, though the fact that the Commentary is simply a revision of the earlier Lectures means that we
find in it more of the ideas of 1513–18 than we would expect in a
new work of 1519.[12]

Luther again interprets the justice of God primarily in terms
of the union of the Christian with Christ. Thus he notes that justice is usually defined as giving to each his own, but according to
Paul, "justice is the faith in Jesus Christ (*fides Christi*), or the
power (*virtus*) by which one believes in Jesus Christ. . . . Hence
it follows that the just man through faith gives no one his own
by himself but through another, namely Jesus Christ, who alone
is so just that he gives to all what should be given them, nay,
all are indebted to him. Moreover, whoever believes in Christ
and by the spirit of faith has become one with Him, he has already
not only satisfied all, but he has further brought it to pass, that
all are indebted to him, since he has all things in common with
Christ. His sins are no longer his but Christ's, and in Christ sins
cannot conquer justice but are themselves conquered by it; therefore in Christ, sins are abolished. Further the justice of Christ
is now not only Christ's but also belongs to His Christian. . . .
This is the inestimable glory of the Christians, this is the ineffable
regard of divine charity toward us, by which such great things
and such precious things are given to us, and concerning which
Paul is rightly vehement lest they be rejected. Hence this justice
is also called the justice of God, as in I Corinthians I,(30) '(in
Jesus Christ), who of God was made for us justice and wisdom
and sanctification and redemption'." [13] Luther quotes a series of

[11] Ibid., II,150,32 f.
[12] For some discussion of the relation of the Commentary of 1519 to the Lectures of 1516–17, see the remarks of K. A. Meissinger in his edition LVII,2 pp. xi f.
[13] Galatians Commentary (1519), henceforth cited as Galatians (1519), II,503,36

scriptural texts and he then adds, "What is the need of more? The justice of God in the scriptures nearly always means faith and grace; only most rarely does it mean the severity by which He damns the impious and saves the just, as it is now commonly interpreted." [14]

As in the Sermo de duplici iustitia, Luther in the Galatians Commentary develops the contrast between two different justices. "One must know first of all that man is justified in two different and entirely contrary ways. The first way is external (*ab extra*), from works, from one's own forces. Such are human justices, gained by use (as it is said) and custom. Such a justice is described by Aristotle and by other philosophers; it is produced by civil laws, by ecclesiastical laws about ceremonies, by the command of reason and by prudence. Thus they suppose that a man becomes just by doing just works, temperate by doing temperate works and so on. This justice is also produced by the Law of Moses, by the Decalogue itself, namely when one serves God by fear of penalty or by promise of reward. . . . This is a servile justice, mercenary, false, specious, external, temporal, and worldly; it is a justice which does nothing for future glory but which receives its reward in this life." [15] On the other hand, there is the justice of Christ which we have already noted. "This is a justice which is free, gratuitous, solid, inward, eternal, true, celestial, and divine; it is a justice which in this life neither merits nor accepts nor seeks anything. Indeed since it is directed to Christ and His name, which is justice, the result is that the justice of Christ and of the Christian are one and the same ineffably joined together." [16]

Luther in the Galatians Commentary is mainly concerned to emphasize the sharp contrast between human and Christian justice, and he has relatively little to say of the positive value of human justice. He declares, for example, "Thus it is clear that Christian justice and human justice are not only entirely different but also entirely contrary, since human justice comes from works, while in the case of Christian justice, works come from it. Hence

---

f. See pp. 29 f., Chapter I, above, with note 132, for some discussion of the comparable passage in Galatians (1516–17).

[14] Ibid., II,504,25.

[15] Ibid., II,489,21.

[16] Galatians (1519), II,491,12.

it is no wonder that Pauline theology was almost completely destroyed and could not be understood, when the teachers of Christians came to be men who falsely asserted that the morals of Aristotle agreed with the doctrine of Christ and of Paul, men who indeed understood neither Aristotle nor Christ." [17] But Luther can also note in passing, "Of course, let the government (*civilis res*) have its justice, let the philosophers have theirs, and let each one have his own. We however must here take justice in its scriptural sense (*ad intellectum scripturae*). . . ." [18]

A significant illustration of Luther's reëvaluation of his older approach to human justice, or the justice of the law, is found in the Resolutiones Lutherianae of 1519. Luther is here defending his thesis that man sins even in good acts, and he argues that all of our justices, even those of grace, are impure and unclean before God. But this very condemnation of all human justice, what one might call a "theological use" of justice, leads to the denial of Luther's early thesis that the justice of the law is imperfect and impure with reference to the higher justice of the Gospel. "Even the ceremonial law was good, and it was instituted by God. Hence its justice was not in itself impure in any way, since the Jews were at that time compelled to obey it no less than the commands of the Decalogue." [19] One can speak of the justice of the law as impure only in relation to the time of the Gospel; it was then abrogated, "not because it was impure, but because it made the foolish confident against the grace of God, as the Apostle teaches in Romans and Galatians." [20]

Luther is here moving further away from his old analysis of justice in the Dictata super Psalterium. He had then recognized two types, the inferior justice of the old law and the superior justice of the Gospel. Toward the end of his early period, Luther tended to depress even more the position of the law, and in con-

---

[17] Ibid., II,493,6.

[18] Ibid., II,503,25. The phrase "iustitia civilis" is rare in this period, but see ibid., II,478,26: "Quare legis opera sunt post Christum sicut divitiae, honor, potestas, iusticia civilis ac quaecunque alia res temporalis"; Ad librum Ambrosii Catharini responsio (1521), VII,761,9.

[19] Resolutiones Lutherianae super propositionibus suis Lipsiae disputatae (1519), II,411,27. Luther later refers back to this passage with approval in the Rationis Latomianae confutatio (1521), VIII,70,9.

[20] Ibid., II,411,31.

sequence also of the justice of the law.[21] But now a new approach appears along with the new distinction between the two realms. The justices of the law and of the Gospel are admittedly always distinct and separate in the Christian's experience; each, however, is perfect in its own realm, and they cannot therefore be related as imperfect and perfect, much less as bad and good. The justice of the Gospel is immeasurably the more important for the Christian, but its realm is heaven. As a consequence it cannot modify or supplant in the world the justice of the law or, more generally, civil justice. And as a further consequence worldly or civil justice gains a positive value and importance in the life of the Christian far beyond that which it possessed in Luther's early thought.

Luther in the long and important Operationes in Psalmos (1519–21) carries a number of these developments on justice forward to further precision; notably he here advances to a more positive interpretation of human justice.

In the Operationes Luther speaks with freedom and assurance of the justice of God. We must learn, he says, to avoid the common misinterpretation as "the justice by which God is Himself just and by which He damns the impious." [22] The true meaning, in accord with Augustine's De spiritu et litera, is that it is the justice "with which God clothes man, as He justifies Him. This is the mercy of God, or justifying grace, by which we are reckoned (*reputamur*) just before God, and of which the Apostle speaks in Romans I,17 . . . and Romans III,(21). . . . It is called God's justice and also our justice, because by His grace it is given to us, like the work of God which He works in us, like the word of God which He speaks in us, like the virtues of God which He works in us, and like many others." [23] Luther cites other biblical passages in support of his statement, and he goes on to note that in Psalm XXIII (XXIV),5 the Hebrew word for justice is translated as mercy: He will accept blessing from the Lord and mercy from God his salvation. Luther approves the translation,

---

[21] See Chapter I, pp. 35 f.

[22] Operationes in Psalmos (1519–21), henceforth cited as Operationes, V,144,2. Compare V,583,27: "Virtus autem et salus Dei, sicut ubique fere pro ea re accipitur, qua nos deus salvos et validos facit, ut sint donorum dei vocabula magis quam autoris, sicut sepius dixi de sapientia dei, de iustitia dei, et similibus."

[23] Ibid., V,144,4.

for "the blessing of God and the justice of God are one and the same, that is, the very mercy and grace of God given us in Christ. And this manner of speaking of the justice of God, since it is different from the usual form of human speech, has caused much difficulty to many people. It is however not entirely to be denied that the justice of God, even in this manner of speaking, is the justice by which God is just, so that we and God are just with the same justice. In like manner with the same word God creates (*facit*) and we are what He is, so that we may be in Him and so that His being may be our being. But these are more profound matters than the present passage allows, and they are intended in a different sense than the others suppose. Though useful and necessary, these things are to be discussed at another time." [24]

In this passage, which comes early in the Operationes, Luther appears to have almost completed his rethinking of the justice of God; at the same time he still makes use of the language of his early period, and he does not give a full statement of his new position. The justice of God is of course declared not to be the justice by which he condemns sinners; Luther here repeats what he had said during his early period and what he will say throughout his life.[25] When Luther speaks of the justice of God as the justifying grace by which we are just before God, it is most natural to understand this in terms of the new justice in Christ; he goes on, however, to explain his point with analogies like the "work of God" which suggest the tropological justice of the Dictata super Psalterium.[26] Finally, Luther adds, in contrast to the general approach of the early period, that the justice of God by which we are justified is the same justice by which God Himself is just, but he reserves a full explanation for later discussion.

Luther offers such an explanation in the Operationes in connection with an analysis of the glory of God. Luther starts from the fact that the glory of God in the Bible is sometimes to be identified with Christ. "The Apostle dares call Him the justice,

[24] Ibid., V,144,15.

[25] See above, Chapter I, p. 10 and for example, Luther's statements in the Preface to the Opera Latina of 1545, LIV,185,17 f.: "Oderam enim vocabulum istud 'Iustitia Dei', quod usu et consuetudine omnium doctorum doctus eram philosophice intelligere de iustitia (ut vocant) formali seu activa, qua deus est iustus et peccatores iniustosque punit."

[26] See pp. 9 f., Chapter I, above.

strength, wisdom, glory, redemption, and sanctification of God, because we justify God through Him as we recognize and confess God as powerful, wise, and glorious. And again (*rursum*), as we worship and honour God by this sacrifice of justice, wisdom, strength and so on, we deserve from Him in return (*rursus*) to be justified, to be strengthened, and to become wise. . . . Nor does anyone offer this sacrifice except one who, having lost his own name, invokes in faith the name of the Lord, that is the wisdom, strength, and justice of God, as I said, in the meantime suffering himself to be held weak, foolish, and bad, knowing nothing of vindication, judgment, or glory, so that we and God might be glorified with the same name, so that we and God might be justified with the same justice, and so that we and God might be wise with the same wisdom. And this is what Peter says, II Peter I,(4). The greatest and most precious things are given to us in Christ, so that we might be sharers (*consortes*) of the divine nature. . . ." [27]

Luther goes on to make similar points in connection with the praise (*laus*) of God, for this praise, by which He is praised in us and we in Him, is far different from human praise. "Our praise, since it is God's praise and from God, is not in the public view nor in the theatre of the world (*in propatulo et theatro mundi*) nor does it appear to men, nor even to us, but like our life, it is hidden with Christ in God." [28]

Thus in summary, says Luther, there is a kind of trade (*mutuum*) between God and men, brought about through the marvellous and most sweet traffic (*commercio*) of Christ. "In this trade (*mutuo*) lies the justice of God, by which we are justified. As we praise and honour Him, thereby giving what we owe, He in return (*rursus*) honours us, thereby giving the reward which we merited." [29]

The argument just noted has certain points in common with Luther's earlier discussion of the ways in which "God is justified in His words," [30] but Luther's further explanation places the dis-

---

[27] Operationes V,252,11.

[28] Ibid., V,252,31.

[29] Ibid., V,253,29. Compare p. 543,4; 608,6; Von der Freiheit eines Christenmenschen (1520), VII,25,34 where Luther speaks of "der fröhlich wechſſel und streytt."

[30] See pp. 9 and 24, Chapter I, above.

cussion clearly in the context of the re-orientation of 1518–19. How he asks, can we praise God so that He may praise us, when we cannot love Him unless He loves us first? Luther replies that the Bible speaks both of the grace of God and of the fruit of His grace; if we confuse them, we fall into the error of Pelagianism, "God alone makes the good tree before us and without us (*ante nos et sine nobis*), and it is necessary that the tree exist before the fruits. But it is also necessary that the fruits exist before the reward. Hence this passage of the Psalms . . . refers not to initial grace but to final grace, that is, to the reward itself which is given to the first grace and to its fruits. . . . Thus, whoever has turned to God and praises Him, that is, whoever having accepted grace lives for the praise of God on earth, him God praises in heaven at the same time and forever (*simul et inaeternum*). At the same time and forever, I say, that is in the present and in the future." [31]

In this discussion Luther preserves something of the approach of his early period, notably in the thesis that the fruits of grace in this life merit God's final grace in the future. Basically, however, he has located the justice of God in a different context. What is primary is the initial grace by which we are just in Christ, and the justice of the fruits of grace is always consequent upon this; this is the direction of thought of his new theory of justification.

In other passages of the Operationes, Luther moves away from his earlier "effective" sense of the justice of God to a greater emphasis on the Christian's union with Christ. On one occasion, he reaches the conclusion: "I do not seek salvation in myself nor in any men, for the salvation of man is vain; I am glad to be deserted by myself and by them, so that I may in Christ your Son be freed from all sins and evils." [32] Luther goes on to quote I Corinthians I,30 on Christ as "our justice, sanctification, wisdom, and redemption." Luther argues that Paul here finely explains the action (*energiam*) of Christ's name and our incorporation into Christ; we should avoid the interpretation of the sophists "who make Christ wisdom and justice for us in such a way that He is always the object or the cause of our justice. Such sophists do not

[31] Operationes, V,254,13.
[32] Operationes, V,311,2.

at all understand the use of Christ, which is through faith in Him, and this is all that Paul is speaking about. Faith in Christ makes Him live and move and act in me, . . . and we become one flesh and one body through the inward (*intimam*) and ineffable transformation of our sin into His justice." [33]

As we have already seen,[34] Luther in the Operationes can distinguish between our justice in Christ and our justice in the world as between grace and the fruits of grace. He can also make this distinction as between faith and charity, two concepts which Luther in his early period virtually identified.[35] "The entering into Christ is faith, which gathers us into the richness of the justice of God. By this justice we are already satisfying God, and we are just, needing no works for the obtaining of justice. The going out from Christ is charity, which takes us clothed with the justice of God and sends us out to the service of our neighbor and for the exercise of our own body in the relief of the poverty of others. . . ."[36] While Luther does not develop a technical terminology, he has in the Operationes gone a long way toward working out the contrast between a "passive" and an "active" justice. For example, he can contrast the theological virtues (in this context, faith, hope, and charity are grouped together) with works. "Perhaps the other virtues can be made perfect by acting, but faith, hope, and charity can be made perfect only by our being passive (*patiendo*) . . . , for the works of the other virtues are the fruits of faith, hope, and charity, as if one saw in them faith incarnate, hope incarnate, and charity incarnate. . . ."[37] In the first case, says Luther, we have nothing but passivity (*mera passio*); in the second, the will which has become incarnate or which has flowed out into the external work may be said to cooperate and to be active (*cooperari et activitatem habere*).[38]

Thus in the Operationes in Psalmos Luther effects a general reconstruction of his earlier doctrine of the justice of God, even

---

[33] Ibid., V,311,8. Compare p. 608,10: ". . . ita ut iam non modo obiective (ut dicunt) sit nostra Christi iustitia, sed et formaliter, sicut non tantum obiective Christi sunt peccata nostra, sed et formaliter."

[34] See above p. 83.

[35] See p. 15, Chapter I, above.

[36] Ibid., V,408,4.

[37] Ibid., V,176,2.

[38] Ibid., V,177,21.

though he has not yet removed all ambiguities. The original concept of the justice of God as that by which God makes us just and which is a stage on the way to salvation, is disappearing. Luther now starts from a contrast between the justice by which we are already just in Christ and the justice with which we act in the world. It will be noted that neither of these can be identified simply as the "justice of God," and in any case the "justice of God" now begins to drop out of Luther's writings as a technical term.

From a somewhat different standpoint, Luther in the Operationes effects a reconstruction of "human justice" and gives it a more positive place in the life of the Christian. In general what happens here is that Luther now reëvaluates human justice as one of the forms which the Christian's justice in Christ takes as it moves into the world in charity.

In some cases, we can trace this change as a modification of Luther's earlier interpretation of the Psalms in the Dictata super Psalterium (1513–15) or in the Unbekannte Fragmente (1518?). For example, Luther early in the Operationes comes to the text of Psalm IV: "When I called on Him, the God of my justice heard me." In the earlier commentaries, Luther understood "my justice" as "the justice of God." In the Operationes Luther still admits this as possible, but his own opinion is now that "my justice" refers to "human justice." He argues that in the Bible, "my justice" does not refer to the justifying grace which is the justice of God, but rather to one's own private right (*causam propriam*). This, says Luther, is justice among men "which God Himself defends (*vindicat*), even though this justice is not enough for anyone before God." [39]

Luther makes similar points in other passages of the Operationes. In his commentary on Psalm VII,9, Luther begins by emphasizing that it is God who rules the peoples, and His rule is defended when innocence is defended. "Thus we see that it is

---

[39] Ibid., V,100,30. Compare Dictata, III,42,12 (1516); Unbekannte Fragmente (1518?), 32,24 f. Luther later refers back to this passage of the Operationes, p. 234,7: "Diximus autem ps.iiij aliud in sacris literis esse iustitiam meam et iustitiam dei, quod illa sit causa cuiusque propria iusta, qua coram hominibus et in conscientia sua sit irreprehensibilis, licet coram dei iudicio non sufficiat; haec vero sit gratia et misericordia iustificans nos etiam coram deo."

not enough, when someone suffers for a just cause or for the truth, that the affair be committed to God and that the sufferer be ready to yield and to be turned to dust with his glory. One must also urgently pray that God judge and justify the cause of truth, not for one's own profit but for the ministry of God and the salvation of the people. . . ." [40] Later in the same discussion Luther notes that the justice of God is not in us, but in God and outside us, "so that no one may be given an opportunity of priding himself on his own justice before God. But for the salvation of others we should . . . always seek to justify our innocence before men." [41]

Finally, in the commentary on Psalm XV,2 Luther identifies this human justice with the morality taught by Christ in the Golden Rule. The phrase "who works justice" does not refer to the justice of God "but to the justice by which we live among men, injuring no one and giving to each his own. . . . What is it that we owe to one another? That which Christ teaches. . . . 'Whatsoever you wish that men should do unto you, do you that unto them'." [42] Luther has thus reached an end-point in his revision of the concept of human justice in the life of the Christian. On the one hand, the Golden Rule, which had once been identified with the new, spiritual law, is now declared to be the basic principle of justice among men ; on the other hand, human justice, once of little importance in the life of the Christian, is now identified with the morality of Christ.

Luther continues of course to assert the over-riding superiority of divine justice in relation to human justice. He speaks, for example, of great kings of the past. "And although they were famous in human and political justice or wisdom, they were all found to be vain, false, and wicked before God and in the things

---

[40] Ibid., V,233,27.

[41] Ibid., V,234,21. Compare 247,28: "Haec omnia mihi dicta et orata . . . pro ignorantia et iustitia mea tuenda secundum conscientiam et quantum est in conspectu hominum. Caeterum non in eam confido nec talem iudico, qua stare coram deo possim, sicut Apostolus i. Cor. iij. . . . Ita et ego aliam habeo iustitiam, in qua glorior, nempe iustitiam dei, misericordiam, et gratiam, qua ignoscit mihi peccata mea et iustificat in conspectu suo. De qua iustitia neque me iacto neque mihi confiteor, quasi sit mea . . . . Quare per iustitiam meam domino et /248 populo quidem libens servierim et impiis restiterim: At in iustitia dei mihi profuerim."

[42] Ibid., V,432,3. Later pp. 516,32 f. Luther brings his distinction into relation with the two positions of Job and of his friends.

which are God's." [43] "There is no comparison between the justice of the flesh (which is the doing of the law) and the justice of the spirit (which is faith in Christ)." [44] Nevertheless each justice has its own positive value in its own area, just as do the two wisdoms, of the spirit and of the flesh. "The wisdom of the spirit preaches to the wisdom of the flesh in such a way that it makes fleshly wisdom foolish and captive to the Word, for the wisdom of the spirit is the day before God, while the wisdom of the flesh is the day before the world, that is to say: each is in its own place famous, bright, and glorious." [45]

In the Operationes in Psalmos Luther has thus established the main outlines of a new doctrine of justice, even though he has not yet filled in all the details. On the one hand, the Christian has a justice in Christ; this is, in later terminology, a passive justice, and the Christian already possesses it completely. On the other hand, the Christian's justice in Christ, his faith, flows out into the world as charity. Further, Luther has gone a long way toward equating this charity with the "human justice" which God establishes and defends in the world.

A Sermon of 1520, on John XVI,5 f., illuminates other new developments in Luther's thinking. As he summarizes his text, "These words are new to our age and not heard before: that sin is not to believe in Christ, that justice is for Christ to go to the Father and to be no longer seen, and that judgment is for the prince of this world to be already judged." [46] The Sermon is of particular interest for its new treatment of the biblical "justice and judgment" which was so important in the early Dictata super Psalterium.[47]

Luther first explains that disbelief is sin, for only faith can purify the heart. He goes on to argue that while justice is usually defined as giving each his own, this definition means the same as

[43] Ibid., V,293,24. For the phrase "politicae virtutes," see De libertate Christiana (1520), VII,54,18.

[44] Operationes, V,518,2. Later, on p. 608,6, Luther speaks first of the marvellous trade (admirabili commertio) by which our sins are no longer ours but Christ's; he then observes, p. 608,21: "In cuius comparatione foedissime sordet, stercus et detrimentum est iustitia, quae ex lege est, etiam sine querela incedens. . . ."

[45] Ibid., V,545,10.

[46] IV,694,25.

[47] See pp. 9 f., Chapter I, above.

Christ's going to His Father and being no longer seen. "By faith one adheres to Christ, and Christ goes out of the world to the Father and thus leaves the world and all things. Hence it is necessary that wherever Christ goes, there also goes the heart of one who believes in Him, as Colossians III,(3). Our life is hidden with Christ in God. . . . Thus the result is that the Christian in his heart is in heaven and with the Father together with Christ (*apud Patrem cum Christo*), and thus he is not seen in the world." [48] In this way the Christian has abandoned and surrendered everything; he no longer owes anything and he has given to each his own, "and he is altogether and entirely just (*est totus omnino iustus*). . . ." [49] He lives and acts in the world, not for the sake of his justice there, "but because one cannot live in the world without these actions (*sine istis negotiis*). . . . He pursues justice here unwillingly for the necessity of this life or for the sake of others and in order to correct their lives." [50] Lastly Luther explains that judgment means that the prince of this world is already condemned. "Just as Christ, the head of all the just and the fountain of justice, by His passage draws with Him to the Father from the world all those who adhere to Him, . . . so the Devil . . . draws with him necessarily, wherever he is himself drawn, all those who adhere to him." [51] Therefore all those who are of the world are already judged. "Moreover every man because of the flesh of sin is still partly in the world and under the rule (*principatu*) of the devil, and by so much the more as he has stronger desires and passions, and since there is no one on the earth who does good and does not sin. . . . Therefore the result is that every man is already judged with the Devil and damned as guilty to eternal hell." [52]

Luther in this Sermon clearly moves away from his earlier interpretation of the tropological justice and judgment of God according to which man achieved justice in the spirit as he condemned his flesh. Luther's position now is that the Christian is already just in heaven, whither he has been drawn by the "going of Christ to

[48] Sermon (1520), IV,697,5.
[49] Ibid., IV,697,25.
[50] Ibid., IV,698,21.
[51] Ibid., IV,698,40 f.
[52] Ibid., IV,699,7.

the Father." On the other hand, he is already totally condemned as he is on earth, for no human justice, whether of nature or grace, can survive God's judgment apart from Christ.

In the writings which we have so far noted for Luther's idea of justice, he has not explicitly discussed the relation of faith to the Christian's justification, and his doctrine of the two justices is therefore still open to misinterpretation. In his early theology, faith or the justice of faith was defined in terms of a vision and love of things spiritual; as such it was one of the causes of salvation. With the re-orientation of 1518–19 the concept of faith changes; it is no longer synonymous with "intellect" but it refers rather to the Christian's trust in the promises of Christ.[53] The question then is whether this new type of faith is a cause of salvation. Luther in the period 1518–22, and also in his later writings, frequently speaks as if it were, or at least so that his statements do not prevent our interpreting them in this way. But in 1521 in the Rationis Latomianae confutatio Luther considers the problem explicitly, and here, as on every later occasion when he essays a precise statement, he denies that human faith is a cause of salvation. He thus preserves the new direction of his thinking about justification, according to which our total justification in Christ is always primary, and he maintains the context within which alone his new doctrine of the two justices of the Christian can survive.

Luther in the argument with which we are concerned makes use of the distinction, established earlier in the Rationis Latomianae confutatio, between grace and gift, and it will be remembered that in this terminology, God's grace is His total favor, while faith and justice are His partial gifts.[54] Luther now maintains that God did not wish us to rest either in ourselves or in His gifts, but only in Christ. Hence the justice, which has been begun (*iustitia illa incepta*), is not enough "unless it cling to Christ's justice and flow from Him." [55] Similarly, "faith is not

[53] Compare, for the new definition, Operationes, V,395,12: "Fides autem esse nullo modo potest, nisi sit vivax quaedam et indubitata opinio, qua homo certus est, super omnem certitudinem sese placere deo, se habere propitium et ignoscentem deum in omnibus . . . ; 399,2 Iusti autem efficimur per fidem, quae credit, deum esse nobis propitium."

[54] See pp. 44 f., Chapter II, above.

[55] Rationis Latomianae confutatio (1521), VIII,111,31.

enough, but (only) faith which hides itself beneath the wings of Christ and glories in His justice." [56] And in summary, Christ is the Christian's atonement, "so that they are safe under His grace, not because they believe and have faith and (His) gift, but because they have them in God's grace." [57]

Luther has accordingly by 1521 completed his first rethinking of the problem of justice in the light of his re-orientation of 1518–19, and one may see the codification of this thought in the Kirchenpostille of 1522. In a passage which we have already noted in part [58] Luther declares that we must accustom ourselves to the usage of Scripture, which sets up two justices. "The one is a human justice, which St. Paul describes here (Titus III,5) and in many other places. The other is a divine justice, that is, the divine grace which justifies us through faith, as St. Paul explains it here and as he says at the end of the Epistle (III,17): so that we, being justified by His grace, are heirs of eternal life. Here you see that God's grace is our justice, which is therefore called God's justice, because He gives it to us out of grace, and which becomes ours, since we receive it." [59] Luther continues, as we have already seen,[60] with an account of the totality of this justice which we have already received. "Therefore, all the life of a good believing Christian after Baptism is nothing more than an awaiting the revelation of a holiness which he already has." [61]

It does not appear that Luther developed these ideas much further in the middle 1520's,[62] and we shall turn immediately to the mature statement of his position as it appears in 1529 and in

---

[56] Ibid., VIII,112,2.

[57] Ibid., VIII,114,19. Compare for Luther's early and transitional positions Galatians (1516–17), LVII,2 p.74,9 and Galatians (1519), II,495,1.

[58] See pp. 58 f., Chapter II, above.

[59] Kirchenpostille (1522), X,1,1 p. 106,2. Compare X,1,2 pp. 36,22 f.

[60] See pp. 55 f., Chapter II, above.

[61] Kirchenpostille (1522), X,1,1 p. 108,6. Compare X,1,1 pp. 325,14 f. where Luther argues that we must distinguish person and work, "Nu gehörtt die rechtfertigung auff die person und nit auff die werck. Denn die person und nit die werck wirt gerechtfertiget, selig, vorurteyllt, odder vordampt."

[62] In the De servo arbitrio (1525) Luther states the doctrine of the two justices somewhat more clearly than in his earlier writings, XVIII,771,37: "Observa quaeso et hic partitionem Pauli, duplicem Abrahae iustitiam recitantis. Una est operum, id est moralis et civilis, sed hac negat eum iustificari coram Deo etiamsi coram hominibus per illam iustus sit. . . . /772,11 Altera est fidei iustitia, quae constat non operibus ullis, sed favente et reputante Deo per gratiam."

the following years. To a large extent this statement is in its essentials simply a more coherent and unified formulation, using the new dualist contrasts of his mature theology, of the ideas which we have already seen in the writings of 1518–22. At one point, however, Luther is able to profit by the intervening development of his thought on a related problem. As we shall see in detail later,[63] Luther during the middle 1520's worked out a new doctrine of God's world-government (*Weltregiment*), and this doctrine helps to bring under a single rubric morality and government. In the writings of 1518–22 Luther after the Sermo de triplici iustitia seems to work with a somewhat hesitant and uneasy identification of the Christian's actual justice with civil justice. The developments of the middle 1520's on world-government, and also on the civil use of the law, make it easier by 1529 to work out the general concept of a worldly justice which may be called indifferently "active justice" or "civil justice."

A convenient introduction to Luther's mature theory of the two justices is found in a Sermon of October 5, 1529. Luther here sets up the basic distinction of the two justices, and he is now able to give a much more adequate account of worldly justice, which he brings into close connection with the two governments of God and with worldly "estates and callings." "You must know that justice is double and that civil and Christian justice are to be carefully distinguished. Civil justice here on earth is (like Christian justice) also a justice which God established and wishes preserved; He placed it in the Ten Commandments in the second table. . . . This is worldly or human justice, and its purpose is that we live together in peace and enjoy the goods which God gives us." [64] Luther links this justice with the estate (*status*) and calling (*vocatio*) of the individual. But this remains in the realm of the world (*in hoc regno mundi*); there must also be a higher saving justice which brings about the remission of sins, and Luther goes on to describe this Christian justice in the second part of the Sermon.

Luther's classic theological statement of the two justices is

[63] See below, Chapter IV,3, pp. 159 f.

[64] XXIX,565,2. It will be noted that here, as so often, Luther states his doctrine most precisely in the context of the thesis that the Christian is at the same time just and a sinner; compare 569,19 f. and specially 573,6 f.

found in the Lectures on Galatians (1531). As we have already seen,[65] Luther argues that Paul's main purpose in Galatians is to distinguish Christian justice from all other justices, for Christian justice is merely passive, while the others are all active.

"Hence Christian justice is to be carefully distinguished from all other justices, for these inferior justices come from laws, precepts, traditions, and works; they constitute a justice which we do ourselves, whether from our natural powers or else from the gift of God. . . . But the justice which is done by us is not Christian justice, and we do not become worthy (*probi*) by it. Christian justice is quite contrary to it, for it is a passive justice, which we simply receive and in which we do not act at all but suffer another, God, to act in us." [66] And Luther argues that just as God carefully separated heaven and earth, so we should carefully separate these two justices.[67]

The two justices are thus absolutely contrasted; at the same time, each has its absolute claim in its own realm. "The highest art of the Christians is to know nothing of all active justice or of the law, just as outside the people of God, it is the highest wisdom to know and to regard the law. A marvellous thing: I ought myself to learn and I should teach other men that they ignore the law and behave as if there were no law, and at the same time in

---

[65] See pp. 62 f. Chapter II, above.

[66] Galatians (1531), XL,1 pp. 40,11 f. Where Luther speaks of the other justices as 'inferior" (*peiores*), it is possible that this is simply a false reading for "the former justices" (*priores*). Compare pp. 44,8 f.: "Si volo docere homines, ut sic legem inspiciant, ut per eam coram deo iustificentur, extra limites legis ivi, ut Papa. Ibi confundo iusticiam activam et passivam. . . . Ibi docendum quod activa iusticia ex oculis removenda. Iam tempus recipiendi alteram iusticiam, quae est passiva, quae non patitur opera, legem; 48,1 Sic dicit iusticia passiva: Sum quidem peccator secundum hanc vitam et eius iusticiam ut filius Adam, ubi accusat me lex, regnat; sed secundum Christum, gloriam, nescio quicquam de lege, peccato, et propter hanc iusticiam passivam tandem in morte sequetur iusticia carnis, quod corpus etiam liberabitur a servitute legis. In hac vita accusatur iusticia operum. Spiritus remittit, regnat, et salvus est iusticia passiva, quia scit se habere dominum sedentem ad dextram patris, qui destruxit mortem et triumphavit, Col. 2,; p. 51,1 Ut sic conscientia possit servari in suo regno, quod est securitas leticiae, Passiva iusticia, i.e. quod praestat Christus."

Luther thus uses "iustitia passiva" as the key concept in his summary of the argument of Galatians, and it is decisive in the development of his own thought. He rarely employs it in the actual commentary on Paul's text, though see XL,1 pp. 69,11 f. and 185,3.

[67] Galatians (1531), XL,1 p. 207,5.

the world, I ought so to emphasize and urge the law, as if there were no grace." [68]

In connection with his description of Christian justice as passive, Luther denies that it may be identified with charity or with any human "quality." As we shall see more clearly in Luther's discussion of law, he insists in his mature period that charity be placed in the realm of the world and of law, not in the heaven of passive justice and the Gospel. [69] On occasion, Luther may say that faith is the "formal justice" of the Christian, but he is careful to add that no man is ever saved because of his faith as a human quality but only because of Christ. [70]

Despite his rigorous distinction between Christian and human justice, Luther can also, as we have seen, [71] declare that the justice of faith and the justice of works are one simple justice. How are we to reconcile these two apparently contradictory approaches? Luther affirms the unity of the two justices since both depend completely on the single will of God. The justice which the Christian has totally in Christ is the same justice which he possesses partially in the world. Luther distinguishes the two justices because the Christian's two realms of existence are distinguished, and as long as the Christian is in this life he may never "mix" them. But while the two realms are thus distinct for Christian experience, the total heavenly justice is in some way primary and active, flowing into the world. "Hence faith is neither the Law nor the doing of the Law, but something else which is prerequisite to the Law. Faith perpetually gives life and justifies. It does not remain idle; it is incarnated and becomes a man." [72] As so often, Luther's final explanation is the parallel of the union of God and man in Christ. "I say that humanity is not divinity, and nevertheless man is

---

[68] Ibid., XL,1 pp.43,9 f.; compare p. 558,6.

[69] See pp. 101 f., below.

[70] Galatians (1531), XL, 1 p. 229,2. Luther's statement is carefully qualified and must be understood in the context of the discussion pp. 225,10 ff.: "Sic formalis mea iustitia est, non est charitas quae informat fidem, sed fiducia cordis mei in rem quam non videt, et tamen habet Christum praesentem. Ideo iustificat fides, dicimus, quia habet illum thesaurum, quia Christus adest; quomodo, non est cogitabile. Qui habet veram fiduciam cordis, — adest ipse in ipsa nebula, fide. Das ist formalis iustitia, propter istam fidem iustificatur, sicut ipsi dicunt: propter charitatem."

[71] See pp.64 f. Chapter II, above.

[72] Galatians (1531), XL,1 pp.426,9 f.

God. Thus law is not faith, but they coincide in the concrete case and the composite." [73]

Luther in the Lectures on Galatians (1531) has relatively little to say about civil justice in itself; he is much more concerned to place it within the proper realm than to describe it for its own sake. In the introduction to the Lectures, he offers a brief classification of the other justices which are to be grouped together as all active justices. There is political justice, treated by rulers and philosophers; there is ceremonial justice, based on human tradition, as in the papacy or, better, in parents and teachers; beyond these there is the moral justice of the Decalogue as taught by Moses. Luther notes that he and his followers teach these other justices too, when once they have laid the proper foundation of Christian justice. All such justice is active in contrast to Christian, passive justice, and it all depends on the Law and on works. While active justice can never lead to salvation and while it makes no claim to salvation, nevertheless God established it and God supports it.[74]

This comparatively brief treatment of civil justice in the Lectures on Galatians (1531) is typical for Luther's mature period. The concept of civil justice plays an essential rôle in Luther's thought as he applies to the idea of justice his basic distinction between the two realms of Christian existence. However, when it comes to describing the worldly realm, Luther makes much more extensive use of other concepts, such as those of God's world-government, or of the estates, callings, and hierarchies. Possibly he felt that any doctrine of civil justice was always open to a new misunderstanding as another "justice of works" leading to salvation. In any case, while the contrast between Christian and civil justice sets the basic context for Luther's theology of society, he works out the details of this theology in other terminology.

2. Law.

The development of Luther's ideas on law in 1518–19 and the following years is comparable to the development of his ideas on

[73] Ibid., XL,1 p. 427,4. Compare also the discussion in Luther's preparation for the Lectures pp. 19,1 f. and spec. lines 19 f.
[74] Ibid., XL,1 p. 40,4; 305,7; 392,6 ff.

justice during the same period. For the most part the development in justice precedes, and the development in law follows; in some cases Luther seems to solve the problem of law by reference to the already solved problem of justice.

The comparability of the two developments results from the fact that in each case Luther is revising similar earlier ideas in the light of his new insights on the two distinct realms of Christian existence. In the case of justice, Luther during 1513–18 had concentrated his attention on the tropological or effective justice of God, and he found in it the basis for the future salvation of the Christian by a God whose mercy will not impute to him the sins that remain. After 1518–19 the problem of justice splits into two problems corresponding to the two realms of Christian existence. Luther accordingly develops the contrast between a Christian, passive justice, by which the Christian is already justified in heaven, and an active civil justice through which the Christian performs good works on earth.

In like manner in the case of law, Luther during 1513–18 argues that God's law makes demands on the sinner and that these demands must be at least partially met so that God may in the future accept him. The basic approach persists despite changes in terminology. Thus in the Dictata super Psalterium (1513–15) Luther emphasizes a spiritual law which both makes the demands and also contains the grace which meets them. In the period 1515–18 he speaks primarily of the contrast between a law, which simply makes demands, and a Gospel or grace, which meets these demands. In each case, however, the fundamental pattern is the same. Demands are made by God, and these demands must be met, at least partially, so that in the future life God will enable the Christian to meet them completely. Consequently neither early form of the doctrine of law is adequate to Luther's new distinction between the Christian's complete justification in Christ and his partial sanctification in the world.

Before looking at the details of Luther's reconstruction of his doctrine of law, we do well to note that while in the period 1513–18 both the concept of justice and the concept of law spanned the whole process of justification, after 1518–19 each concept is limited to certain specific contexts. Roughly speaking, Luther after 1518–19 needs three basic propositions to cover his theory of justification and sanctification: I. The Christian is totally just in Christ; II. The Christian, like all other men, is totally a sinner before God apart from Christ; III. The Christian in the world is engaged in the process of sanctification. As we have already seen, Luther's doctrine of justice after 1518–19 is relevant only to the first and third propositions; through passive justice, the Christian is totally just in Christ, and through active justice he moves forward in sanctification in the world. On the other hand, his doctrine of law after 1518–19 will be relevant only to the second and third propositions; through the theological use of the law, God shows all men that they are condemned absolutely apart from Christ, and through the civil use of the law, He provides for the order and discipline of the world.

As in the case of justice, Luther works out the essential changes in his doctrine of law during the years immediately following 1518–19, and he has completed them by about 1522. Accordingly we shall again study the transition period first and then turn to the more general statement which appears toward 1530.

It will be remembered that in the years 1515–18 Luther had moved to an increasingly sharp contrast between any law and the Gospel.[75] The Law, when spiritually understood, can do nothing but condemn and kill; only the Gospel's grace can free men and save them, and those thus saved are no longer under the law. Luther repeats many of these statements in the writings of 1518–19, but we also find signs of the emergence of a new position.

In the Galatians Commentary (1519) Luther maintains most of the positions of the earlier Lectures on Galatians (1515–16) and of the Sermons of 1516–17.[76] In some cases, however, he moves even further away from his first position of the Dictata super Psalterium. Thus on one occasion he denies "that the Old Law is fulfilled by the New Law in the sense that the New Law is spiritual understanding and spiritual words. Grace alone is the fullness of the Law, and words do not fulfill words, but things fulfill words." [77] On another occasion, Luther points out that Paul

---

[75] See pp. 34 ff., Chapter I, above.

[76] See pp. 38 f., Chapter I, above.

[77] Galatians Commentary (1519), II,575,38 f. Compare the Sermon from the

is implicitly comparing Moses and Christ; he goes on to comment, "Therefore Christ is not a legislator but a fulfiller of the law. Every legislator is a minister of sin, since through law he gives occasion for sin."[78] In his early period Luther had commonly referred to Christ as legislator; now he is moving slowly toward his later violent attack on any such description.

In another passage of the Galatians Commentary, Luther brings the law into relation with the Christian who is both just and sinful. The passage is difficultly transitional, and it is sometimes hard to be sure whether Luther is speaking of total justice or of partial justice. He begins by explaining that Paul attacks the works of the law, so that no one will attempt through them to introduce justice into the heart; the Christian is already just in his heart through the justice of faith, from which works and the fullness of the law flow into his flesh.[79] But the Law is still important even for the Christian. "Hence the precepts of the Law are necessary only for sinners. But the just are sinners too because of their flesh. . . . Accordingly the precepts are necessary, not that we might be justified through their works, but that being already just we might know in what way (*qua ratione*) our spirit should crucify our flesh and direct it in the things of this life. . . ."[80] Thus by 1519 Luther clearly rejects some of the "antinomian" tendencies of his early period. Less clearly, he moves away from the interpretation of the Law as serving only to kill and condemn, an interpretation which had been dominant in his writings of 1515–18; the Law also serves in some way to direct us "in the things of this life."

One may see signs of a similar change in a remark of the Resolutiones Lutherianae (1519). Luther here reasserts the familiar doctrine of 1515–18, that the Law without grace simply kills and makes sinful. However, he adds the qualification, "although it does restrain the hand externally."[81] The notion of the law as restraining the hand was important in the Dictata super Psalterium

---

Poliander Codex (1519), IX,437,4 where Luther attacks the interpretation of the Gospel as "leges quedam, quas secundum spiritum Christus intelligendas docuit."
[78] Ibid., II,494,9.
[79] Ibid., II,497,25.
[80] Ibid., II,497,36 f.
[81] Resolutiones (1519), II,422,6.

as a characteristic of the literal law of Moses, but it had almost disappeared in the writings of 1515–18 as Luther concentrated on the absolute contrast between Law and grace. Now with the re-orientation of 1518–19 Luther begins to feel the need for some recognition of a "worldly" function of the Law, and he moves very tentatively toward this in the Galatians Commentary and in the Resolutiones Lutherianae.

Luther reaches clarity on the main outlines of a new doctrine of law in a Sermon of November 30, 1520, where he adapts some of the concepts of his early period to the new context produced by the re-orientation of 1518–19. In his early period Luther had worked with a double division of God's message to man, though he did not always explain it in the same way. In the Dictata super Psalterium, he had contrasted the literal law of Moses with the spiritual law of the Gospel which contains grace; in the period 1515–18 he had concentrated on the contrast between a law without grace, which always condemns, and the Gospel, which alone saves without law. In the Sermon of 1520 Luther preserves both these contrasts and reinterprets them, as he proclaims a triple division of God's message to man.

Luther starts from the three wells dug by Isaac (Genesis XXVI, 19 f.), and he goes on to compare these with the three "preachings" of Moses, Elias, and Christ. "Moses is preached, when the Law is set forth; Elias is preached when the spirit is added; Christ is preached, when the forgiveness of sins is proclaimed." [82] Or, in another reporting of the same Sermon: "The preaching of Moses is to preach the Law and external works. The preaching of Elias is the exposition in the Spirit. The preaching of Christ is the Gospel. . . ." [83] In his further discussion Luther explains that the Mosaic Law is a veiled doctrine. Moses had to veil himself (Exodus XXXIV,33; II Corinthians III,13), since the Jews could not bear his open countenance. Elias then removed the veil and revealed the spiritual demands of the Law; he showed that "we are all alike and that we are all equally sinners." [84] In the Dictata super Psalterium Luther had spoken of the veil of Moses,

---

[82] Sermon, IX,387, 14.

[83] Sermon, IX,486, 21.

[84] Ibid., 487, 5. Compare Operationes, V,603,28; Rationis Latomianae confutatio (1521), VIII,70,20.

but here the removal of the veil regularly reveals the spiritual law which saves.[85] In the period 1515–18 Luther speaks instead of the revealing of a spiritual law which damns, and he gives little importance to the original veiled law. Now after 1518–19 Luther of course preserves the concept of a spiritual law which damns, but he also goes back to reëstablish the positive function of the veiled law as a law of external works and civil order.

While Luther by 1520 had clearly established a triple division of God's message to man, it is not yet evident how this division is to be related to the basic contrast between the Law and the Gospel. In other words, will he place Elias on the side of Moses or on the side of Christ? We have seen that even in the early period Luther had developed the doctrine of a double office of the Gospel, first the spiritual interpretation of the Law and second the giving of grace.[86] Further, Luther repeats this doctrine in the Enarrationes of 1521.[87] But while such a solution is always theoretically possible and while the problem is one of terminology not substance, Luther's regular approach in his mature period is first to set up the primary division between the Law and the Gospel, and second to explain that the Law has a double office, eventually to be described as the two uses of the law, the civil use and the theological use.

The contrast between the two uses of the law is clearly explained in the Kirchenpostille of 1522. In the Sermon on Galatians III, 23–29 Luther asks what is the purpose of the law, and he replies that it has two functions. "The first is, that it maintains discipline among us and urges us to an honest way of life externally, so that we can live together and not devour one another, as would happen if there were no law, no fear, no punishment. . . . The second function is, that man learn through the Law how false and evil is his heart, how far he still is from God. . . ."[88] Luther in the Kirchenpostille also sets up a close connection between the

---

[85] See pp. 14 f., Chapter I, above. Compare also III,33,10: ". . . quia est lex Euangelii revelata veritas: illi autem suas tabulas invelatas, i.e. legis onera magis significativa quam expletiva, etc."

[86] See pp. 38 f., Chapter I, above.

[87] Enarrationes epistolarum et euangeliorum, quas postillas vocant (1521), VII, 508,31 f.

[88] Kirchenpostille (1522), X,1,1 p. 454,10.

civil use of the Law and the "worldly sword" which maintains order.[89]

Luther does not appear to have introduced any notable changes in the doctrine of the two uses of the Law during the 1520's, and we shall therefore turn immediately to his more general statement of the doctrine as it is found in the Lectures on Galatians (1531) and in the Disputations (1535 f.).[90]

Luther in the Lectures on Galatians (1531) starts from the basic contrast between the Law and the Gospel, and we have seen that the absolute distinction between these two is equivalent to the absolute distinction between Christian, passive justice and any other kind of justice.[91] More strongly than ever before, Luther attacks any identification of the Gospel with a law or of Christ with a legislator. There are many parallels to his well-known exclamation, "If I hold Christ to be a legislator, then I am damned." [92] Even if the Law were to be fulfilled, it would not justify. On the other hand, "If we are outside the realm (*locum*) of justification, the law is in every way to be exalted." [93]

In the discussion of the law itself, Luther presents a general statement of its double office. If the law cannot justify, then what

[80] Ibid., X,1,1 p.454,19; compare also 344,24 f.; 460,1 f.; 467,20. For a comparable statement from 1523, see Sermon (Feb. 24, 1523), XI,31,6 f.; this is discussed by G. Ebeling "Zur Lehre vom triplex usus legis in der reformatorischen Theologie," Theologische Literaturzeitung, 75 (1950), 235–46.

[90] For an analysis of Luther's doctrine of law, the most ambitious recent work, with full bibliography, is J. Heckel, Lex charitatis . . . (note 2, Chapter I, above); on the position of Heckel, see Appendix. H. Beyer, Luther und das Recht (Die Lehre Luthers IV), München, 1935, is a useful anthology of Luther's scattered observations on the law. On the place of the law in Luther's theology, see particularly the penetrating studies of Ernst Wolf, " 'Natürliches Gesetz' und 'Gesetz Christi' bei Luther," Evangelische Theologie, 2 (1935) 305–30; "Gesetz und Evangelium in Luthers Auseinandersetzung mit den Schwärmern," ibid. 5 (1938), 96–109. For Luther's general doctrine of the Law and the Gospel, the most impressive presentation is still that of Theodosius Harnack, Luthers Theologie, 2 vols., originally published 1862–86, Neuausgabe with references to the Weimar Kritische Gesamtausgabe, München, 1927. I have not seen P. Husfeldt, Studien zum Problem des Gesetzes in der Theologie Luthers (Diss. Kiel, 1939).

[91] See p. 62, Chapter II, above.

[92] Galatians (1531), XL,1 p. 50,4. Compare pp. 91,7; 259,6; 297,9 f.; 533,11; 540,9 f.; 560,3; 562,6. See also the significant statement in Luther's preparation for the Lectures, with its sharp contrast to Luther's early position in the Dictata: XL,1 p. 15,25: "Est ridiculum Christum facere legis latorem et promissionem de eo intelligere de lege alia. Cum nihil possit altius tradi quam lex Mosi in coelo et terra, quam nec intelligit homo, tantum abest ut faciat."

[93] Galatians (1531), XL,1 p. 558,6.

is its purpose? In the first place it serves civilly as a restraining and ordering force; this is its civil use. In the second place, it serves spiritually to reveal to man his total sin apart from Christ; this is its theological use.[94]

As Luther in the Lectures separates charity from faith and from Christian justice, so he insists that charity belongs on the side of the Law and not on the side of the Gospel. He accuses the papists of not understanding the Gospel, for "They make of the Gospel a law of charity." [95] Luther's own position is that the precept of charity is a legal precept and that charity itself is accordingly a work of the Law.[96] "The true Gospel: charity is not the adornment nor the perfection of faith nor its works, but faith is in itself a divine work in the heart which justifies because it apprehends the Saviour Himself. Faith, in its proper sense, justifies; it does not speculate about charity, for whoever does so is lost." [97] Here again we see Luther separating what had been equivalent in his early period, for he is now working with the distinction between the two realms of Christian existence. In the period 1513–18 charity and faith had both pointed to the partial spiritual justice of the Christian. Now in 1531 charity has been restricted to the realm of partial sanctification and the Law; faith has been centered in the realm of total justification and passive justice.

In the Lectures on Galatians (1531) Luther is free to relate his doctrine of the law to the various general dualisms which he had not yet had available in the period 1518–22. Thus he can move easily, for example, from the contrasts between the civil and theological uses of the Law to the contrast between civil and Christian justice, or to the more general contrast between heaven and earth, or polity and religion. "Paul is not now talking of civil laws and customs, but of the justice by which we are justified in

[94] Ibid., XL,1 pp. 487,10 f.; compare 429,10 f.; 491,1; 501,5 f.
[95] Ibid., XL,1 p. 141,6.
[96] Ibid., XL,1 p. 424,1. Compare Disputations (1542), XXXIX,2 p. 201,17: "Legale dictum est. Nam cum de charitate dicitur, opus legis proponitur. Est autem distinguendum; aliud genus doctrinae est promissio, aliud praeceptum."
[97] Ibid., XL,1 p. 164,2. Luther in his mature period regularly denies that the law even if, *per impossibile*, it were fulfilled, would justify. Compare Disputations (1542), XXXIX,2 p. 188,28; TR, §2066 (1531), II,309,18; §6720–21, VI, 144,30 f.

the realm of heaven. . . . Let civil laws remain in their own sphere (*in suo ordine*), let the magistrate and the house-father (*oeconomus*) arrange their laws. Nevertheless their best types of law do not free us from condemnation before God. . . . It is not in vain that I urge this distinction: few observe it, and it is very easy to confuse heavenly justice with political justice. As I said above, in political justice one must pay attention to laws and works, but in divine, spiritual, and heavenly justice one must disregard all laws and all works, and notice only the promises and blessings of Abraham." [98] "Paul is here discussing the law in the higher realm and not in the political realm (*in superiori loco, non politico*). Polity and economics are subject to reason. There reason is primary, and there one finds civil laws and civil justice. . . . On the other hand, there is a (different) justice before God, by which we are made free by God." [99]

In his Disputations (1535 f.), notably in those against the Antinomians (1537–38), Luther carries his thought further on a few points of detail, but he makes no material changes. As he notes in an interesting autobiographical passage, the Antinomians had forced him to concentrate on an aspect of his doctrine of law which he had previously little emphasized. Originally, he had been writing against the papists and the scholastics, and he spoke to men already terrified by a too exclusive emphasis on the Law. Hence in the early writings he stressed the overwhelming importance of grace and faith as the only way to salvation, and he found it unnecessary to speak at length about the Law. But now the Antinomians have fallen into an error exactly the opposite of Luther's early opponents. They accept much of what Luther has to say of grace and of the Gospel, but they reject the Law entirely for the saved, and they deny Luther's central thesis that the preaching of Christianity must always include the two aspects of the Law and the Gospel, not merely the Gospel alone.[100]

In the various Disputations against the Antinomians, Luther reasserts strongly the double aspect of God's word to man; God speaks to man not only through the Gospel but also through the

[98] Galatians (1531), XL,1 pp. 392,10 f.
[99] Ibid., XL,1 p. 305,7 f.
[100] Disputations (1538), XXXIX,1 pp. 571,10 f.

Law, and the Law continues to be necessary for Christians.[101] As in the Lectures on Galatians (1531) Luther goes on to distinguish two uses of the Law: "You know that there is a double use of the Law, in the first place for restraining crimes (*coercendi delicta*), in the second place for revealing crimes (*ostendendi delicta*). . . . The justice of the world has its glory and its reward in this life among men, but not before God." [102] More than in his earlier writings, Luther in the Disputations relates the theological use of the Law to the "hidden God" of majesty; in contrast, the Gospel is the message of the "revealed God" in Christ.[103]

Luther is particularly successful in the Disputations in bringing his doctrine of the Law into harmony with the other major dualisms of his mature period, such as the contrast between civil and Christian justice or the contrast between the realms of earth and heaven. Thus in the Promotion-Disputation of Palladius and Tilemann (1537), Luther again considers the fruitful paradox that our works are both good and at the same time not good. His reply,

[101] Disputations (1537), XXXIX,1 p. 361,1 f.

[102] Disputations (1538), XXXIX,1 p. 441,2. Compare the other recension of the same passage. "Primus (sc. usus legis) est coercere delicta, atque haec coercitio est mundi seu carnis iustitia, quae habet suum praemium et gloriam." For other references to the double use in the Disputations, see p. 209,11; 483,14 and 26; 485,16; see also TR, §6695, VI,128,26 f. In Disputations (1538), XXXIX,1 p. 485,22 Luther apparently teaches a "triplex usus legis," and the problem has been much discussed recently. This text itself is probably an interpolation from Melanchthon: see W. Elert, "Eine theologische Fälschung zur Lehre vom tertius usus legis," Zeitschrift für Religions- und Geistesgeschichte 1 (1948), 168–70, and his Zwischen Gnade und Ungnade (München, 1948), pp. 161–9; and G. Ebeling, "Zur Lehre . . ." (note 89, above). On the more general problem, whether the *triplex usus* is consistent with Luther's theology, see R. Bring, "Gesetz und Evangelium und der dritte Gebrauch des Gesetzes in der lutherischen Theologie," in: Zur Theologie Luthers I (= Schriften der Luther-Agricola Gesellschaft in Finland 4), Helsinki, 1943, pp. 43–97; W. Joest, Gesetz und Freiheit (note 125, Chapter I); W. Geppert, "Zur gegenseitigen Diskussion über Problem und Bedeutung der Tertius usus Legis," Evangelisch-Lutherische Kirchenzeitung, 9 (1955), 387–93. In general it would seem that there is no need for a "tertius usus" in Luther's thinking. Those who argue in its favor have not realized sufficiently that the civil use of the law, like civil justice, is enough and more than enough for the "world" and that the Gospel has nothing to add to it.

[103] Disputations (1538), XXXIX,1 p. 484,5 and particularly, line 12: "Sic quoque Spiritus sanctus in sua maiestate est incomprehensibilis, et quando in hac maiestate sua ut Deus revelat legem, non potest non occidere et vehementer terrere"; compare pp. 370, 12 f.; 389,2. Luther elsewhere relates the double use of the law to the old contrast between the law as veiled or unveiled; Disputations (1540), XXXIX,2 p. 133,30; 140,25.

which we have noted in part above,[104] is that terms have different meanings in different realms. "While we are on earth, one must speak to us in our own language. Therefore in terms of natural philosophy (*physice*) or of law (*iuridice*), I rightly say: civil institutions (*ordinationes*) and the works of the Law are good, just, and necessary. God wills that we should live according to these laws in this human and civil society. But before Him and in heaven, He wishes us to have another good, His mercy, which is in Christ Jesus, and which because of Him and by Him is given to us. Thus you have heard that our works are good and not good, that they are justice and not justice. Both statements are true, but each in its own realm (*foro*). There are two different justices; the one is of the law, achieved by our own forces or works, while the other is imputed to us by God's mercy through faith." [105]

We must be cautious not to misinterpret the contrast between the civil and the theological uses of the law as if it were a contrast between two different kinds of law. Luther is here talking about law in general, and what he says can apply to the Mosaic law, the natural law, or an ordinary civil law. God uses law in general, or anyone of these particular laws, in two ways. In the first case, He uses it for the realm of the world to prevent crime; the pagan accepts this use only unwillingly, in the final analysis, but the Christian tries to affirm it as a standard of sanctification (it will be remembered that the law extends to the ultimate demands of charity). In the second case, God through the Holy Spirit uses the law to show the individual his complete sinfulness before God. This is not a question primarily of any stricter interpretation of the demands of the law. It is rather a revelation of the law as the absolute command of the creator to the creature, for no creature can accept such a command unless he believes the Gospel that God has already accepted him in Christ. And God can make this use of a natural or of a political law. Thus we read in the theses which Luther proposed for a sixth Disputation against the

---

[104] See pp.66 f. Chapter II, above.

[105] Disputations (1537), XXXIX,1 pp.232,7 f. I have quoted the text as it appears in Recension A I, but the other three recensions (A II, A III, and B) are also of independent interest.

Antinomians (1540). "§15. A law which does not damn is a fictitious and painted law, like a chimera or a trageleph. §16. Nor is a political or natural law anything unless it damns and terrifies sinners."[106]

The theological use of the law serves much the same purpose as the thesis that every man, even the best of Christians, is totally a sinner before God apart from Christ. In each case Luther prevents any reversal of the direction of our thought about justification and sanctification. We are totally justified in Christ first, and we then move into the world and work toward sanctification through civil justice and the civil use of the Law. But lest the Christian be tempted at any time to assume that his civil justice or his civil obedience of the law constitutes the slightest movement toward justification, there remains the fact that apart from Christ he is still a sinner before God and that apart from Christ the law still condemns him utterly before God.

In his thinking after 1518–19 Luther is concerned primarily with the "law" in general rather than with the special types of law. He does, however, have a good deal to say about natural law, and it is in this connection that he best indicates the source and content of law for the Christian.[107]

It will be remembered that Luther in his early period of 1513–18 never dealt with the natural law at length. He ignored it almost completely in the Dictata super Psalterium (1513–15).[108] In the period 1515–18 he pays more attention to it, but it is still relatively unimportant. On the one hand, in the context of the

[106] Disputations (1540), XXXIX,1 p. 358,26. Compare Disputations (1540), XXXIX,2 pp. 133,30 and 139,28 f.

[107] There is a large and controversial literature on natural law in Luther. For some general account of the literature see J. T. McNeill, "Natural Law in the Thought of Luther," Church History 10 (1941), 211–27; and F. Lau, 'Äusserliche Ordnung' und 'Weltlich Ding' in Luthers Theologie (Studien zur systematischen Theologie, Heft 12), Göttingen, 1933, pp. 33 f. See also the articles by Ernst Wolf cited in note 90, above, and also his "Naturrecht und Gerechtigkeit," Evangelische Theologie 7 (1947–48), 233–53, and "Zur Frage des Naturrechts bei Thomas von Aquin und bei Luther," Jahrbuch der Gesellschaft für die Geschichte des Protestantismus in Österreich, 67 (1951), 186–204 (this appeared in a slightly revised form in E. Wolf, Peregrinatio (München, 1954), 183–213; H. M. Müller, "Das christliche Liebesgebot und die lex naturae," Zeitschrift für Theologie und Kirche, N.F. 9 (1928), 161–83; R. Nürnberger, "Die lex naturae also Problem der vita Christiana bei Luther," Archiv für Reformationsgeschichte, 37 (1940), 1–12.

[108] See pp.18 f., Chapter I, above.

unity of all law against grace, he emphasizes that the Mosaic, natural, and evangelical laws are in fundamental agreement; [109] on the other hand, as long as he worked with the notion of a spiritual law of grace, Luther tended to equate this with the natural law. In the Lectures on Romans (1515–16), for example, Luther glosses the "law of the mind" (Romans VII,23) as identical with charity or the spiritual law,[110] and he elsewhere in the Lectures identifies the spiritual law with the law of nature.[111]

After the re-orientation, Luther immediately drops the identification of the law of nature with a spiritual law of grace; the natural law, like charity, will never appear on the side of the Gospel and passive justice, but always on the side of the Law and its justice. Thus in the Rationis Latomianae confutatio, Luther again has occasion to gloss the "law of the mind" of Romans VII,23, and he now denies his early position. "Moreover Paul by the ' law of the mind' does not mean what they call natural law, but he opposes it to the law of the members. . . ." [112]

But the re-orientation of 1518–19 simply strengthened Luther's thesis on the essential unity of all law, and he makes frequent mention of the natural law as the most common embodiment of law. We must remember, however, that Luther regards the details of natural law, like the details of civil justice or of polity, as not within his proper competence as a theologian, and what he has to say about it is limited. He must as a theologian see that it remains within its proper realm, but it is finally up to reason and philosophy to determine its content. Hence Luther for the most part assumes that his readers already know what natural law is, and he speaks of it incidentally. He discusses it in detail only in opposition to some false theology such as that of the Mosaicizers who would impose the law of Moses on sixteenth century Europe.

For the general concept of the natural law, two remarks from the Table-Talk may be taken as typical. "The law of nature is inborn in us as heat in fire, and it is within us as the fire within

---

[109] See pp. 33 f., Chapter I, above.

[110] Romans, LVI,72,10: *"legi mentis meae*: i.e. charitati, que est lex spiritualis, immo spiritus. . . ."* Compare p. 34 Chapter I, above.

[111] See, e.g., Romans, LVI,197,19 f. and other passages cited note 147, Chapter I, above.

[112] Rationis Latomianae confutatio (1521), VIII,122,29.

the flint. Its use is like that of a mirror (compare *Sachsenspiegel* or *speculum principis*); further it cannot be separated from the divine law." [113] "It is imposible that even a most impious man should entirely destroy the law, since it is in nature and in natural right in the souls of men. However the law of nature itself is somewhat obscure and speaks only of works in general. Therefore Moses and the Holy Spirit explained it more clearly and made the works specific." [114] As in his early period, Luther continues throughout his life to see the basic content of the natural law as charity and the Golden Rule. He observes in the Lectures on Galatians (1531), in a discussion of charity: "This doctrine the philosophers also transmitted. They call it the law of nature, Do unto others . . . and, Do not unto others. . . ." [115]

Luther's most careful analysis of the natural law appears in his argument against those who argued that the Old Testament law of Moses is still binding for Christians. Luther's reply is clear, and he works it out most precisely in Wider die himmlischen Propheten (1525).[116] In the first place, as he had often done before,[117] Luther here denies any fundamental distinction within the law of Moses and asserts its fundamental unity; when Paul speaks of the "Law" he means the whole Law.[118] In the second place, Luther argues that Moses spoke with authority only to the Jews, whether in the ceremonial law or in the Decalogue. The

---

[113] TR, §2243 (1531), II,374,17. Compare §2151 (1531), II,338,3. "Porro ego optarem videre aliquem, qui proprie posset distinguere inter legem naturae et legem divinam." In TR, §581, (1533), I,267,22 f. Luther defends the notion of a specifically human *ius naturae* as against the position of the Roman jurists that this *ius naturae* is common to both animals and men.

[114] TR, §3650 d (1537), III,484,8.

[115] Galatians (1531), XL,2 p. 65,9; Galatians Commentary (1519), II,580,15; Operationes V,434,26; 435,14; Responsio ad condemnationem per Lovanienses et Colonienses factam (1520), VI,185,30.

[116] For the general problem of the relation between the natural law and the law of Moses, see H. Bornkamm, Luther und das Alte Testament (Tübingen, 1948), Chapter IV; W. Dress, "Die Zehn Gebote in Luthers theologischem Denken," Wissenschaftliche Zeitschrift der Humboldt-Universität zu Berlin, Gesellschafts- und sprachwissenschaftliche Reihe, 3 (1953–4), 213–18; Hayo Gerdes, Luthers Streit mit den Schwärmern um das rechte Verständnis des Gesetzes Mose, (Göttingen, 1955); K. G. Steck, Luther und die Schwärmer (Theologische Studien hgg. von K. Barth, Heft 44), Zürich, 1955.

[117] E.g., p. 33, Chapter I, above.

[118] XVIII,76,19 f.

Mosaic Law is not universal but a national law for Israel, in the well-known phrase, the *Sachsenspiegel* of the Jews.[119]

Hence the law of Moses as such does not bind the Christians at all; it binds them accidentally where it coincides with the law of nature. In Wider die himmlischen Propheten Luther repeats his usual description of the natural law. It is written in everyone's heart; the Bible mentions it in Romans II,14 and states its content in the Golden Rule of Matthew VII,12. Paul summarizes it in Romans XIII, "where he comprehends all the commands of Moses under love, and the natural law teaches this love naturally." [120] But though the Christians are bound only by the natural law and though the law of Moses has been abrogated, nevertheless the law of Moses remains of unique value to them since nowhere else is the law of nature so finely expressed.[121]

In this discussion of the different relation of Jews and Christians to the law of Moses, Luther makes use of ideas which he will develop more fully in connection with the idea of God's world-government (*Weltregiment*). Thus, for example, in the Sermons on Exodus (1524–27) Luther analyzes the different ways in which God rules His people before and after Christ. Luther explains that God exercised a triple government of the Jews: 1. A secular government of things; 2. A spiritual government of ceremonies; 3. A government before God through the Ten Commandments.[122] In New Testament times, however, God separated the first two governments from His people. He transferred the government of the sword to Caesar, the Turk, and the king of France; he gave the Christians no ceremonies by divine law.[123] Hence, says Luther, there remains for the Christians only God's direct rule through the Ten Commandments insofar as these coincide with natural law. In a slightly different account elsewhere in the Sermons on Exodus, Luther speaks of the triple commandments given the Jews as divine, ceremonial, and judicial. Of these three, for the

---

[119] Ibid., XVIII,81,14. Compare Unterrichtung wie sich die Christen in Mosen sollen schicken (1525), XVI,378,23.

[120] Wider die himmlischen Propheten (1525), XVIII,80,18 f.

[121] Ibid., XVIII,81,18.

[122] XVI,588,17.

[123] Ibid., XVI,588,22.

Christians and the heathen, "there remains only the divine commandments which pertain to the law of nature." [124]

How does man learn of this law of nature which is the most important part of divine government and law for the Christians? Luther's regular answer in his mature period is that reason discovers the law of nature. In the early period of 1513–18 "reason" had played no significant rôle in Luther's thought, for the crucial doctrine of the spiritual law was regularly ascribed to the "intellect" as contrasted to the "senses." [125] In his mature period, the "intellect" virtually disappears as an active religious faculty of man, for faith now depends on passive justice. On the other hand, reason becomes of central importance as the all-embracing term which best refers to man's principle of action in the realm of the world of civil justice, natural law, and polity. [126]

There is consequently no need for specifically Christian revelation in the area of natural law, and Luther recommends that the Christians make use of the insights here of Aristotle and Cicero. [127] But if natural law does not require revelation, it is nevertheless far from being accessible to the reason of "everyman." An understanding of the natural law is a particular gift, and those who possess it are in the class of Luther's "heroic men" and his "miracle-workers" (*Wunderleute*). [128]

Ordinary positive law is regularly derived from the natural law through reason. [129] As against natural law, Luther has little regard for written law, and he will go so far as to call the written law "sick" in contrast to the natural law which is "healthy." [130] Nevertheless Luther comes more and more to feel that in the sad state of the present world written laws are probably the best possible solution.

We have now seen the main outlines of Luther's mature theory of law; like his mature theory of justice, this is a revision and

---

[124] XVI,528,17.
[125] See pp.6 f., Chapter I, above.
[126] Compare e.g., Galatians (1531), XL,1 pp. 292,6 f.; 305, 7 ff.
[127] E.g., Auslegung des 101 Psalms (1534–35), LI,214,35 f.
[128] Ibid., LI,212,14 f.
[129] Ibid., LI,211,36.
[130] Ibid., LI,214,14.

transformation of his ideas of 1513–18 in the light of his fundamental re-orientation of 1518–19. In the period 1513–18 Luther starts from a doctrine of law which can explain man's justification as he moves through grace from the limited law of the letter to the higher spiritual law. Toward the end of his early period, Luther concentrates more on the contrast between any law, which simply makes demands, and grace, which alone satisfies the demands, but this new approach does not lead to any fundamental re-orientation.

Toward 1518–19, however, Luther begins to recognize two distinct realms of Christian existence, and in the light of these he must now effect a general re-organization of his earlier ideas on law. The idea of the law as always condemning is given free rein in the total realm of heaven as the theological use of the law; even the best of Christians in the world is in heaven apart from Christ totally condemned by God's Law. On the other hand, Luther now needs a new statement on the positive importance of the law in the realm of the world; to meet this need he works out the doctrine of the civil use of the law, comparable to civil justice, by which God brings about a measure of order and goodness here on earth. To some extent this civil use of the law represents the re-appearance in a new context of Luther's early ideas on the law of Moses as a literal law which restrains only the hand.

In his subtle and difficult theory, Luther is thus able to maintain for law the distinction between the two simultaneous realms of Christian existence. Likewise, in the same way that the justices of faith and of works are finally one simple justice,[131] so the law which God uses either civilly or theologically is one and the same law. The Christian, as Christian, knows no more about the law in its civil use than does the pagan. When the Holy Spirit reveals to him its spiritual use, this tells him nothing about the content of the law as such; it simply reveals what in modern language might be called the nature of the commitment demanded. Creaturely man must totally accept the command of the "hidden God" of majesty, who is his creator. But all men fail of this

---

[131] See pp. 64 f., Chapter II, above.

acceptance and therefore all men are without Christ utterly condemned before God.[132]

[132] It has been debated to what extent Luther's doctrine of natural law agrees
with that of St. Thomas. F. X. Arnold, Zur Frage des Naturrechts bei Martin
Luther (München, 1937), has argued for extensive agreement; for a more careful
statement, see Ernst Wolf, "Zur Frage des Naturrechts . . ." (note 107, above).
If one compares the doctrines of Thomas and Luther on the most specific level,
their descriptive statements about the natural law are similar; both mean by it a
law given to man by God through reason for the government of his life on earth.
On the other hand, Thomas and Luther place these similar descriptive statements
in such different contexts that a comparison of their doctrines of natural law
involves a comparison of two whole theologies. Notably, Thomas always defines
a natural law in contrast to a divine, supernatural law which leads man to a higher
goal; after his early period Luther recognizes no such higher law, and hence the
natural law is a divine law for him. Secondly, Thomas always treats the natural
law as a command which man can obey, and when he obeys it he advances toward
salvation; there is no need for a distinction between a civil and a theological use
of natural law. Luther, however, maintains that man can never obey the natural
law when it is spiritually understood, and the natural law therefore never leads
men to salvation. In its civil use it simply provides for the restraint of crime
in this world; in its theological use, as it is understood spiritually, it reveals to
man his total condemnation apart from Christ.

CHAPTER IV

THE CHURCH AND SOCIETY.

IN HIS GENERAL THEOLOGY and in his theories of justice and of law, Luther established the broad context for a new theology of society.[1] We have now to consider how he develops ideas through which he can give content to this theology of society. In the first place, he will work out a general dualism, roughly comparable to those we have already studied, between church and polity. In the second place, for the more specific analysis of society, Luther will transform certain traditional concepts in the light of the distinction between two realms of Christian existence, and three essentially new doctrines will emerge: first, of the estates and callings; second, of God's two governments, His spiritual gov-

---

[1] For a full bibliography on Luther's ideas on society, see the notes in J. Heckel, "Lex charitatis . . ." (note 2, Chapter I, above), and for a brief discussion of Heckel's own studies, see Appendix. Among the more significant books on Luther's general theory of society may be mentioned: Hermann Jordan, Luthers Staatsauffassung. Ein Beitrag zu der Frage des Verhältnisses von Religion und Politik (München, 1917). Specially valuable for its full citations from Luther's scattered Sermons; Georges de Lagarde, Recherches sur l'esprit politique de la Réforme (Paris, 1926). A brilliant essay but with no appreciation of the theological context of Luther's social ideas. The author places particular theses of Luther within the framework of a Thomistic world-view and, as might be expected, finds that the consequences are disastrous; K. Matthes, Luther und die Obrigkeit. Die Obrigkeitsanschauung des reifen Luther in systematischer Darstellung (Aus der Welt christlicher Frömmigkeit 12), München, 1937; Franz Lau, 'Äusserliche Ordnung' und 'Weltlich Ding' in Luthers Theologie (Studien zur systematischen Theologie, Heft 12), Göttingen, 1933. An important but difficult study. Lau relies for his evidence primarily on the Genesis Commentary (1535-45); Gunnar Hillerdal, Gehorsam gegen Gott und Menschen (Göttingen, 1954); G. F. Forell, Faith Active in Love. An Investigation of the Principles Underlying Luther's Social Ethics (New York, 1954).

Articles on Luther's general idea of society are too numerous to list. Two of the most recent "interpretations" may be mentioned: C. Trinkaus, "The Religious Foundations of Luther's Social Views," A. P. Evans Festschrift (New York, 1955), 71-87; S. S. Wolin, "Politics and Religion: Luther's Simplistic Imperative," American Political Science Review 50 (1956), 24-42.

For books on special aspects of Luther's ideas of society, see below notes 2 (the church), 125 (estates and callings), 144 (God's two governments), and 199 (the three hierarchies).

ernment and His world-government (*Weltregiment*); and third, of the three hierarchies.

The development of these various ideas on society differs in two main ways from that of Luther's ideas on justice and law. In the first place, the ideas on society are not so immediately connected with the all-important problem of justification. In the second place, with the exception of the church, these ideas play no significant rôle in Luther's early thought.

Nevertheless, Luther after 1518–19 was more and more drawn to consider the theology of society. His new insight on justification has consequences for the Christian church as well as for the Christian individual, and his re-orientation gives to the "world" and its society a positive importance which they lacked in Luther's early thought. And Luther himself felt that some of his achievements in this area, notably the doctrine of the two governments of God, ranked with his best work.

Luther's thinking about these problems after 1518–19, as in the cases of justice and of law, involves the modification and reconstruction of earlier ideas in the light of the new distinction between the two realms of Christian existence. In the discussion of church and society, however, the "earlier ideas" are not so specifically connected with Luther's early theology; they are rather the received opinions of the late fifteenth and early sixteenth centuries.

In anticipation and summary, it may be noted that Luther's thought here follows the same general course which we have seen in his general theology and in his ideas of justice and law. In the early idea of the church, for example, Luther works with a church militant which is proportional and antecedent to the church triumphant, as partial justice had been proportional and antecedent to total justification. After 1518–19, however, Luther will move to redefine the church primarily in terms of the Christian's heavenly realm of existence and of his total justice; what happens on earth is always in a different realm of existence and is always only consequent. But the church, like the Christian individual, exists in both realms, and therefore the full doctrine of the church must also take account of its existence in the new "world."

Similarly in the case of society, Luther starts from received ideas which set up important religious distinctions within the Christian society on earth; the spiritual estate of the clergy is to be contrasted with and distinguished from the secular estate of the laity. One might relate this distinction to the contrast in Luther's early thought between the literal law and the spiritual law. But after 1518–19 Luther's new distinction between the two realms of Christian existence changes these older ideas in two ways. On the one hand, the only true "spiritual estate" of the Christians is their existence in heaven, and this cannot set up any distinctions within the human society of the world, even if that society is Christian. On the other hand, as this new "spiritual estate" is separated from the world all the estates of human society, including that of the clergy, will be re-interpreted as estates of the world, or in Luther's special terminology, "callings" (*Berufe*).

Further the traditional view of government had distinguished between two types of rule, spiritual and secular, within the Christian society on earth. But when Luther has achieved the concept of passive justice, he must assert that there can be no human rule, as there can be no human estate, which is spiritual in the full meaning of the word. Hence Luther revises the older doctrine of government in the light of the distinction of the two realms. The result is the new theory of the two governments of God; there is His spiritual government through Christ (in the realm of passive justice), and there is His world-government through kings and, more generally, through all the aspects of civil justice, the civil use of the law, and of polity.

Luther's doctrine of the two governments of God establishes within government the basic distinction between the two realms; in particular it separates God's rule of the church in heaven from any earthly rule. But as we have seen, the church like the Christian individual, exists in both realms. How is it to be ruled "in the world"? Insofar as Luther answers this question, he does so in terms of the last of his new developments on society, the theory of the three hierarchies. The traditional theory had separated three ruling estates; there was the spiritual estate of the clergy and there were the secular estates of kingship and of the household. After 1518–19 Luther finds the older concept of the spiritual estate an unwarranted mixing of heaven and earth and he rejects it; on the other hand the older view of kingship and the household failed to recognize their significance as God's ordinances for the Christian. Hence he develops a new doctrine in which all three are placed on the same level as "worldly" but nevertheless "holy" rules or, to use his own technical term, "hierarchies."

We shall treat the development of Luther's theology of society under the following headings:

Section 1. Church and Polity.
Section 2. Estates and Callings.
Section 3. God's Two Governments.
Section 4. The Three Hierarchies.

1. *Church and Polity.*

Our main source for Luther's early idea of the church[2] is the Dictata super Psalterium, for he has relatively little to say about it in the Lectures on Romans, on Galatians, and on Hebrews. A new phase begins with the publication of the 95 Theses in 1517 and with the consequent controversy, but this does not immediately lead to any fundamental re-orientation. In the case of the church, as in the case of justice, Luther is carrying on an "Augustinian" attack on certain features of Aristotelian scholas-

---

[2] There is a tremendous bibliography on Luther's doctrine of the church. Among the best introductions to the problem may be mentioned: F. Kattenbusch, "Die Doppelschichtigkeit in Luthers Kirchenbegriff," Theologische Studien und Kritiken, 100 (1927–28), 197–347; E. Kohlmeyer, "Die Bedeutung der Kirche für Luther," Zeitschrift für Kirchengeschichte, 47 (1928), 466–511; P. Althaus, Communio Sanctorum (Forschungen zur Geschichte und Lehre des Protestantismus I,1), München, 1929; M. Doerne, "Gottes Volk und Gottes Wort," Luther-Jahrbuch 1932, pp. 61–98; E. Rietschel, "Das Problem der unsichtbar-sichtbaren Kirche bei Luther (Schriften des Vereins für Reformationsgeschichte, 50,2 Nr. 154), Leipzig, 1932; A. Oepke, Das neue Gottesvolk (Gütersloh, 1950), Chapter XIII: Wilhelm Pauck, The Heritage of the Reformation (Glencoe, Illinois, 1950), Chapter III. For a discussion with bibliography of the institutional problem of church government in Luther, see L. W. Spitz, "Luther's ecclesiology and his concept of the prince as Notbischoff," Church History, 22 (1953), 113–41.

For special discussion of Luther's early idea of the church, see K. Holl "Die Entstehung von Luthers Kirchenbegriff," in his: Gesammelte Aufsätze I 6th. ed. (Tübingen, 1932), pp.288–325; J. Heckel, "Gesetz und Recht. . ." (note 10, Chapter I, above), and "Initia iuris ecclesiastici Protestantium," Bayerische Akademie der Wissenschaften, SB, phil.-hist. Kl. 1949, Heft 5; W. Wagner, "Die Kirche als Corpus Christi mysticum beim jungen Luther," Zeitschrift für katholische Theologie 61(1937),29–98; H. Fagerberg, "Die Kirche in Luthers Psalmenvorlesung 1513–15," Werner Elert Festschrift (Berlin, 1955),109–118.

ticism well before the general change of 1518–19 introduces a development which will result in an attack on "Augustinianism" as well as on "Aristotelianism." Hence we shall notice the Indulgence Dispute only briefly, and our main attention will be devoted to the emergence and codification of Luther's new position after 1518–19.

In some ways Luther's development of the idea of the church presents more difficulties than the development of his idea of justice or law. In the first place, during the early period and notably in the Dictata, Luther does not relate his statements about the church to his ideas about human society and government, and our account of his "theology of society" is necessarily incomplete. In the second place, during his mature period Luther seems in the case of the church to have early reached a point where he shies away from any systematic statement of his position. To some extent we can construct such a position by combining what he has to say of the church and the polity with what he has to say of God's two governments and of the three hierarchies, but we must be very cautious in constructing a system where Luther declined to do so.

The general stages in Luther's thinking about the church after 1518–19 correspond roughly to those for justice and law. There is a comparatively brief period of transition and reconstruction; this culminates in Von dem Papsttum zu Rom (1520) and in the Ad librum Ambrosii Catharini responsio (1521). As in the case of justice, Luther seems to feel by about 1521 that he has clarified for himself the absolutely essential points about the church, and there is a slackening of the theoretical development during the next years. A second period, of more general statement, begins toward 1530, and Luther here works out the basic contrast of church and polity as a pendant to the comparable dualisms on justice and law.

In his early period Luther had occasion to mention the church frequently in the Dictata super Psalterium (1513–15), for as we have seen, he believes that the Psalms consist primarily of prophecies about Christ and His followers.[3] What Luther has to say about the church is for the most part traditional; he usually de-

[3] See pp.11 f., Chapter I, above.

scribes it in the familiar terminology of Christ's body and people.[4]

Luther also relates these traditional ideas of the church to the other parts of his early theology. Thus for example, he speaks of the church in terms of the fourfold meaning of scripture; as the justice of Christ has its tropological sense in the Christian individual, so it has its allegorical sense in the church.[5] Similarly he defines the church in terms of his early contrast between visible and invisible. "Therefore one should note that the world or the creature is double: 1. the visible world, which God first made and with which He then acted and worked. . . . 2. the invisible world, intelligible through faith, is the church, which is called the new heaven and the new earth."[6] Or Luther in the Dictata can describe the church as one of the spiritual realities imaged by things sensible, for it is "signified by the synagogue and by the other nations."[7]

Luther also discusses the church in the Dictata in terms of his increasing emphasis on the theology of the cross; the church is another illustration of the way in which God reveals spiritual truth under its opposite image. Thus Luther explains that fools never recognize the church. "This happens because the church, the work and creation of Christ, does not appear to be anything outwardly (foris) but its whole structure is within, before God, and invisible. Therefore these things are not known by carnal eyes, but only by spiritual eyes which see in intellect and faith. The foolish condemn the church, for they value only the things that are outwardly fair."[8] Luther elsewhere speaks of the "glorious things" of the church as hidden, "not only hidden and pro-

---

[4] See the articles by Wagner and by Fagenberg cited in note 2, above.

[5] See Dictata, III,532,9; compare also 359,27; 369,7.

[6] Dictata, IV,189,11. Compare III,429,24 f.; IV,444,26; Hebrews, LVII,3 p. 197, 20. "Tertio alii cum Apostolo hoc loco tabernaculum intelligunt mundum quendam spiritualem, quae est ecclesia sancta Dei." (Compare pp.83,8 f.)

[7] Dictata, III,369,7: "Opus dei allegorice est ecclesia per synagogam et alias nationes significata." Compare also III,395,3: "Quia ecclesia olim in synagoga erat abscondita, nunc autem manifestata"; 524,19: "Non sic in synagoga: illi enim in figura pugnabant et expulerunt carnem et sanguinem. Quia erant populus carnalis et figurativus futurorum"; IV,171,29: "Opus Domini est Christus et ecclesia, scilicet nova creatura per veterem et visibilem significata."

[8] Ibid., IV,81,11. Compare III,124,35; IV,38,34.

found but even too profound (*nimis profunda*), since they seem to hide under their opposites." [9]

In Luther's early thought the existence of the church is comparable to that of the tropological justice of God or of the spiritual law of grace; it is found where man participates through intellect and faith the higher reality of things invisible and divine. For example, Luther discusses the passive sense of the "sight of God" (Psalm XCV (XCVI) 6) as the sight by which God is seen. "And in this sight is the true abode of the church. . . . Here all the saints are in one place, however much they may be separated in space and in the sight of men. . . . They are here . . . by the eyes of the soul through the sight of faith. . . . There are two things in man, the spirit and the flesh. . . . To be in the sight of God properly pertains to the church according to the soul, and not according to the body. In the soul moreover there is intelligence and will. . ." [10] Luther thus brings the church into relation with his basic division of man into spirit and flesh, and he can also relate it to his early theory of justification in which the flesh is condemned as the spirit is justified. "The flesh and its movements are condemned and not justified; the soul (*anima*), however, is justified, from which the flesh is separated. But since the flesh and soul are one man, therefore both are finally saved. But the whole world is as one man before God; in this man the bad are in the place of the flesh and its movements, the good in the place of the soul and its movements. But since the world is not 'personally' one (*personale unum*), in this case the judgment of God abides to eternity. And as the flesh is manifest while the spirit is hidden, so the church is hidden in this life, while the world is manifest." [11]

As Luther in his early theory of justification argues that the Christian is partly just, in the spirit, and partly sinful, in the

---

[9] Ibid., IV,77,37; III,547,5. This notion of hiddenness is also prominent in the early biblical commentaries, notably in Romans (e.g., LVI,290,20 with Ficker's notes), but Luther does not often relate it explicitly to the church; but compare Galatians, LVII,2 p. 85,15; Hebrews, LVII,3 pp. 107,5 f.

[10] Dictata, IV,108,24 f.; compare III,106,25 f.; 150,27 f. " 'Absconditum' ergo ecclesie est ipsa fides seu spiritus, quod idem est. Quia in fide et spiritu vivunt, id est in cognitione et amore invisibilium"; IV,127,2.

[11] Ibid., III,203,17. Compare Sermon (1516), I,106,16; Auslegung des 109 (110), Psalms (1518), I,704,25.

flesh, so he argues that the church is partly in heaven and partly in the world. "With its heart, the church is in heaven and has its spirit in the right-hand things of Christ; with its flesh it is in the world, and this is its side or left part." [12] "The congregation of the holy or the church is manifest according to the flesh, where or when they exist, but according to the spirit they are placed in the treasuries (*thezauris*) that is, in the hidden places. . . . They are placed and established in things invisible, which no man can see, though he can believe." [13]

The church which is only partly just and only partly in heaven is of course the church militant, and Luther often contrasts it as the present imperfect church of earth with the perfect church triumphant to which the Christians will belong in the future in heaven.[14] During Luther's early period, he also makes use of a comparable contrast between two kingdoms of Christ, His kingdom as man and His kingdom as God; Christ's rule as man is the kingdom of the church militant.[15]

Luther accepts the traditional view that the church militant is a mixture of good men and bad, and he employs various terms to distinguish the two groups within it. Most commonly he contrasts those who are in the church only by number with those who are in it not only by number but also by merit.[16] There is a

---

[12] Dictata, IV,73,8. Compare IV,38,34; 112,10; 167,23.

[13] Ibid., III,184,2.

[14] E.g., III,101,4; 242,16; 370,3; 475,5; 642,26; IV,287,22; 399,32. In an isolated passage Luther suggests that in some sense the church in this life is both militant and triumphant, III,85,26. "Facta dicit (sc. Psalmista), que tamen fienda petit, quia semper Ecclesia est militans et triumphans in hac vita."

[15] Ibid., IV,406,22: "Vocatur autem Ecclesia militans domus David propter humanitatem Christi, Quia nunc regnat Christus inquantum homo et per fidem humanitatis sue, quam habet ex David." Compare IV,85,5; 105,34; 113,38 f.; 454,32; Galatians, LVII,2 p. 55,15; Sermon (1517?), IV,645,2 f.; Hebrews, LVII,3 pp. 104,17 f.; 202,13. In the Operationes, V,128,36 f. Luther relates the reign of Christ as man to the theology of the cross. "Humanitatis seu (ut Apostolus loquitur) carnis regno, quod in fide agitur, nos sibi conformes facit et crucifigit, faciens ex infoelicibus et superbis diis homines veros, idest miseros et peccatores."

[16] E.g., Dictata, III,632,9: "Sicut illi Iudei et Israel carnales et nomine tantum, loco et numero: Ita Christiani carnales nomine, loco, et numero tantum. Advene enim et hospites sunt eiusdem civitatis participes, sed non sunt cives." IV,24,35: "Quia alii, qui tantum numero sunt fideles, non habitant sed hospitantur in Ecclesia, immo transeunt, i.e. secundum corpus sunt in Ecclesia, quod transit, non secundum animam, que permanet"; 240,13: "Qui enim tantum numero est in Ecclesia sine merito, tantum in congregatione est"; 129,7: ". . . ut heretici, qui

parallel contrast between the mixed and bodily "congregation," which includes both the good and the bad, and the spiritual "council" (*concilium*), which includes only the just.[17] But Luther has no intention of setting up a purely spiritual church, and he insists that no one can be in the council who is not also in the congregation.[18]

Luther's early theology of the church is thus strictly comparable to his early theology of justice, and it does not make use of the later distinction between two simultaneous realms of Christian existence. In Luther's early thought he argues rather that there is a contrast between the partial justice of the church and its partial sinfulness, or between its partial justice now and its complete justice of the future.

When Luther discusses the actual organization of the church, which he does infrequently, he greatly emphasizes the importance of preaching and of the word, and he has notably little to say about the sacraments.[19] He regularly recognizes a hierarchy of superior and subordinate within the church, and he stresses the obligation of complete obedience due to all prelates.[20] In a Sermon of 1516, Luther explains Matthew XVI,18: "Unless Christ had given all His power to a man, there would have been no complete church, since there would have been no order (*ordo*), as everyone wants to say he is touched by the Holy Spirit." [21] Likewise in the Dictata, he speaks of the pontiffs of the church as powerful with the spiritual power of the keys which was granted to Peter.[22]

---

sunt in ecclesia tantum numero et litera, non autem merito et spiritu," Unbekannte Fragmente (1518?), p.39,4.

[17] Dictata, IV,236,7; 239,36 f.

[18] Ibid., IV,240,17: "Ita potest quis esse in congregatione et non in concilio &c., sed non potest esse in concilio iustorum et tamen non in congregatione."

[19] See K. Holl, op. cit. (note 2, above), pp. 292 f.; Wagner, op. cit. (note 2, above), pp.49 f.

[20] E.g., Dictata, III,244,28 f.; IV,404,28: ". . . inspice Ecclesiam, et videbis eam ita sine dubio dispositam in ordinibus secundum sub et supra, sicut iste versus descripsit. Ecclesiam inquam militantem. Secus erit de triumphante"; Romans LVI, 251,24: "Sed non credunt in ea que sunt ipsius (sc. Christi). Quę sunt illa? Ecclesia scil. et omne verbum, quod ex ore prelati Ecclesie procedit Vel boni et sancti viri, Christi verbum est"; Die sieben Busspsalmen (1517), I,193,35 f.; 206,1.

[21] Sermon (1516), I,69,11.

[22] Dictata, IV,165,26. See also III,647,32.

How is Luther's early idea of the church related to the idea of human society in general and of the Christian society in particular? Luther does not face the problem directly, and human society as such, like human justice, has little religious interest for him during 1513–18. One may, however, recognize two different tendencies in his thought. On the one hand, the theology of the cross moved toward an absolute opposition between the hidden church and the persecuting world. In this approach, the world often approximates the "body of the devil," and the secular powers (*potestates saeculi*) are simply the gates of hell.[23] But the theology of the cross is not finally intended to solve the problem of human society any more than it solves the problem of human justice. On the other hand, when Luther speaks in a more practical context, he regularly assumes that the secular powers, while distinct from the spiritual powers, have been Christianized and made subject to Christ.[24] Luther thus implies some sort of unified Christian society, but he does not discuss it explicitly. In this area, he seems in his early writings simply to repeat the phrases of his time, and he does not come to grips with the many problems involved in the already badly shaken medieval tradition.

The indulgence controversy, running from 1517 to about 1520, introduces a new phase in Luther's thinking about the church, and this phase overlaps the fundamental re-orientation of 1518–19. In terms of Luther's general development, the controversy rising out of the 95 Theses has less positive importance than one might expect. Luther here adopts for the most part the terminology of his opponents, notably the concept of divine right; using this somewhat alien terminology, he rejects his opponents' conclusions and he denies the hierarchic church which they were defending. But when it comes to working out his own idea of the church, Luther makes almost no use of any such concept as divine right. He does what we have already seen in the case of justice and law; he rethinks and reconstructs his earlier ideas in terms of the new distinction between the two realms of Christian existence. Hence in analyzing his development we shall first notice briefly the way

[23] Ibid., IV,25,31. Connected with this is his doctrine of the "two generations" among mankind, the good and the bad, Jerusalem and Babylon; compare III,273,31; 400,16.

[24] E.g., Dictata, III,78,22; 117,38; 139,29; 443,32.

in which Luther rejects his opponents' ideas of the church in the indulgence controversy; we shall then turn back to notice in greater detail the positive changes coming out of the re-orientation of 1518–19.

In its relation to the idea of the church, the indulgence controversy turned essentially on the position of the pope.[25] Luther's critics, notably Eck, quickly saw that Luther could not maintain his particular theses about indulgences unless he were to deny the validity of certain papal decretals. Hence they established a chain of arguments leading from the divine right of the pope as head of the church to the validity of his decretals and finally to the rejection of Luther's theses. Luther, though slowly, accepted the challenge in terms of divine right. He rethought his own position in terms of it, and he eventually turned the concept of divine right not only against the papacy but against the whole hierarchical organization of the church.

In the Resolutiones disputationum de virtute indulgentiarum (1518), Luther moves hesitantly and cautiously into the problem of church organization, and he has a good deal to say about divine right (*ius divinum*), a concept which does not appear at all in the Dictata super Psalterium. "Christ is without doubt a divine legislator, and his teaching is divine right." [26] In the Resolutiones Luther assumes that divine right as we can know it is to be found only in the Bible, and in the somewhat later Leipzig Disputation with Eck in 1519 he explicitly identifies divine right with the Bible.[27] Luther in the Resolutiones also has a good deal to say about divine law. His main point about divine right and divine law is that both are immutable and that not even the pope can change them, "But evangelical penance is a divine law, and at no time to be changed." [28]

Luther discusses the power of the pope only incidentally in the

---

[25] For a summary account of Luther's development during the controversy, see R. Seeberg, Lehrbuch der Dogmengeschichte, Vol. IV,1, 5th ed. (Basel, 1953), pp.344 ff.

[26] Resolutiones disputationum de virtute indulgentiarum (1518), henceforth cited as Resolutiones (1518), I,533,15.

[27] Disputation with Eck (1519), II,279,23: "Nec potest fidelis Christianus cogi ultra sacram scripturam, que est proprie ius divinum. . . ."

[28] Resolutiones (1518), I,531,36; compare 536,18, and Resolutiones (1519), II,433,19.

Resolutiones. He notes, for example, that at the time of Gregory the Great (590–604) the Roman church was not supreme over the other churches.[29] He urges that one should yield to the pope with all reverence, but he justifies this in terms of Romans XIII as obedience to one of the powers that be.[30] Further, he attacks the two-swords allegory which places both swords in the hands of the pope, and he strongly emphasizes the biblical duty of obeying the secular powers.[31]

Luther's attitude toward the papacy was soon denounced, and in defense he issued the Resolutio Lutheriana super propositione sua XIII de potestate papae (1519). Luther here continues to urge the acceptance of the pope's power in the church, but he is now explicit that such power does not exist by divine right (*iure divino*) but only on the basis of history and long custom.[32] On the other hand, all men including the clergy, are by divine right subject to the emperor in things temporal.[33] If the Roman church possesses any power by divine right, all other churches possess the same power.[34]

Once Luther has denied the divine right of the papacy, he has taken the decisive step, and he soon goes on to reject the rest of the older hierarchic idea of the church. In the Leipzig Disputation (1519), he argues that the pope can err and he calls into question the infallibility of a council. Shortly after the Disputation, he asserted that universal councils had in fact erred; Luther is therefore no more able to build his church on councils than on

[29] Resolutiones (1518), I,571,16.
[30] Ibid., I,618,24: "Quia auctoritati papali in omnibus cum reverentia cedendum est. Qui enim potestati resistit, resistit Dei ordinationi. . ."; compare Acta Augustana (1518), II, 20,28.
[31] Resolutiones (1518), I,621,12: "Sic enim omnes sancti potestatem saeculi, quam etiam Dei vocat Apostolus, sustinuerunt et honorarunt . . ." For the two swords allegory, see I,624,10; for the combination of both powers in the pope, see Ad Dialogum Silvestri Prieratis de potestate papae responsio (1518), I,677,27; 685,29; Operationes, V,278,25.
[32] Resolutiones (1519), II,201,36: "Sequitur ergo quod non verbis evangelicis et iure divino iste primatus stet, Sed iure hominum et usu. . ."; compare 227,28 and 238,6.
[33] Ibid., II,220,9: "Imperator in temporalibus omnibus praecellit, etiam sacris, idque iure divino, ut haec Petri verba (I Peter II,13) cogunt . . . potest hanc praecellentiam ipse sponte vel retinere vel dimittere, et in utroque habet ius divinum." Compare 205,6 and for the "translatio imperii," see Operationes, V,649, 23.
[34] Resolutiones (1519), II,208,17.

the papacy.[35] The results of the controversy about indulgences which began with the publication of the 95 Theses in 1517 are to a large extent codified in the Resolutiones Lutherianae super propositionibus suis Lipsiae disputatis (1519). By divine right, Luther maintains, there is no distinction between priests and bishops; similarly by divine right there is no distinction between bishops and archbishops, patriarchs, or popes.[36] Thus Luther finally reaches a position where the whole hierarchy of the church loses its basis in divine right and appears as resting simply on history, custom, and law. And while Luther was himself for a long time ready to accept the papacy as one of the historical "ordinances of God," such an attitude had little relevance in the actual situation. One could not for long accept on the basis of history a papacy which defined itself as grounded in divine right and above historical judgment. First in his private letters and then in his public writings, Luther identified the papacy and the hierarchical structure of the church with the reign of Antichrist.[37]

In summary therefore, Luther in the indulgence controversy accepted his opponents' terminology of divine right and then used it to destroy the whole institutional structure of the hierarchical church. On its negative side, this is doubtless of crucial importance. Luther is no longer bound by the medieval idea of the church, and he has cleared the ground for his own thinking. On the positive side, as we have already indicated, the results of the indulgence controversy are less significant, for Luther does not use the concept of divine right as a starting-point for a new idea of the church. What he does, and he had begun this even during the controversy, is to rethink and reconstruct his early theology of the church in the light of the general re-orientation of 1518–19.

The change of 1518–19 impinges on Luther's early idea of the church primarily through the new doctrine of justification. In the Dictata super Psalterium, it will be remembered, the tropological justification of the individual implies and involves the

---

[35] Resolutiones (1519), II,404,1 f.; compare Acta Augustana (1518), II,10,18; Ad Dialogum Silvestri Prieratis de potestate papae responsio (1518), I,656,30; 685,19.

[36] Resolutiones (1519), II,432,16 ff.

[37] See R. Seeberg, op. cit. (note 25, above), pp. 350 f.; H. Preuss, Die Vorstellung vom Antichrist im späterem Mittelalter, bei Luther, und in der konfessionellen Polemik (Leipzig, 1906).

allegorical justification of the church. The individual through God's grace is placed in the right relation to things invisible and eternal; here in the sight of these things is the "place of the church." Because the individual is justified in his spirit, God in His mercy will accept him in the final judgment; similarly one can say that the members by merit of the church militant will at the final judgment join the church triumphant.

Luther in 1518–19 reversed the order of this early doctrine of justification as he asserted the distinction between the two realms of Christian existence. In one realm of existence, the Christian is in Christ already saved and totally just, not piece-meal but all at once. In the other realm, which is always consequent and never antecedent to the first, the Christian is gradually being sanctified; here he is partly just and partly unjust.

It is clear that Luther, if he is to achieve a coherent theology, must somehow effect a comparable reconstruction of his early idea of the church. In its primary and antecedent form, the church must be placed in the realm of total justice. And when Luther has done this, he will have to turn with increased attention to the problem of the church or the Christian society in the world. Partly he will be able to do this in terms of the new contrast between church and polity; on a more detailed level, he will do so in terms of his new theories of the world-government of God, of the estates and callings, and of the hierarchies.

One can see the first beginnings of such a reconstruction in the Resolutiones disputationum de indulgentiarum virtute (1518). Luther starts, for example, from Thesis §37: "Every true Christian, whether alive or dead, has the participation of all the goods of Christ and of the church given him by God even without letters of pardon." In explanation, Luther moves toward a new idea of the justice of the Christian in Christ and toward a definition of the church in terms of it. "It is impossible to be a Christian, without having Christ, and if Christ, then at the same time all the things of Christ. . . . And this is the trust (*fiducia*) of the Christians and the joy of our conscience, that by faith our sins are not ours but Christ's, in whom God placed the sins of all of us, and He bore our sins . . . and again all the justice of Christ becomes ours." [38] And in the course of this argument about Christ's justice, Luther notes how Paul describes the Christians. "We are all one body and one bread in Christ, all the members one of another . . . since by the faith of Christ a Christian is made one spirit and a unity (*unum*) with Christ." [39]

In the roughly contemporary Sermo de virtute excommunicationis (1518), Luther turns more directly to the problem of the church as a society. He starts from a definition of excommunication as an expulsion from the communion of the faithful; "communion" is here used in the general sense of sharing, and Luther can employ "participation" as an explanation of it.[40] But the communion of the faithful is double. "One is internal and spiritual, the other is external and bodily. The spiritual communion is one faith, love, and charity toward God. The corporal communion is the participation of the sacraments of these things, that is of the signs of faith, hope, and charity. This communion is however further extended to the communion of things and of their use, of communication, of dwelling together, and of other bodily actions." [41] In the Sermo de virtute excommunicationis, Luther does not use the phrase "communion of the saints," but it is clearly present in his thought. In the Resolutio Lutheriana super propositione XIII de potestate papae (1519) Luther explicitly defends "communion of the saints" as a synonym for "church," and it is thereafter the key phrase in his writing about the church.[42] It is a phrase which, somewhat surprisingly, played no significant rôle in the Dictata super Psalterium; perhaps it was therefore better fitted to serve as the crystallizing point for a new doctrine.

Here in the Sermo de virtute excommunicationis, we see Luther

---

[38] Resolutiones (1518), I,593,7. Compare I,616,39 f.

[39] Ibid., I,593,12.

[40] I,639,4. (For a later German version of the Sermon, see the Sermon von dem Bann (1520), VI,63,1 ff.) Compare also Ein Sermon vom Sakrament des Leichnams Christi und von den Brüderschaften (1519), II,743,11; 752,36 f.; 756,17.

[41] Sermo de virtute excommunicationis, I,639,2; compare VI,64,1.

[42] Resolutio Lutheriana super propositione sua de potestate papae (1519), II, 190,16. See Holl, op. cit. (note 2, above), p. 312, note 3 for other early passages on the *communio sanctorum*, and for a more general discussion, see Althaus, op. cit. (note 2, above), pp. 54 f. On Luther's translation of *communio* as *Gemeinschaft*, see T. Pauls, " 'Gemeinschaft' der Heiligen bei Luther, das Wort und die Sache," Theologische Studien und Kritiken, 102 (1930), 31–60.

moving toward a more complete statement of the problem of the church as it will appear in his mature theology. In the first place, the concept of a "spiritual and internal communion" will later develop into an explanation of the existence of the church in Christ. In the second place, the concept of the "external communion" points to the different aspect of the church's existence in the world. And thus the problem of the church in Luther's mature thought is revealed as strictly comparable to the problem of the Christian individual. Like the individual, the church has two distinct realms of existence, and it lives at the same time both in heaven and on earth.

In solving the problem, Luther can make some use of his earlier thought. This is particularly true for the church's existence in heaven. In the Dictata super Psalterium, for example, Luther had spoken of a spiritual and invisible church; he had meant this in the context of his early theology with its basic dualism of invisible and visible, spiritual and sensible.[43] Now in the Resolutiones (1518) and in the Sermo de virtute excommunicationis he continues to use some of the same terms, but he begins to give them new meanings as they are understood in the context of the distinction between two realms of Christian existence. And as time goes on this new context will dominate completely, as Luther speaks primarily of the church in Christ or of the hidden church.

On the other hand, the problem of the "external communion" of the church is essentially new, and one detects hesitations in Luther's treatment of it in the Sermo de virtute excommunicationis. Luther here finds little that is relevant in his early thought, and his starting point is rather a reconsideration of the traditional idea of the church as the Christian society or commonwealth. In part Luther will continue to affirm this idea throughout his life; the Christian individual exists on earth as well as in heaven and so does the Christian society. But Luther must also attack and then reconstruct the traditional form of the idea. In the first place, he must scrupulously avoid the "mixing" of heaven and earth found in the late medieval idea of the church, and in the second place he must make sure that the church in heaven is

---

[43] See p. 118, above.

always primary and antecedent to the church on earth, as passive justice must always be antecedent to active justice.

Luther deals with these questions in several Sermons of the spring of 1520, and he here tries to analyze the church as a commonwealth (*respublica*). In the first Sermon, of April 8, he does this only in passing. Christ, he declares, founded His new people, and He gave it only two marks or ceremonies: Baptism and the Eucharist. "Henceforth these ceremonies should be in the Christian commonwealth what watchwords (*tesserae*) are in war." [44] Luther goes on to note that there are only a few Christian ceremonies, since the best method of administering commonwealths is to have as few laws and ceremonies as possible.

Somewhat later, in May 1520, Luther preached two Sermons dealing more directly with the problem of the Christian society. In the first, of May 17, Luther explains that Christ withdrew to heaven so that He might draw our heart heavenward. He goes on to note man's double nature, as body and soul; according to the body man has civil magistrates, but according to the soul his only magistrate is Christ. "Hence the church is nothing but a congregation of spirits and their agreement together." [45] In the second Sermon, of May 18, Luther starts from the concept of a Christian commonwealth. Christ, he declares, wished to establish a certain communion and commonwealth (*rempublicam*) of his followers, and accordingly He ascended to heaven. But no one should suppose that the Christian commonwealth is comparable to a profane one, for the two differ as soul and body. Luther then suggests that we establish a triple classification of all human commonwealths. "First, there is the profane and secular commonwealth which, since it is multiple, has many heads and rulers. Second there is the commonwealth which is properly that of the Christians, who through one faith are subject to Christ as one head. Third, there is the indifferent commonwealth (*adiaphoram*), properly neither the one nor the other, in which we must place priests, monks, and that sort of religious; this is a commonwealth attached to ceremonies." [46] In another recension of the same

---

[44] Sermon (1520), IX,445,10.

[45] Sermon (1520), IX,457,1.

[46] Ibid., IX,457,24. There are some connections between this Sermon and the discussion of ceremonies in Operationes, V,401,5 ff.

Sermon, Luther's argument makes more use of the terminology of the church. He again separates three groups, which he calls communities (*communitates*). The first is secular; the second is the external churchly community of ceremonies or the *ecclesia larvalis*; and the third is the spiritual church of Christ.[47]

In the first part of the Sermon Luther thus appears to set up three separate commonwealths or communities, but the remainder of the Sermon rephrases these distinctions as if between three classes in a single commonwealth. A prince in a civil polity, says Luther, possesses first of all citizens, secondly lictors for punishments, and thirdly court-fools (*moriones*). "Similarly Christ, the prince of the celestial commonwealth, which is the church, has as His citizens all believers; secondly, because human affairs are as they are, so that the tares of the wicked always arise among the good, He gave the sword to earthly rulers (*principibus terrenis*), and He uses them as torturers and lictors to restrain the evil; thirdly, in the place of court-fools, he has the ceremonious religious." [48] The description of the external ecclesiastical community of ceremonies as comparable to that of the court-fools may seem to suggest that it should be abolished entirely. Luther goes on, however, to explain that the proper office of the priest, as of bishop and pope, is that of legate. "Thus no other office was imposed on the pontiffs by Christ, except that they should announce to Christians the word of Christ." [49]

These Sermons of early 1520 reveal much of the problematic of Luther's new approach to the church and society. On the one hand, Luther is concerned to distinguish the true spiritual church from any external community and of course from any merely profane or secular community. On the other hand, he does not wish to isolate a "spiritual church," and he also wishes to call the actual Christian society the church. In the background of the problematic we can see first of all the new distinction between the two realms of Christian existence, for this tends to remove

[47] Sermon (1520), IV,716,7. For Luther's terminology of the church in his early period, see Ad dialogum Silvestri Prieratis de potestate papae responsio (1518), I,656,30 f.; Galatians Commentary (1519), II, 446,27; 447,28 f.; Operationes V,450,12 f.

[48] Sermon (1520), IX,457,32.

[49] Ibid., IX,458,34.

the primary reality of the church, its existence in Christ, from the world. But in the second place, the church, like the Christian, exists on earth as well as in heaven, and hence there must be a worldly church too. In the longer writings of 1520 and 1521, Luther's main interest is in working out a precise statement on the spiritual church in Christ; we shall study this in Von dem Papsttum zu Rom (1520) and in the Ad librum Ambrosii Catharini responsio (1521). However, he also continues to speak of the unity of the Christian society in the world, and we shall notice this briefly as it appears in An den christlichen Adel (1520).

The work Von dem Papsttum zu Rom is in form a refutation of a writing of Augustin Alveld in defense of the divine right of the papacy, but Luther goes far beyond the needs of refutation to develop an important statement of his own position. Alveld had, for example, argued on the basis of natural reason that every community (*gemeine*) on earth must have a bodily head under the true head Christ and that the church therefore needs the pope as its head on earth.[50] Luther first attacks the argument as based only on natural reason, for reason cannot deal with God's ordinances unless it be first illumined by faith.[51] Further he notes that the argument does not hold even on the level of reason, since there are many earthly communities ruled by more than one person, and since in worldly government (*im weltlichem regiment*) there is no single sovereign but many independent rulers such as the kings of France or of Hungary.[52]

More important, Luther undertakes to refute Alveld by explaining the true nature of the Christian community or Christendom (*Christenheit*). Christendom, according to biblical usage, is to be absolutely distinguished from any worldly community, for it is the community of saints, "an assembly (*vorsamlunge*) of

---

[50] Von dem Papsttum zu Rom (1520), VI,290,20. For a special discussion of this work, see J. Heckel, " 'Die zwo Kirchen,' Eine juristische Betrachtung über Luthers Schrift 'Von dem Papsttum zu Rom,' " Evangelisch-Lutherische Kirchenzeitung, 10 (1956), 221–26.

[51] Von dem Papsttum, VI,291,4.

[52] Ibid., VI,292,9. Luther here speaks of the secular communities as within Christendom; see 292,15: "Das kunigreich von Franckreich hot seinen kunig, Ungern seinen, Polen, Denen und ein iglich seynen eygen, und seyn doch alle ein volck des weltlichen stands in der Christenheit on ein eyniges heubt. . . ."

all believers in Christ on earth." [53] Christendom is therefore "an assembly of hearts in one faith" [54] and not any bodily assembly. Thus the communion of saints has a spiritual unity, and this alone constitutes Christendom, not any unity of city, time, person, or work. Christ's kingdom is not of this world (John XVIII,36), and His Christendom is never to be confused with any bodily community. Christ Himself removed its unity from all outward or bodily location and transferred it to the place of the spirit (*in die geystliche ort*).[55] The bodily community can never be more than a figure of this spiritual community.[56]

In addition to this strictly biblical sense of Christendom or the church, Luther admits another sense, according to which it is "an assembly in a house, parish, bishopric, archbishopric, or papacy." [57] But he maintains strongly that there is not a syllable in the Bible to show that this Christendom or church as it stands by itself is divinely ordained.[58] In a careful statement, Luther argues that we should give two different names to these two churches. "The first one, which is natural, primary, essential, and true, let us call a spiritual, inward Christendom. The second, which is artificial (*gemacht*) and outward, let us call a bodily, outward Christendom. We do not of course wish to separate them one from the other; it is just as when I speak of a man and call him spiritual according to his soul and bodily according to his body, or when the Apostle speaks of the inner and of the outer man (Romans VII,21). So also the Christian assembly, according to the soul, is a communion in accord with one faith; even though it cannot be assembled according to the body in one place, yet every group (of it) is assembled in its own place." [59]

Christ is the one head of the first and essential Christendom.

[53] Ibid., VI,292,37.

[54] Ibid., VI,293,4.

[55] Ibid., VI,293,37. Luther here uses Luke XVII,20 to explain the distinction of the church from the world; this text appears frequently in other writings of the period, e.g., Romans, LVI,493,15 f.; Acta Augustana (1518), II,19,37 f. Operationes, V,450,24 f.; Auf das überchristlich usw. Buch Bocks Emsers Antwort (1521), VII, 683,8 f.

[56] Von dem Papsttum zu Rom, VI,295,25.

[57] Ibid., VI,296,17.

[58] Ibid., VI,296,30. "Von disser kirchen, wo sie allein ist, stet nit ein buchstab in der heyligenn schrifft, das sie von got geordenet sey, ..."

[59] Ibid., VI,296,39 f.

There can be no human head on earth; all priests, or bishops, or apostles are equally messengers of this spiritual Christendom. There are three outward marks (*zeichenn*) by which one can recognize the appearance of the true spiritual church in the world: baptism, the sacrament, and the Gospel.[60]

In respect of the second, external Christendom, Luther is quite willing to recognize that "one is superior to another on the basis of human ordinance (*ausz menschlicher ordenung*).[61] But he cannot admit that anyone is a Christian or justified because of this second, external Christendom.

We are perhaps in danger of giving too much emphasis to the polemic and anti-papal character of Von dem Papsttum zu Rom and of thus failing to see that Luther has here established the positive principles which will always be basic to his thinking about the church. Luther must attack Alveld in the first place, because the movement of Alveld's thought, like that of the early Luther, is from the present church with its graces to the future perfect church of triumph and salvation. Luther after 1518–19 reverses this direction of thought in the case of the church as in the case of justice and law. What must always be primary is the existence of the spiritual church in Christ; here is the communion of the saints and the participation in all the goods of Christ. As a corollary of this reversal of Alveld's direction of thought, so Luther must deny Alveld's starting point, the foundation of the external church in divine right.

But if Luther denies that the external church leads to divine justice or follows from divine right, he has no intention of reducing the Christian society to a merely spiritual church. The church, like the Christian, also lives in the world. And in Von dem Papsttum zu Rom, Luther moves slowly toward a statement of the principles of organization for the external church. On the negative side, as we have already indicated, divine right plays no significant part in its construction; Luther does not even make much use of his theory of the universal priesthood of all believers, though this may be regarded as the one positive result which finally emerges from the long work of destruction

---

[60] Ibid., VI,301,3. Compare Operationes, V,504,13.
[61] Von dem Papsttum zu Rom, VI,300,26.

which began with the questioning of the divine right of the papacy.[62] On the positive side, Luther's first and main point is the
doctrine of the signs of the true church, such as baptism, the
sacrament, and above all the word. Here are the essential marks
of the earthly existence of the church whose primary reality is in
heaven. Luther's second point in Von dem Papsttum zu Rom
is that whatever organization the church needs for the use of
these signs it derives from human ordinance and reason. It is
true that Luther often seems to belittle the papacy when he calls
it a merely human ordinance in contrast to its own claim to
absolute divine right. On the other hand, Luther in 1520, and
indeed much later,[63] is prepared to accept the papacy on this basis;
when he rejects the papacy, he never intends to reject the idea of
an external church; and in the absence of any divine right which
defines church organization, he entrusts this organization to
reason.

Luther does not say much in Von dem Papsttum zu Rom about
human society in general, and he is not explicit on the relation
of the external church to the secular community. He does, however, introduce some interesting observation on secular authority
(*weltliche ubirkeit*). Luther argues that now in the time of the
New Testament God does not publicly invest anyone with secular rule, even though there is no human power without His secret
ordinance. For this reason, Peter (I Peter II,13) speaks of
"human ordinances"; such men rule without God's word, though
not without His counsel.[64] Here Luther seems to be moving
toward his later distinction between God's spiritual government
by the word and His world-government (*Weltregiment*).[65] In
Von dem Papsttum zu Rom, as already indicated, Luther is still
prepared to accept the papacy as a human ordinance; as such
it too is the result of God's counsel, but of wrath not of grace.[66]

The Ad librum Ambrosii Catharini responsio (1521) remains
within the general position of Vom dem Papsttum zu Rom (1520),
but Luther develops his ideas further at several important points.

---

[62] On the universal priesthood, see Holl. op. cit. (note 2, above), p. 318 f.
[63] Compare his statements in the Schmalkaldische Artikel (1538), L,213,1 f.
[64] Von dem Papsttum zu Rom, VI,318,27.
[65] See pp.159 f. below.
[66] Von dem Papsttum zu Rom, VI,321,31 f.

Thus he makes explicit the concept of the church without sin which corresponds to the Christian who is already totally just in Christ. When Christ promises in Matthew XVI,18 that He will build His church upon a rock and that the gates of hell shall not prevail against it, He is necessarily speaking of a church without sin. Hence the promise can apply to no external church, specifically not to the Roman church.[67] Hence Peter cannot be the rock "but only Christ, who alone certainly is and remains without sin, as with Him His holy church in the spirit is without sin." [68] And from this standpoint, in contrast to that of his early period, Luther reaffirms the spirituality and the invisibility of the church. "Therefore just as the rock which is without sin, invisible, and spiritual, can be perceived only by faith, so it is necessary that the church which is without sin, invisible, and spiritual, should also be perceived only by faith." [69]

Catharinus on one occasion had argued that it would be impossible to recognize a purely spiritual church, and Luther's reply helps to clarify the existence of the church in the world. The church, explains Luther, lives in the flesh but not according to the flesh (*in carne, non secundum carnem*). "The church does not exist without body and location, and yet body and location are not the church and do not pertain to it." [70] All such things are indifferent and free; any place is suitable for a Christian; no place is necessary to him. How then does one recognize the church? As earlier, Luther points to its sensible and visible signs: baptism, the bread, and above all the Gospel.[71]

---

[67] Ad librum Ambrosii Catharini responsio (1521), VII,709,20.

[68] Ibid., VII,709,31.

[69] Ibid., VII,710,1. Compare with this statement on the invisible, spiritual church, Luther's remarks in Auf das überchristlich usw. Buch Bocks Emsers Antwort (1521), VII,683,9: "Da ich die Christliche kirch ein geystlich vorsammlung genennet het, spottistu meyn, als wolt ich ein kirch bawen wie Plato ein statt, die nyndert were." In reply Luther makes use of the usual texts such as Romans II,11 (that God is no "respecter of persons"), and Luke XVII,20 (that the kingdom of God does not come "cum observatione"). "Ich meyn yhe, du heyssist das reych gottis die Christenliche kirche odder uns, yn wilchen gott lebt und regiert." Hence one may not follow Emser's "reason," for Christ clearly says, "Es sey kein statt, rawm, noch eusserliche weysse am reych gottis, und sey nit hie noch da, sondern eyn geyst ynn unsserm ynwendigen."

[70] Ad librum Ambrosii Catharini responsio, VII,720,2.

[71] Ibid., VII,720,32 f. Compare Operationes, V,57,1: "Atque ita Ecclesia iam nullum locum et omnem locum habet."

In the Ad librum Ambrosii Catharini responsio, Luther also does something toward developing in relation to the church and society a contrast comparable to that between Christian and civil justice or, ultimately, between the two realms of Christian existence. There are, however, special difficulties in the case of the church, for Luther begins to shy away from any contrast, such as the "two churches" of Von dem Papsttum zu Rom, which might threaten the church's fundamental unity, either by splitting it into two parts or by restricting it to heaven alone. Nevertheless Luther gradually moves to increased clarity as he works out more limited contrasts, which do not have the church as one of the members, or as he again attacks "mixing" in this area. Thus in one case he contrasts the kingdom of Christ with those of the world. "The kingdoms of the world are ruled by human laws which evidently have to do with things temporal; the kingdom of Christ is ruled by the pure and simple word of the Gospel." [72] Luther goes on to argue that the papacy is neither the one nor the other; it pretends to deal with things spiritual and actually deals with things worldly.[73] On another occasion, Luther attacks the papacy for being concerned with laws rather than with the Gospel; even worse, he argues, is the fact that the papacy makes laws within the area which belongs to the Gospel. "If they had established their laws in the works of the virtues such as are commanded by the Decalogue or are dictated by the philosophers and by natural reason . . . perhaps they might only have constituted a synagogue (and not the reign of Antichrist) and have spread some sort of civil justice in the world." [74] In each of these passages, Luther is developing a contrast between the church as spiritual and invisible on the one side and the kingdoms of the world and civil justice on the other side; in neither passage is he explicit on the way in which the external church fits into the contrast.

In Von dem Papsttum zu Rom and in the Ad librum Ambrosii Catharini responsio Luther's main concern was to reach clarity on the primary, spiritual church which is without sin. But Luther

[72] Ad librum Ambrosii Catharini responsio, VII,743,6.
[73] Ibid., VII,743,8.
[74] Ibid., VII,761,9.

will never limit the title "church" to this alone, for there is also an external church, which is not properly another church but rather another mode of existence, in the world and in the flesh, of the one true church. Furthermore, Luther always assumed that there would be only one church within one earthly society; hence there is the closest connection between the invisible mode of existence of the church, its external existence with its "signs," and the secular commonwealth which includes the same Christians. And whether for the whole of Christendom or for a particular part of it such as a nation or a city, Luther is always willing to call the actual society the church. To some extent this is simply a matter of terminology, but it is also more. The title "church" is of tremendous importance in Luther's experience of Christianity; further it is most closely connected not only with his sense of total justice in Christ but also with his sense of belonging to a particular Christian community on earth. Hence Luther will not let the concept of the church disintegrate into a number of special concepts such as the church in Christ, the church in its external existence and so on, even when he has the distinctions which seem to involve such special concepts. In his mature period, Luther can to some extent make explicit the different standpoints from which he can either make precise distinctions or overlook them in the interest of unity; in 1520–21 Luther still seems to make the shift from one standpoint to another less consciously. Thus in Von dem Papsttum zu Rom and in the Ad librum Ambrosii Catharini responsio Luther concentrated mainly on the distinctions; on the other hand in the contemporary An den christlichen Adel (1520) Luther with a different purpose emphasizes the unity of the whole Christian society.

In the Preface to An den christlichen Adel Luther explains that he is proposing several matters "touching on the improvement of the Christian estate, in the hope that God may deign to help His church through the lay estate, since the spiritual estate, to which this properly pertains, has become indifferent to its duty." [75] Luther here uses "Christian estate" as a synonym for the church or Christendom, as will appear from the course of the argument and as is indicated by Luther's summary of the

---

[75] An den christlichen Adel, VI,404,13.

work in his letters as concerning the improvement and reform of the church (*de statu ecclesiae emendando, de reformanda ecclesia*).[76]

Luther's general position on Christian unity is involved in the main thesis, that the temporal power has jurisdiction over the so-called "spiritual estate." Luther begins by attacking the claim of the clergy to be in a special sense the spiritual estate (*geistlicher Stand*); all Christians are of the spiritual estate, and the differences between them are simply those of office (*Amt*). We shall have to notice Luther's position on estates in more detail later,[77] but the general basis of his argument here is clear. Christians are constituted by their membership in the primary, spiritual church of heaven, and this is the only true spiritual estate; in contrast to it all differences in the world or in the external church are simply differences of office. "From all this it follows that there is really no difference between laymen and priests, princes and bishops, and, as they say, 'spiritual' and 'worldly,' except that of office and work. There is no difference of estate, for they are all of the same estate, true bishops, priests, and popes. . . . This is the teaching of St. Paul . . . and of St. Peter . . . that we are all one body, of Christ the head, all members one of another. Christ does not have two bodies or two kinds of body, the one worldly and the other spiritual. He is one head and has one body." [78]

[76] The phrases are taken from letters cited by J. Heckel, "Lex charitatis . . ." (note 2, Chapter I, above), p. 169, note 1355a.

[77] See pp. 153 f. below.

[78] An den christlichen Adel, VI,408,26. For the general context of the passage, see W. Köhler, "Zu Luthers Schrift, An den christlichen Adel deutscher Nation," Zeitschrift für Rechtsgeschichte, kan. Abt. XIV (1925), 1–38. The passage cited is best understood as equivalent to Luther's preceding statements in the terminology of estate (*Stand*). There is only one *Christenstand* and its unity is not affected by the existence in the world of the *geistlicher Stand* and the *weltlicher Stand*. Similarly there is only one "body of Christ," and one cannot split this into two parts because of the existence of a "spiritual" body of the clergy and a "worldly" body of secular rulers. Luther is not here talking about the "zwo Kirchen" of Von dem Papsttum zu Rom, p.132 above.

The passage has often been discussed in relation to the problem of the *corpus Christianum* (on which, see pp. 152 f. below); for an excellent survey of this literature see K. Matthes, Das Corpus Christianum bei Luther im Lichte seiner Erforschung (Studien zur Geschichte der Wirtschaft und Geisteskultur V), Berlin, 1929. See also O. Scheel, Evangelium, Kirche, und Volk bei Luther (Schriften der Vereins für Reformationsgeschichte, Nr. 156), Leipzig, 1934; H. Liermann "Studien zur Geschichte des corpus christianum in der Neuzeit," Zeitschrift für Rechtsgeschichte,

In this first part of the argument, Luther is still within the context of Von dem Papsttum zu Rom, and he is using the concept of the true spiritual church of heaven to destroy any notion of a specially "spiritual" estate in the world. But he goes on from a different standpoint to locate the secular estate very definitely within the "Christendom" of the world. Luther argues that since God ordained the worldly power and since the members of the body are to help one another "so one should allow the office of the worldly power to proceed without hindrance throughout the entire body of Christendom (*durch den gantzen corper der Christenheit*), whether it affect pope, bishops, priests, monks, nuns, or anybody else." [79] And Luther makes essentially the same point later in the work. "Worldly rule (*hirschafft*) has become a member of the Christian body (*des Christlichen Corpers*), and even though it has a bodily work, nevertheless it is of the spiritual estate. Hence its work should extend freely and without check to all members of the body; it should punish and use force whenever guilt deserves it or necessity demands it." [80]

It is clear on careful reading that An den christlichen Adel does not deny any of the distinctions of Von dem Papsttum zu Rom. The concept of the spiritual estate implies all of the primacy of the spiritual, invisible church; no one is a member of the spiritual estate because he is a king or because he is a priest. On the other hand, An den christlichen Adel goes further than the other works we have noted in its assertion of a Christian unity of society. The true and primary spiritual church is not any earthly commonwealth, but it must appear in an earthly commonwealth. When it does so appear, Luther will call the commonwealth as a whole the church, the Christian body, and Christendom.

---

kan. Abt. XXVII (1938), 486–529; E. G. Schwiebert, "The Medieval Pattern in Luther's Views of the State," Church History 12 (1943), 98–117.

[79] An den christlichen Adel VI,409,17. One may find similar ideas in a roughly contemporary Sermon (1519–20), IV,669,10: "In una fide sumus omnes, alter alterius membrum: et quemadmodum in nativo corpore membrum membro servit, ita quoque in mystico fiat, ut quodvis suum habeat actum. . . . Quod si colonus rebus ecclesiasticis est intentus aut presbyter negotiis prophanis aut maritus religioni inhiet aut caelibitui, aut cuiuscunque conditionis fuerit, si suae quemque sortis pigeat, verum ecclesiae corpus constare non potest."

[80] An den christlichen Adel, VI,410,3.

Toward 1521, Luther seems to feel that for the church, as for his other key concepts, he has achieved clarity on the points which are absolutely essential, and there is a slackening of the theoretical development for almost a decade. But the church, like justice and law, was included in Luther's new attempt, beginning toward 1529, to work out a general statement of his theology. In such works as the Lectures on Galatians (1531) and in the Disputations (1535 f.) we find, not any new theory of the church, but a significant restatement of the doctrines of 1520–21 in a new and more general context.

Luther in his mature period of course preserves his basic distinction between the church in its primary spiritual sense and the church as it appears in the world. He is, however, more keenly aware that this is the same church in two different realms of existence, and he avoids the terminology of two churches found, for example, in Von dem Papsttum zu Rom (1520). Thus he explains in the Preface to a Disputation of 1542, "The church is such an assembly (*congregatio*) that we could not comprehend it unless the Holy Spirit had revealed it. The church is in the flesh and appears as visible; it is in the world and appears in the world. Nevertheless it is not the world nor in the world, and no one sees it. Therefore those who do not proceed in the proper meaning of the words are easily deceived." [81] Or in a contemporary letter to Nicholas Amsdorf, who had qualms of conscience about the pomp and circumstances of his episcopate, Luther writes that God does not care for such persons or masks (*personas seu larvas*) as the episcopate, and they are not His kingdom. On the other hand, adds Luther, "The church must appear in the world. But it cannot appear except in a mask, person, shell, husk, or some sort of costume, in which it can be heard, seen, and grasped; otherwise it could never be found. Such masks are a husband, a ruler, a servant, John, Peter, Luther, Amsdorf; and yet the church is none of these, for the church is neither Jew nor Greek. . . ." [82]

Luther after 1530 is also able to bring his idea of the church,

[81] Disputations (1542), XXXIX,2 p. 149,8. The other recension of the argument is slightly more explicit at one point, with its phrasing "Est et apparet in carne et tamen non est caro," p. 149,22.

[82] Briefe (Feb.? 1542), IX,610,47.

even more clearly than in 1520–21, into relation with his basic thesis that the Christian is at the same time totally just in Christ and also a sinner. Luther does this most explicitly as he denies the Antinomian claim to set up in the world a church without sin. In the first place, argues Luther, the church in the world is "mixed," and it here includes also the wicked and the hypocrites.[83] In the second place, and of more fundamental importance, even the true members of the church are all sinners. "I say moreover that the church is to be taught and admonished (I speak of the true and holy church) concerning sin which is present and still clinging to our flesh. . . ."[84] But what of the communion of the saints? Is there no holy church without sin? Luther replies with the paradoxical distinctions which we have already seen in the case of the individual Christian; [85] the church too is at the same time just and sinful. "And so it is true, that the church is pure and that sin is removed, but take care that you distinguish rightly. We are such with reference to Christ (*quoad Christum*) but with reference to ourselves (*quoad nos*) we struggle perpetually with the devil and the flesh and with all sorts of vice and evil. . . ."[86]

Luther makes the same point more briefly in the Lectures on Galatians (1531). "And I believe in the holy church, that is, in the church I see no death, no sin, but merely holy Christians, not sinners nor guilty to death, living forever, holy and just as Christ. This I see by faith. But when I turn my eyes the other way, there I see my brother distressed and sinning. And is the church therefore not holy? I deny the conclusion. If I look at my own person, it is never holy. If I look at Christ, then it is

---

[83] E.g., Disputations (1538), XXXIX,1 p.490,24; 496,3; 514,13.

[84] Disputations (1538), XXXIX,1 p. 491,15.

[85] See p.69, Chapter II, above.

[86] Disputations (1538), XXXIX,1 p. 493,14. For another comparable statement, see XXXIX,1 pp. 514,13 f. and specially p. 515,2: ". . . quod deus, cum sit mirificator sanctorum suorum, haec perpetuo miscet in Ecclesia, ut Ecclesia sit sancta, et tamen non sancta, aliquis sit iustus, et tamen non sit iustus, beatus alius et non beatus. Et hoc bene notandum est: Etsi id rationi, quae ubique in rebus et operibus Dei vult sapere, non probatur, duo contraria esse in uno eodemque subiecto. Sed tamen reipsa sic est et sic in hoc regno et scriptura sic loquitur, ut Psalmus: Beati, quorum remissae sunt iniquitates, Hic est sanctus et beatus, statimque subiicit: Pro hoc orabit ad te omnis sanctus. Hic vides peccatorem. Item videre est Ro. 7. Sanctus es et ora pro iniquitate. Reime du es zusammen."

holy, for the sins of the whole world do not exist where we are looking." [87]

As we saw earlier,[88] Luther in the Lectures on Galatians (1531) worked out a general theological statement of the two realms of Christian existence, and this had implications not only for justice and law but also for society. How does Luther apply this statement to the church? In a few cases Luther attempts to translate the distinction between the two realms directly into a contrast between church and polity, or between ecclesiastical and political statements.[89] But such simple contrasts require a good deal of qualification, since the church like the individual Christian exists not only in one but in both realms. On the other hand, society here and now in the world can be analyzed apart from Christian existence in Christ, and Luther does so in terms of polity. The key concept of polity thus serves to describe and affirm a whole aspect of human existence which is God-ordained, though it is not specifically Christian and though it is out of relation to salvation. As in the cases of justice and law, Luther can here use ideas he had worked out during the 1520's on the world-government of God, and these ideas now help him better to grasp and express the general unity of morality, law, and government.

The new concept of polity furnishes a kind of counterpoint to the idea of the spiritual church. In the case of the spiritual church, Luther starts from his apprehension of the total realm of Christian existence in Christ. From this standpoint he re-

[87] Galatians (1531), XL,1 pp. 444,9 f. One might also compare Luther's interesting argument on Galatians, IV, 26 pp. 662,6 f. with its conclusions 662,13 f.: "ergo ecclesia est in terra et tamen spiritualis," and 663,5: "ne ergo spacir, quasi non in terris, 'sursum' intelligamus non localiter sed spiritualiter, ut distinguantur, quae coelestia, temporalia, quia spiritualia sunt sursum et temporalia deorsum. Sunt distincta bona, sed non in diversis locis." The distinction, Luther is saying, is between two realms of existence, not between two cosmological realms.

[88] See pp. 65 f., Chapter II, above.

[89] See p. 66, Chapter II, above. Luther in Galatians (1531) also contrasts polity with religion; see p. 65, Chapter II, above. This is not entirely unambiguous, since *religio* itself can be contrasted with the Christian's existence in Christ. XL,1 p. 347,10: "quicquid in homine est praestantissimum extra spiritum, vocatur caro, etiam ipsa religio" (see also De servo arbitrio (1525), XVIII,740,19). Hence Luther's most precise contrast is between speaking in polity and speaking in theology or before God. XL,1 p. 392,7: "quia Paulus versatur non in loco politico, sed theologico et spirituali coram Deo"; compare pp. 394,11 f.; 397,11. It must then be recognized that the church "appears" in the political realm as well as the theological realm.

constructs and fuses the older ideas of the church militant and church triumphant. The church militant had an actual, present justice, but only a partial justice. The church triumphant had a total, perfect justice, but the Christian would not share it until the future. Luther's spiritual church transcends these distinctions since it is totally just now in Christ.

In the case of polity, Luther starts from his apprehension of the existence of the Christian in the world. From this standpoint he reconstructs and fuses the older ideas of the church militant once again and of the secular community. The church militant had claimed a justice which was Christianly significant, but it also argued that this justice was in some way an antecedent of salvation. The secular community had been granted a justice which made no such false claim of salvation, but earlier thought had not recognized its significance for the Christian. Luther now defends the concept of polity, whose justice is not in any sense an antecedent of salvation but is nevertheless of vital and positive significance for the Christian as an ordinance of God.

Man, declares Luther in evident paraphrase of Aristotle's Politics, is naturally made for civil life and for society (*naturaliter constitutus ad civilitatem et societatem*).[90] But what is "natural" in society for Luther is at the same time divinely ordained. "You have often heard that economic and political ordinances are divine; God ordained them as He ordained the sun, the moon, and the other creatures." [91]

While polity, like civil justice and the civil use of the law, is divinely ordained, it is of course of no use for justification. Caesar has his corporal blessing, and the Christians stand in awe of it but only in the civil realm; in the realm of theology one needs the very different spiritual blessing of Christ. "We say that the creatures of God are good, and political ordinance is a creature of God. Thus to have a wife, wealth, and dwelling-places is a divine blessing, but in its own realm (*in suo loco.*) [92]

In his description of polity as a realm of human existence, Luther emphasizes two main characteristics. In the first place

---

[90] Galatians (1531), XL,2 p. 72,4.
[91] Ibid., XL,1 p.460,7.
[92] Ibid., XL,1 p.395,3.

it is as a whole subject to reason. "The polity and economics are subject to reason. Reason there has first place, and there one finds civil laws and civil justice."[93] In the second place, man in polity always deals only with the masks (*larvae*) of God, while God Himself remains hidden. "Kingship, empire, the magistrate, the teacher, the pupil, father, mother, lord, mistress, slave, maid-servant — these are all masks and persons which God wills us to cherish and recognize as His creatures."[94] However, man without Christianity, the political man, cannot make this distinction between the masks and God, and in consequence he falsely endows the mask with divinity and with power to save. It might further be noted that in Luther's thought the concept of God's masks extends beyond the sphere of government and that it finally embraces all of man's life apart from Christ and the whole visible world. "What I live in the flesh . . . I do not hold to be life; it is rather a mask of life."[95] "Hence the whole creation is God's mask. Accordingly our knowledge is how to distinguish divinity from the mask, and this the world does not do."[96]

Through his concept of polity and its masks, Luther has established a general statement of the "world" in which the Christian exists apart from Christ. The world is God's good creature, and in its aspects of law and authority it contains God's commands to man. Nevertheless Luther has "creaturized" the world, so that it cannot in any way appear as an antecedent to salvation or justification, for salvation and justification are found only in the Christian's existence in Christ, not in his existence in the world.

Man's life in polity is as such not specifically Christian. "Hence the Christian in the world (*in orbe terrarum*) uses all creatures

[93] Ibid., XL,1 p. 305,7.
[94] Ibid., XL,1 p. 175,3.
[95] Ibid., XL,1 p. 288,5. Luther goes on to say that his true life is Christ. The brief notes of Rörer seem to be correctly expanded in the printed version of 1535,XL,1 p.288,24: "Non enim est vere vita, sed tantum larva vitae, sub qua vivit alius, nempe Christus, qui est vere vita mea, quam non vides, sed tantum audis." I have not seen the article by W. J. Kooiman, "Gods Maskenspiel in de Theologie van Luther" in: Maskenspiel (= W. Lundertz Festschrift), Amsterdam, 1955, pp. 49–83.
[96] Ibid., XL,1 p. 174,3. Compare pp. 463,9 f., and p. 173,9: "Hoc videre non est hominis politici, naturaliter conditi. . . ."

in such a way that there is no difference between him and the heathen (*inter pium et impium*)."[97] Accordingly it is true in one sense that pagans such as Cicero and Aristotle knew as much as any Christians, or more, about the content of polity, or what Luther in scholastic terminology calls its formal and material causes. Hence Luther urges that the Christians profit by the political wisdom found in such pagan writers.[98] But no pagan can perceive the efficient and final causes of polity; only the Christian can begin to see and accept it as a creature of God and a command of the creator to man.[99]

Thus in the case of polity as elsewhere Luther revises traditional notions in the light of the distinction between two realms of Christian existence and of the unity of the Christian individual. Christianity leaves unchanged the content of polity as it leaves unchanged the civil use of the law and civil justice; the heavenly realm of existence is not "mixed" with the world, and lest mixture take place in the opposite direction Luther firmly denies that any polity ever leads to salvation. But the Christian as Christian has also his heavenly realm of existence, apprehended only through faith. Here he realizes that polity is God's creature and here he accepts it as such. The two realms are thus distinct but they do not threaten the ultimate unity of the Christian individual, since in each case there is only one polity, as the justices of works and of faith are one justice, and as the civil and theological uses apply to one law. The total justice of the Christian in heaven, or its partial appearance in his sanctification on earth does not change polity as such at all; it merely changes the individual's evaluation and acceptance of it. In modern jargon one might say that for polity as for the "world" in general, Christianity affects the nature of the Christian's commitment; it does not affect that to which he is committed.

We have now seen Luther's general doctrine of the church

---

[97] Ibid., XL,1 p. 289,12.

[98] Compare Enarratio capitis noni Esaiae (1543–44), XL,3 p. 607,22; 608,11.

[99] Compare In XV Psalmos graduum (1532–33), XL,3 pp. 202,15 f.: "Aristoteles in Aethicis /203 et politicis, qui tamen optime, Cicero et Plato, de legibus. Efficientem et finalem causam non attingunt"; p. 204,9: "Et concedo, quod apud gentes non minus bonae formales causae reipublicae et magistratus meliores, sed hoc tantum est materia et forma." Compare Enarratio capitis noni Esaiae XL,3 pp. 612,31 f.

and of polity, and we have seen that because the church exists both in heaven and earth Luther does not reach a simple contrast between church and polity comparable to that between passive and civil justice or between the theological and civil uses of the law. The only way to reach such a contrast is to limit the church to the spiritual church in heaven, and Luther in his mature period, much more than in 1520–21, is deeply suspicious of any such limitation. Consequently Luther's doctrine of church and polity must also take up the difficult problem of the interaction between church and polity in the world. We shall notice two aspects of the problem. In the first place, on the individual level, as Luther had made a general distinction between the world-person and the Christian person of the individual,[100] so he will separate the "political person" from the Christian as such. In the second place, on the social level, Luther will suggest and imply that the church in the world, what we may call the church as masked, in this phase of its existence takes on many of the aspects of polity.

On the distinction between the Christian in the polity and the Christian as such, Luther argues, in connection with the problem of resisting the emperor, that the prince as prince is a political person. When he acts, he therefore does not act as a Christian "who is neither prince, nor male, nor any other of the persons in the world."[101] He makes the same point in one of his Table-Talks. The emperor is head in the political body and realm, and every private man is a part and member of this body. Among the special members are the seven electoral princes, but "so far as they are members of the polity and of Caesar, they are political and not Christian."[102] Luther concludes with the general distinction that the Christian is a "double person," both a believer and at the same time a political person. And in one

[100] See pp. 68 f., Chapter II, above.

[101] Briefe (Jan., 1531), VI,17,10. Compare TR, §7007, VI,323,9. For Luther's various positions on armed resistance to the emperor, see K. Müller, "Luthers Äusserungen über das Recht des bewaffneten Widerstands gegen den Kaiser," Bayerische Akademie der Wissenschaften, SB, phil.-hist. Kl. 1915, Abh. VIII.

[102] TR, §4342 (1539), IV,237,2. Compare Enarratio capitis noni Esaiae (1543–44, printed edition 1546), XL,3 646,29: "Omnes Christiani sumus fide 'unum corpus' . . . sed secundum corpus quod circumferimus, subiecti sumus potestati et rebus politicis. Ecclesia, regnum Christi, concors et unanimis est per omnia. In politico regno aliter se res habet et secus omnia geruntur quam in illo spirituali."

of his Disputations, in a passage noted above, Luther explains how the Christian both has his polity in heaven and is also a citizen of the world.[103]

In such distinctions between the political person and the Christian, Luther has simply applied his general distinction between the two realms of Christian existence to a specific context. The Christian as such, the Christian hidden in Christ who is totally just, is to be distinguished from the Christian existing in the world or in the polity which is the general concept for the social aspect of the world. It is to be noted that in all these cases where Luther sets up a simple contrast, he is thinking of the Christian in heaven, not of the churchman or of the pastor; we shall see later that the office of the pastor is in Luther's thought, if not political, at least worldly along with the other callings.[104]

On the relationship between the masked church and the polity, Luther is less explicit. Here as on a number of comparable questions, he seems to hesitate to give full rein to certain logical possibilities of his theology. Thus he will suggest that the church in the world is in some way an aspect of polity, but this is always an end-point or an implication of his argument; it never appears as starting point or principle. Similarly, as we shall see later,[105] Luther will suggest that the church in the world is in some way a part of God's world-government and that the hierarchy of the church is strictly comparable to the hierarchies of the household and of polity. Here again, Luther seems, however, to feel that this is not an entirely satisfactory end-point to the argument. In all these cases, therefore, we must be cautious in drawing final conclusions where Luther does not draw them, and we must try to discover something of the reasons for his hesitation.

Luther links the church in the world to polity first of all by its masks, for the masks which are connected with the church in the world appear to be quite comparable to those which are connected with polity in general. We have already seen Luther's letter to

[103] See p.68, Chapter II, above. Compare Briefe (March, 1531), VI,56,13: "Wir reden de membris Christi et corporis ecclesiastici; wissen sonst wohl, dass ein Christ als ein Bürger oder membrum corporis politici, müge das Schwert und weltlich Amt führen, davon wir oft geschrieben."

[104] See p. 156, below, with note 135.

[105] See pp. 173 and 176, below.

Amsdorf, where he notes that the church cannot appear in the world, except as masked; among the masks Luther lists Amsdorf as bishop along with a husband or a ruler.[106] Similarly in the Lectures on Galatians (1531) Luther dwells at some length on the proposition that God is no respecter of persons (Galatians, II,6); throughout the discussion the persons or masks of the bishop, the apostle, and the pastor are used indiscriminately along with those of the prince or the magistrate.[107]

Luther further links the church in the world with polity in terms of reason. Reason is the general principle of polity, and it can even serve as a synonym for polity; the realm of reason is the same as the political realm. But in terms of its organization and government, the church in the world is likewise subject to reason.[108]

As early as in Von dem Papsttum zu Rom (1520) Luther had described the "external church" as of human ordinance and linked to reason. We find much the same position restated and elaborated in Von den Konziliis und Kirchen (1539) which, along with Wider Hans Worst (1541), constitutes the fullest statement of Luther's mature doctrine of the church.

Luther in Von den Konziliis und Kirchen has a good deal to say about church government in his discussion of the early ecumenical councils. Thus, for example, he notes that the Council of Nicaea dealt not only with articles of faith, though these were its main concern; it also reached decisions concerning the external, temporal government of the church (*von eusserlichem zeitlichem Regiment der Kirchen*), e.g., on the rights and powers of bishops. Luther argues that it was not absolutely necessary to have a universal council for dealing with such questions "since for these external matters (of the church) reason, given by God, is enough for their ordering. There is here no need for the Holy Spirit, which should proclaim Christ and not be concerned with such questions that are subject to reason. Unless one wishes to

---

[106] See p. 140, above.

[107] Galatians (1531) XL,1 pp. 172,8 ff. See specially 172,11; 176,4; 177,7.

[108] In analyzing this problem, the remarks of R. Sohm, Kirchenrecht, 2 vols., anastatischer Neudruck (München und Leipzig, 1923), Vol. I,460 f. are still of value, even if Sohm's general thesis cannot be accepted without qualification.

say that the Holy Spirit does everything that pious Christians do, even when they eat or drink." [109]

Luther makes essentially the same point in connection with the Council of Constantinople. The Council did three things. First, and this was its main business, it declared as an article of faith that the Holy Spirit was in truth God. Secondly, it deposed some heretical bishops and appointed orthodox Christians to replace them. This action was no article of faith "but an external, perceptible work, which reason can and should do" and for which we do not need the extraordinary assistance of the Holy Spirit.[110] Thirdly, the Council of Constantinople established the patriarchate of Constantinople. This again was merely "an external, perceptible work of reason, or of flesh and blood. What does the Holy Spirit care which bishops are promoted or demoted? It has other things to do than such worldly childsplay." [111] Thus Luther gives reason a large part in the organization of the church in the world, and he can go so far as to assert, "The governing of the church (*Kirchen zu regieren*) is nothing but reason." [112]

But if Luther can go a long way toward describing the church in the world in terms of masks and reason, the full argument of Von den Konziliis und Kirchen also shows the limits to such an approach. In Part III of the work, Luther considers the general meaning of "church." He starts from the creed and from the church as the communion of saints. As he had done on earlier

[109] Von den Konziliis und Kirchen, L,552,21.

[110] Ibid., L,579,28.

[111] Ibid., L,580,13. Speaking of the Nicaean council, Luther declares that it first determined articles of faith, "Daneben haben sie etlich zufellige, leibliche, eusserliche, zeitliche stücke gehandelt, die billich weltlich zu achten sind," p. 559,33. Later, speaking of the times of worship, etc., he declares, pp. 649,34 f. "Denn solche stück sind gantz und gar eusserlich, auch der vernunft zu regieren (wie es die zeit, stet, und person foddern) mechtiglich und gentzlich unterworffen. Gott, Christus, und der Heilige Geist fragen nichts darnach, eben so wenig, als was und wo wir essen, trincken, kleiden, wonen, freyen, gehen oder stehen wollen. . . ."

[112] Sermon (May 16, 1529), XXIX,355,9: "Ideo non indigeo spiritu sancto ut dicam: Episcopus Moguntinus sol hoher sitzen quam Brandenbergensis. Spiritus sanctus confirmat wol quod iam ordinatum et positum. Sic kirchen zu regieren et pueros in scolis, sic canere ist eitel ratio." Compare also De potestate leges ferendi in ecclesia (1530), where Luther asks whether the church can pass any laws. He replies that it can pass none which bind the conscience, and he limits its legislation to the "civil" sphere. XXX,2 p. 684,15: "Foris tamen constituit pro pace et concordia inter homines, ceu aliae civiles aut oeconomicae leges. Talia sunt summo honore amplectenda, quia non nocet fidei et prosunt paci."

occasions, Luther attacks the word church (*Kirche*) as unclear in German, and he prefers community (*Gemeine*) or people (*Volk*) as a more meaningful term.[113] There are many peoples on earth, but the Christians are a special holy people, and Luther explains their holiness in terms of his basic doctrines of justification and sanctification.[114]

But how can anyone recognize this church, which is in the world but which is not the world? Luther replies with the same general answer as in Von dem Papsttum zu Rom, with a doctrine of "signs." In Von den Konziliis und Kirchen, Luther lists seven of these outward signs as most important, as "the seven main parts of the holy possession (*heilthum*) through which the Holy Spirit works in us a daily sanctification and life-giving in Christ." [115] Luther goes on to notice that "beyond these outward signs and holy possessions, the church has other outward customs (*weise*), by which and through which it is not made holy, either in body or soul; and yet, as has been said of them at length above (in the discussion of the councils) they are of great necessity and usefulness and are fine and proper." [116] In illustration, Luther mentions the time of services and the ways in which church buildings shall be used, and he again states that all these things are "entirely outward and are for reason to rule." [117]

Thus Luther's doctrine of "outward signs" remains a central part of the idea of the church in the world, and it can never be entirely subsumed under polity. Hence one might say that the church in the world has two aspects. First, there are the outward signs. These are of course not subject to reason, and they are to be precisely distinguished from any "masks," for God hides Himself in masks and reveals Himself in signs. Second, there are the organizations and arrangements for making these outward signs available to Christians. Luther would entrust this

---

[113] Von den Konziliis und Kirchen, L,624,15.

[114] Ibid., L,624,26 f.

[115] Ibid., L,642,32. For another statement of these same ideas from Luther's mature period, see Wider Hans Worst (1541), LI,479,4 f. In Von den Konziliis und Kirchen, L,643,6 Luther goes on to note other "signs" which are not peculiar to the church though characteristic of it.

[116] Ibid., L,649,7.

[117] Ibid., L,649,34 cited note 111, above; compare 651,12 where Luther says of feasts that they practically belong "ins weltlich regiment."

second aspect completely to reason, and he is quite prepared to discuss the authority of any person in the organization, such as a pastor or a bishop, as one of God's masks. Luther seems to have no desire to develop his thought further in this area, and it is characteristic of him to show little interest in systematic completeness for its own sake. In describing Luther's thought, we do well here as elsewhere to remain within the limits which he himself chose.[118]

The last point to be noted on Luther's mature theory of the church is that he continues to give the title of church to actual Christian society, either as a whole or in one of its territorial sub-divisions. The approach is well illustrated in Luther's writings dealing with the Turks, for he here employs it in close connection with the various distinctions we have already noted between a political person and a Christian, between the realm of polity and the realm of Christian justice. Thus in Vom Kriege wider die Türken (1528) Luther attacks the notion that any war against the Turks can be a crusade or a Christian war. There are two fighters against the Turk; the one is called "Christian," and the other "Emperor Carolus." The first can "fight" through prayers alone; the second does not, strictly speaking, fight as a Christian but as an Emperor or as a political person. "The Emperor is not the head of Christendom, nor the Protector of the Gospel or of the Faith. The church and the faith must have another pro-tector than emperors and kings. . . ."[119] But in the Heerpredigt wider den Türken (1529) Luther speaks of Daniel's prophecy (VII,17 f.) of a war to be waged against "the saints of the most high," and he explains this as the Turkish war against Europe. There may be many false Christians in the West; nevertheless where we find the Gospel and the sacraments, there must be some true Christians present. Because of them, the whole land may be called "Christianland (*Christenland*) and the true saints of

---

[118] Compare in this context the penetrating remarks of R. Prenter, Spiritus Creator (Forschungen zur Geschichte und Lehre des Protestantismus X,6), Mün-chen, 1954, p. 26 on the importance of the "hiatus" in Luther's thought.

[119] Vom Kriege wider die Türken (1528), XXX,2 p. 130,27. On Luther's writings about the Turks, see H. Lamparter, Luthers Stellung zum Türkenkrieg (For-schungen zur Geschichte und Lehre des Protestantismus IX,4), München, 1940. R. Lind, Luthers Stellung zum Kreuz- und Türkenkrieg (Diss. Giessen, 1940) ; G. W. Forell, "Luther and the War against the Turks," Church History 14 (1945), 256–71.

God." [120] Or again, somewhat later, "But there must be some Christians present, since Christ's name, Baptism, and Gospel have remained. Because of them the whole land is called Christianland, and the people are called Christendom (*Christenheit*) or Christ's people or God's saints." [121]

Luther can make the same point in the more technical language of polity. Thus in his Lectures on the Song of Songs (1530–31), Luther explains that the main intent of Solomon is to offer thanksgiving for the blessing of polity, and in particular of a polity where God is known and worshipped. "Every kingdom, principality, or polity which has the word of God and His true worship is compelled to suffer many troubles . . . and such a kingdom or polity is rightly called the people of God." [122] But Luther can also make it clear that the basic distinction between church and polity is in no way to be ignored. "Thus every polity, in which is the church and a pious ruler, may assume that the Song of Solomon refers to it. . . . It is a song for all polities, which are the people of God, that is, which have the word of God and reverently worship it, and which recognize and truly believe that the power of the magistrates is from God." [123] Thus church and polity remain distinct, but to paraphrase what Luther says of the prince and the Christian, they are "most tightly joined together." [124]

Luther's doctrine of church and polity thus provides the basis for a new theology of society consistent with his insight into the distinction between the two realms of Christian existence. It is a fundamentally new theology in relation to the medieval tradition, and it is perhaps pointless to quarrel about whether or not Luther is thinking in terms of a *corpus Christianum*. What the *corpus Christianum* meant in the Middle Ages, whether as a pri-

---

[120] Heerpredigt wider den Türken, XXX,2 p. 169,15.

[121] Ibid., XXX,2 p. 169,28.

[122] Lectures on the Song of Songs, XXXI,2 p. 586,22.

[123] Ibid., XXXI,2 p. 587,6.

[124] TR, §4342 (1539), IV,237,11 f.: "Christianus est duplex persona, sc. fidelis et politica. . . / 238. . . Sed nunc cum principes sunt Christiani, difficile est concludere quia principes et Christiani sunt coniunctissimae personae." One might also compare the close relationship between the Law and faith: Galatians (1531), XL,1 p.427,1: "Ut si dico de Christo homine, tamen duae naturae distinctae: . . . Dico: humanitas non est divinitas et tamen homo est Deus. Sic lex non est fides. in concreto et composito kommen sie zusammen."

mary unity or as resulting from the completion of the natural by the supernatural, was the unity of a society which in its ideal form was antecedent to salvation. Luther has broken this unity by his distinction between the church which is totally just in Christ and the church which is still partly sinful on earth. He has re-established a unity of the Christian society, as of the Christian individual, because it is one church which exists in these two realms; he is further willing to call the whole society the church, where by its outward signs he believes that the church is present. But whatever terminology we use, it must be made clear that his distinction within society is new and that accordingly the unity which he recognizes is new too.

2. *Estates and Callings.*

Luther's ideas on estates and callings [125] have a simpler history than his ideas of justice, law, or the church; and we shall notice them more briefly. Ultimately the problem of the estates and callings concerns the relation of the offices and duties of this life to Christianity. The problem has little interest for Luther in the Dictata super Psalterium (1513–15) or in the early biblical commentaries, since Luther here interpreted Christianity largely as a turning away from the world and this life.[126] The indulgence controversy, however, forced Luther to consider more closely the practical problems of Christian life in this world. In his first statements dealing with such questions, Luther appears to adopt a traditional view according to which some of the estates of this

[125] For an excellent introduction to Luther's doctrine of callings, with full bibliography, see Gustaf Wingren, Luthers Lehre vom Beruf (Forschungen zur Geschichte und Lehre des Protestantismus X,3), München, 1952.

[126] See above pp.32 f., Chapter I. Even in his early period, however, Luther of course recognizes the duty of all men to labor in their callings, and he can contrast all callings as works with the spiritual justice of faith. Compare Dictata, IV,311,22 f.: "Primo ante omnia scire oportet, quod secundum Apostolum I Corin. 13, differentes sunt donationes spiritus, ex quibus quoque differentes sunt status fidelium. . . . Exempli gratia, mihi docere et orare fideliter est iustificatio; /312 . . . Rustico autem non est: cui audire et laborare fideliter est salus et iustitia"; Romans, LVI,418,19: "Ecce in suo statu ille sic et sic vivit, tibi in Exemplum, ut in tuo statu similiter facias, Non autem, ut illius eadem facias Et tuo statu neglecto in illius transilias"; Galatians, LVII,2 p. 28,16: "Ergo non est sacerdos neque laicus, non est canonicus neque vicarius, non est dives neque pauper, non est Benedictinensis neque Carthusiensis neque Minor neque Augustinensis, non est huius vel huius cuiuscunque status, gradus, aut ordinis. Omnia enim hec talia sunt, ut non faciant fidelem, si assint, nec infidelem, si desint. . ."; 63,25 f.

life are specifically Christian or spiritual while others are not. But as Luther sees more clearly the significance of his general re-orientation of 1518–19, he realizes that the traditional view represents the very "mixing" which he was attacking with his distinction between the two realms of Christian existence.

Luther accordingly modifies and reconstructs the traditional view in a relatively short time. No one of the estates or callings of the world can be specifically Christian and spiritual as against the others, for what is Christian in the primary sense is heavenly and not worldly. On the other hand, the world is the place where all Christians live their active lives of sanctification, and a Christian can live equally well in any one of the God-ordained callings and estates of the world. Hence the older ideas both of estate and of calling are divided into two parts in accord with Luther's basic distinction between the two realms of Christian existence. There is an estate and a calling which is invisible and spiritual, and this belongs in heaven where the Christian is totally just in Christ. There are others which are visible and active, and these belong in the world of the Christian's existence in the flesh.

Luther first speaks of the estates at significant length in Ein Sermon von dem Sakrament der Taufe (1519), and his thought here is already a mixture of tradition and his own new insights. Luther exalts the importance of baptism in terms of a theology of the cross. "Such is the grace and power of God that sin, which brought death, is driven out again through death which was its own work." [127] But many, who wish to become righteous, do not yet understand this. "Therefore God has ordained several estates (stend), in which men are to learn to exercise themselves and to suffer. To some He commanded the estate of marriage, to some the spiritual estate, and to others the ruling estate; He ordered them all to toil and labour to kill the flesh and accustom it to death, for baptism has made the rest of this life, to all those who are baptized, a very poison and hindrance to its work. . ." [128]

Luther goes on to ask whether baptism and its vows are greater or less than the vows of chastity, of the priesthood, and of the clergy (geystlichkeit). He replies with a strong assertion on the

[127] Ein Sermon vom dem Sakrament der Taufe, II,734,19.
[128] Ibid., II,734,24.

primacy of baptism as common to all Christians and as equal
for all Christians. But there is no one way or estate for following baptism, and here each one must ask himself in which estate
he can himself best kill sin, though no other vow can be greater
than that of baptism. Luther returns to a rough classification of
the estates, but this time he suggests that they may be arranged
in an order of increasing perfection. Some Christians are in the
estate of marriage and have taken upon themselves its labors and
sufferings. Those who wish more suffering and who would achieve
the work of baptism more speedily, should bind themselves to
chastity or to the spiritual order (*geystlichen orden*) "for the
spiritual estate, if it is as it ought to be, is full of suffering and
martyrdom." [129] But above the spiritual estate, there is one
still higher, which is "the ruling estate in the spiritual government
(*regiment*), such as that of bishop or pastor." [130] But Luther once
more emphasizes the over-riding importance of baptism; all the
estates exist simply for the fulfilling of baptism.

It is clear that Luther's distinction between the two realms of
Christian existence must soon lead to a sharper attack on the
traditional concept of the "spiritual estate," and this takes form
in the writings of 1520. In Ein Sermon von dem Neuen Testament
(1520), Luther denies the existence of a special priestly estate
in the old sense, for all those who partake of the sacraments with
faith are priests. "Therefore all Christian men are priests, the
women priestesses, be they young or old, masters or servants,
mistresses or maids, learned or unlearned. Here there are no
differences unless faith be unequal." [131]

In An den christlichen Adel (1520), as we have already seen
in part,[132] Luther carries these ideas on to a general reconstruction of the concept of the spiritual estate. In the first place, all
Christians are truly of the spiritual estate in its primary and
proper sense, and there is no distinction between them except
that of office (*Amt*).[133] Thus the old title of the "spiritual estate"
is taken out of the world; it belongs in heaven, along with Chris-

---

[129] Ibid., II,736,14.
[130] Ibid., II,736,18.
[131] VI,370,25.
[132] See pp.138 f. above.
[133] An den christlichen Adel, VI,407,13.

tian and passive justice, and Luther sometimes calls it simply the
"Christian estate." [134] In the second place, within the worldly
realm, the priesthood and the clergy lose the special place which
they had once held as the "spiritual estate," and they are rele-
gated to the worldly realm of offices. "Therefore the estate of a
priest (*ein priester stand*) is nothing else in Christendom than
an office. . . . Hence it follows from this that layman, priest,
prince, bishop, and as they say, spiritual and worldly, have no
other difference at bottom than that of office and work, not of
estate, for they are all of the spiritual estate, truly priests, bishops,
and popes, but they are not all equally of one work, just as
among priests and monks each does not have the same work." [135]

Luther has thus applied his basic distinction between the two
realms of Christian existence to the traditional concept of the
spiritual estate. As a result he now argues for the essential contrast between the heavenly "spiritual estate" of the Christian in
Christ and his "worldly estate" or office here on earth. While
Luther never thereafter denies this essential contrast, he does not
intend to make "spiritual estate" simply a technical term for
the Christian's existence in heaven, and he continues to give it
different meanings in different contexts. He can argue, for example, that in some sense all the worldly estates are, for a Christian, also spiritual. In Das siebente Kapitel S. Pauli zu den
Corinthern (1523) he writes: "Nothing should rightly be called
spiritual except the inward life of faith in the heart, where the
spirit rules. But since we now also call that spiritual, which happens outwardly in the body through the spirit of faith, so let us
here recognize and decide with clarity and firmness, that the estate
of marriage shall in all right be called spiritual. . . ." [136] And,

---

[134] Ibid., VI,408,3.

[135] Ibid., VI,408,18. Compare for a foreshadowing of this position Galatians
Commentary (1519), II,482,32 f.; also De abroganda miisa privata (1521), VIII,
429,30: ". . . Christianum populum esse simplicem, in quo prorsus nulla secta,
nulla differentia personarum, nullus laicus, nullus clericus . . . Episcopi vero, seu
presbyteri, seu seniores, seu diaconi nulla re differi a caeteris Christianis debent
nisi solo officio verbi et sacramenti." As V. Vajta rightly points out, Die Theologie
des Gottesdienstes bei Luther (Lund, 1952), p. 201, note 18 "Auch als Pfarrer ist
man 'Weltperson,' denn *alle* Ämter gehören dem irdischen Leben zu."

[136] XII,105,27. Compare 126,16: "Will also sagen: Der glaube und Christlicher
stand ist so eyn frey ding, das er an keynen stand verbunden ist, sondern ist uber
allen stenden, ynn allen stenden, und durch allen stenden. . . ."

when there is no danger of misunderstanding, Luther can continue to use "spiritual estate" in its traditional sense as a synonym for the clergy. Thus he remarks in 1530, that reason always objects to the truth that "the spiritual estate and the worldly estate should be as nothing in contrast to the Christian estate." [137]

Luther's fullest discussion of the problem of the "worldly estates" is found in his doctrine of "callings," and his modification of the traditional meaning of *Beruf* is well-known. In developing his new concept of the "spiritual estate," Luther had started from the traditional notion of a special spiritual class in the world; he modified it in two ways, by making the spiritual estate common to all Christians and by transferring it to heaven. In developing his doctrine of the "callings," Luther starts from a comparable traditional concept, that of the special religious calling of the clergy; he again modifies this in two ways, by making the callings common to all men and by placing them in the world.

Luther establishes his new doctrine clearly in a Sermon from the Kirchenpostille (1522) on John XXI,19–24: "And Jesus said to Peter, Follow me. . . ." Luther expounds this in an anti-ascetic and anti-monastic interpretation. "Regardless of the lives and examples of the saints, everyone should await what is commanded him and take heed of his calling (*wahrnehmen seynis beruffis*). Oh, what a necessary, saving doctrine this is." [138] Many Christians, however, do the exact opposite; they fail to do what is commanded them, and they devote themselves instead to practices of human invention, such as going on pilgrimages or entering monasteries.

But what if someone says he has no calling? "I reply: how is it possible that you should not be called. You will always be in some estate (*stand*), you will be a husband, or wife, or child, or daughter, or maid." [139] In any one of these callings, a man has enough and more than enough to do. "Thus everyone should take care, that he remain in his estate, looks to himself, realizes his calling, and in it serves God and keeps His command." [140]

Luther's doctrine of the callings is thus essentially a doctrine

[137] Commentary on Psalm 117 (1530), XXXI,1 p. 241,25.
[138] Kirchenpostille (1522), X,1,1 p. 306,17.
[139] Ibid., X,1,1 p. 308,7.
[140] Ibid., X,1,1 p. 309,15.

of the worldly estates, and in the world "calling" (*Beruf*) and
estate (*Stand*) are largely synonymous. In general "estate" is
the more formal term; it refers to "offices" or "classes" which
are clearly defined and socially recognized. On the other hand,
"calling" is a more fluid concept, capable of extension to all the
obligations of the worldly realm; it includes not only social
classes but also biological stages in human life, such as that of
the young man or of the old man, and even God's general command to Saul, "Do whatsoever your hand shall find" (I Samuel
X,7). For the special case of the estates and callings which
involve rule and government, Luther's most careful discussion
will appear in the doctrine of the three hierarchies, which we
shall notice later.[141]

Luther's main treatment of the callings thus analyzes them
as part of the worldly realm. They are, like polity in general,
God-ordained, but they do not lead to justification nor is one
more spiritual than another. It is, however, typical of the movement of Luther's thought that just as his general dualism of
two realms of Christian existence leads to the distinction between spiritual and worldly estates so it can lead to the distinction
between spiritual and external callings.

Luther develops this contrast clearly in a Sermon of October,
1531, and one may regard this as a restatement of the doctrine
of callings of 1522 in the light of his general theology of the
early 1530's. All of us, declares Luther, have a double calling;
the one is spiritual, the other external. "Our spiritual calling is
that we are all through the Gospel called to baptism and the
Christian faith, so that through the word and baptism we are
incorporated into Christ. . . . This calling (*vocatio*) is common
and alike, for the son of a king does not obtain any better baptism
than the son of a slave." [142] In his spiritual calling the Christian
is a member of Christ; his estate (*status*) is holy, and his order
(*ordo*) is heavenly. On the other hand the Christian has also an
external calling, and here there are distinctions among Christians,
for the prince is better than the peasant. "Therefore let everyone
attend to what his heavenly and Christian order through baptism

---

[141] See pp. 173 f., below.
[142] Sermon (1531), XXXIV,2 p. 300,8.

calls him. Afterwards let him look to his outward estate, and he will so live rightly. This is the observation of the good Paul, when he urges everyone to abide in his estate, both spiritual and bodily." [143]

3. God's Two Governments.

Luther had high regard for his works on secular government, and he reckoned his theory of God's two governments as one of his main contributions to a restoration of true biblical theology.[144] For the most part, the theory of the two governments is a product of the middle 1520's, and it is closely connected with Luther's involvement in the Peasants' Wars.

The problem of government did not much concern Luther in his early period of 1513–18 nor even in the immediately following years, and what he has to say of it is largely incidental and traditional. Thus in his discussion of Romans XIII and of the powers that be, he distinguishes the ecclesiastical and the secular powers, and he defines their duties in terms of his early theology. "In the preceding chapter (=XII), Paul taught that the ecclesiastical order (ordinem) should not be thrown into confusion. In the present chapter, he teaches that the secular order is also to be preserved. Both these orders are from God; the former for the direction and peace of the inner man (interioris hominis) and

[143] Ibid., XXXIV,2 p. 308,9.

[144] E.g., Ob Kriegsleute auch in seligem Stande sein können (1526), XIX,625,15: "Denn ich mich schier rhümen möchte, das sint der Apostel zeit das weltliche schwerd und oberkeit nie so klerlich beschrieben und herrlich gepreiset ist . . . also durch mich." Vom Kriege wider die Türken (1528), XXX,2 p. 110,1.

Of modern works on Luther's doctrine of the two governments, the best introduction is G. Törnvall, Geistliches und weltliches Regiment bei Luther (Forschungen zur Geschichte und Lehre des Protestantismus X,2), München, 1947; see also F. Lau, Luthers Lehre von den beiden Reichen (Luthertum, Heft 8), Berlin, 1953. Among the numerous shorter treatments the following may be mentioned: Harald Diem, Luthers Lehre von den zwei Reichen (Evangelische Theologie, Beiheft 5), München, 1938; Hermann Diem, Luthers Predigt in den zwei Reichen (Theologische Existenz Heute, N.F. VI), München, 1947; E. M. Carlson, "Luther's Conception of Government," Church History 15 (1946), 257–70; G. Wingren, "Geistliches und weltliches Regiment bei Luther," Theologische Zeitschrift 3 (1947), 263–73; A. Nygren, "Luthers Lehre von den Zwei Reichen," Theologische Literaturzeitung, LXXIV (1949), 1–8; G. Törnvall, "Der Christ in den zwei Reichen," Evangelische Theologie 10 (1950–51), 66–77; E. Kinder, "Gottesreich und Weltreich bei Augustin und bei Luther," Werner Elert Festschrift (Berlin, 1955), 24–42.

his affairs, the latter for the direction of the outer man and his affairs." [145]

Luther in his early period discusses God's government primarily in terms of the kingdom of Christ, and he sets up a number of distinctions and contrasts here. He is interested first of all in the church which is Christ's kingdom of faith and insofar as He was man.[146] Christ has also two other kingdoms as He is God. There is His heavenly kingdom of the future church triumphant, and there is His natural kingdom by which the whole universe is subject to Him.[147]

With the indulgence controversy and with his increased attention to the moral problems of the Christian in the world, Luther begins to have more to say about government, but through about 1520 he remains largely in a traditional context. He regularly starts from the fourth commandment, and he explains that it includes honor not only to parents but also to ecclesiastical and secular rulers. Thus Luther in Eine kurze Erklärung der zehn Gebote (1518) lists the various violators of the fourth commandment; he begins with those who dishonor their parents and continues, "Whoever does not obey the commands of the church, in fasting, holy days, etc. Whoever dishonours the priestly estate, speaks disrespectively of it or slanders it. Whoever does not obey his lords and magistracy (uberkeyt), or whoever is not loyal and obedient, whether they be good or bad." [148] Somewhat later, in the (Grosser) Sermon von dem Wucher (1520) Luther makes the same point in terms of the two magistracies or two powers. "And yet it is true that God instituted the worldly sword and in addition the spiritual power of the church; he ordained

---

[145] Romans, LVI,124,9. Compare the somewhat later statement in Operationes, V,526,15: "Non enim Christus Caesaris regnum sustulit, sed sublimius regnum veritatis condidit. Et Paulus subiicit omnem animam potestatibus sublimioribus. Ro. 13, secundum carnem, qui tamen secundum spiritum omnes asserit liberos esse in Christo."

[146] See p.120 above.

[147] Compare Dictata, IV,433,38. "Mihi putatur, quod in iis versibus describitur regni Christi latitudo, altitudo, profunditas, quia omnia ei subiecta sunt. . . . Vel saltem de utroque intelligitur, scilicet de regimine nature et gratie"; 454,32; Sermon (1519-20), IV,645,10 ff. with 650,5; Auslegung des 109 (110), Psalms (1518), I,692,6 (the distinction between the right and left hands of God).

[148] I,252,35 f.; compare 254,30. For the Latin version, see I,260,37 f. Compare also Eine kurze Unterweisung wie man beichten soll (1519), II,62,15; Decem Praecepta (1518), I,460,1; Sermon (1519), IV,607,16 f.

both magistracies (*ubirkeyten*) to punish evil-doers and to rescue the oppressed, as Paul teaches in Romans XIII and many other places. . . ." [149] Insofar as Luther takes any polemic position during these years, it is against the combination of the two powers in the pope or in the clergy, not against the two powers as such.[150]

But these traditional ideas of government and kingdom are not in harmony with Luther's new distinction between the two realms of Christian existence. He must therefore modify them or create new ones so that he can distinguish in the area of government and kingdom between what God does in the realm of Christian, passive justice as against what He does in the realm of civil justice and polity. The need for some sort of change is therefore clear; it is not clear just how the change should be made, and Luther moves only slowly to a new position.

On the simplest level, we find during 1521 a movement away from a spiritual "power" such as Luther had previously accepted. In Das Magnificat verdeutschet (1521) Luther notes that "in the scriptures we do not find any spiritual magistracy or power but only service and subjection." [151]

More important, in 1521 and 1522, Luther begins to reconsider the whole question of kingdom and government, and the outlines of a new position appear gradually. The Sermon an der Heiligen Drei Könige Tag (Jan. 6, 1521) is a good illustration of Luther's first attempts toward such a reconsideration. Luther here works out at some length the contrast between King Christ and King Herod, and he suggests that this corresponds to a contrast between the two "peoples" in the world. Herod is strong without and weak within; Christ is weak outwardly but strong inwardly. Further the two kingdoms may be compared as Herod's kingdom of works against Christ's kingdom of forgiveness of sins as defined by David. "He has made a continuous reign (*regiment*) over us, as forgivenesses of sins, grace, and mercy for eternal life." [152]

---

[149] VI,39,23. See also Von den guten Werken (1520), VI,255,18 f.

[150] See p. 124, above.

[151] VII,578,22. Compare De captivitate Babylonica, VI,564,11.

[152] Sermon an der Heiligen Drei Könige Tag (1521), VII,240,31. There is a variant edition of the same Sermon, IX,501–03. For a roughly contemporary contrast of the two kingdoms, see Sermon (1520), IV,706,29 f.

Luther goes on to discuss the somewhat different contrast between Christ's kingdom and that of the pope, finally the contrast between the kingdoms of Christ and Antichrist.[153] In this Sermon Luther appears to be hindered by the confusion of two different contrasts. In the first place, there is the contrast between a kingdom of works and a kingdom of forgiveness; this corresponds to the distinction between two realms of Christian existence and each kingdom has positive value. In the second place, there is the contrast between the kingdoms of Christ and Antichrist, and this is a simple opposition of good and evil.

Luther continues to wrestle with the problem of these kingdoms in various Sermons of 1522. On April 18, for example, he again attempts to state the spiritual nature of Christ's kingdom, although he here recognizes that Christians must live in the world too. Christ's kingdom is in faith and truth. "Here lies the kingdom and holiness, not in the outward kingdom. The outward kingdom is only a mask and a carnival play (*ain larven und fassnacht spil*) and nothing right, although those who are in God's kingdom must nevertheless live outwardly in eating and drinking and using the world, but with moderation, for the true kingdom is within." [154]

In later Sermons of May and June, Luther re-examines the problem from the standpoint of the two magistracies, worldly and spiritual. In the Sermon of May he discusses worldly magistracy much as he had done before, in a summary of Romans XIII. On the spiritual power, however, he continues his movement away from the recognition of any human "spiritual magistracy" in the usual sense of the term.[155] In a Sermon of June 22, 1522, Luther takes the important step of defining the two authorities, as he had earlier defined the two kingdoms of Christ and of Herod, in terms of the two groups within mankind. "These are the two governments, of the pious and of the wicked. One gathers the pious together with the word, and one drives the wicked to orderly behavior with the sword." [156]

The most careful discussion of the two kingdoms and govern-

[153] Sermon an der Heiligen Drei Könige Tag, VII,242,13.
[154] Sermon (1522), X,3 p. 79,3.
[155] Sermon (1522), X,3 pp. 121,10 f.
[156] Sermon (1522), X,3 p. 175,30.

ments in 1522 is found in two connected Sermons of October 24 and 25. Luther starts with the kingdom of God, and he identifies it as "the Christian believing people of Christ." [157] He goes on to make an important distinction between the spiritual and the worldy kingdom of Christ. Up to the time of His incarnation, says Luther, Christ possessed not only the spiritual but also the worldly kingdom or government of Israel, for He gave them laws on diet, dress, and so on.[158] But when Christ appeared on earth He gave up this worldly kingdom of Israel and retained only the spiritual. He did not, of course, wish to abolish the worldly kingdom; He simply transferred it to kings and princes.[159] In the remainder of this first Sermon Luther treats only of the spiritual kingdom, and he concludes it to be one in which God must rule alone; its human representatives are simply legates or ambassadors, whose only business is to preach Christ's word.[160]

In the second Sermon of October 25, Luther concentrates on the worldly kingdom. The terminology is difficult and suggests Luther's gradual transition to a new position. Luther's basic contrast is between the kingdom of God or of Christ as against the opposed kingdom of the sophists or the pope or the devil. Within the kingdom of God, he distinguishes a spiritual and a worldly government (*regiment*).[161] These two governments may be connected with Christian faith and Christian works respectively, and in each government God rules alone, "for where the kingdom and government (*das reich und Regiment*) of God is, there one needs no sword nor law, which elsewhere belongs to the magistracy (*öberkeit*)." [162] God will eventually bring about such a kingdom of Christ, and men shall beat their swords into ploughshares. But meanwhile the devil has most of mankind under his control and rule, "Hence one needs another government; hence comes the worldly sword, and one needs princes and officials. . . ." [163] Thus Luther in this Sermon distinguishes two "worldly governments." The first is part of God's future

---

[157] Sermon (1522), X,3 p. 371,14.
[158] Ibid., X,3 p. 371,19.
[159] Ibid., X,3 p.371,23. Compare Sermons on Exodus (1524–27), XVI,352, 1 f.
[160] Sermon (1522), X,3 pp. 372,3 ff.
[161] Sermon (1522), X,3 p. 379,14.
[162] Ibid., X,3 p.379,19.
[163] Ibid., X,3 p. 379,29.

kingdom where He will rule alone; the second is embodied in the worldly sword which is necessary because of the devil and man's wickedness. The distinction is not maintained in Luther's later thought, and the problem of worldly government takes its start from the problem of the worldly sword.

In the remainder of the Sermon of October 25 Luther speaks primarily to the worldly rulers. He will not give them detailed advice anymore than he would to a tailor, and for the princes he refers all such matters to the control of reason. Luther's purpose is simply to show them how to use their office in a Christian fashion. They should act only from love and for the sake of their neighbors; they should always recognize that they themselves are powerless unless God acts through them.[164] As usual, Luther bases his discussion on the familiar biblical passages, Romans XIII, 1 f. and I Peter II, 13. The function of the prince is to protect the good and punish the evil. Throughout Luther discusses princely rule in the context of a Christian society, and he declares, "The princes are also the executioners and jailors (*hencker und Stockblöcher*) of Christ, and they must punish and judge His people for Him. . . ." [165]

Luther modified and expanded these ideas of 1522 in the important tract of 1523, Von weltlicher Obrigkeit, wie weit man ihr Gehorsam schuldig sei. Here Luther more definitely than before takes as his starting-point the division of all mankind into two kingdoms. "We must divide Adam's children and all men into two groups: the first belong to the kingdom of God, the others to the kingdom of the world." [166] Those who belong to the first kingdom are the believing Christians in Christ and under Christ; these need no worldly sword or worldly law. In contrast the kingdom of the world along with subjection to the law extends to the vast majority who are not Christians. Hence in addition to the Christian estate and the kingdom of God, "God set up another government (*regiment*) and placed it under the sword." [167]

Luther then relates the two governments to these two groups.

[164] Ibid., X,3 p. 380,18.
[165] Ibid., X,3 p. 381,31.
[166] Von weltlicher Obrigkeit, XI,249,24.
[167] Ibid., XI,251,5.

"God ordered two governments: the spiritual government, which makes Christians and pious men through the Holy Spirit under Christ, and the worldly government, which controls the wicked, so that they must keep peace outwardly and be quiet whether they will or not." [168] "Therefore one must carefully separate the two governments and allow both to remain: one which makes pious men, and the other which keeps the peace outwardly and checks evil deeds. Neither one without the other is enough in the world." [169]

While Luther justifies the worldly government of the sword primarily in terms of the wicked and the non-Christian, he also explicitly defends Christian exercise of the sword. The office of a ruler is a "divine estate" (*gottlicher stand*), and the Christian may be active in it as in the other offices and estates which God has ordained.[170] But worldly government is limited, as the law of its kingdom is limited, "to body and goods and what is outward on earth"; [171] it has no power over the soul.

Luther's basic contrast in Von weltlicher Obrigkeit is between God's spiritual government and the worldly government of the sword, and he has relatively little to say about any spiritual power of the clergy. As he had done earlier, he denies that priests or bishops have any magistracy (*uberkeytt*) or power, for Christ alone rules the Christians and they have no other magistracy at all.[172] The government (*regiment*) of priests and bishops is simply a service and an office; what is called their rule is simply the carrying out of God's word. And the bishops have no more power over the soul, which is under God alone, than do the worldly magistrates.[173]

Luther's discussion of the problem of government represents a considerable advance over his ideas of 1521-22, but ambiguities still remain. On the positive side, Luther has achieved a clear division between the two governments of God, His spiritual

[168] Ibid., XI,251,15.
[169] Ibid., XI,252,12.
[170] Ibid., XI,248,27.
[171] Ibid., XI,262, 8; 266,14.
[172] Ibid., XI,271,11.
[173] Ibid., XI,271,11 f.

government exercised by God alone, and the worldly government exercised through the worldly sword. Luther has thus successfully disentangled this contrast from its earlier confusion with the contrast between God's kingdom and Satan.[174] On the other hand, it does not seem that Luther has yet achieved an adequate statement of the relation of God's government to the two groups of mankind. In some passages Luther suggests that he is endeavoring to translate into a theory of government his basic distinction between the two realms of Christian existence and that he means to contrast the Christians in Christ with the same Christians, together with the non-Christians, in the world. But in other passages he seems perfectly explicit that the Christians and the non-Christians are two mutually exclusive groups, and that the Christians even in the world would need no coërcive government.

In the years immediately following Von weltlicher Obrigkeit (1523) Luther was much concerned with the practical problems of government,[175] but he did not develop his theory of the two governments of God further until 1526 in Ob Kriegsleute auch in seligem Stande sein können. In the meantime he had in the important De servo arbitrio reached greater clarity on certain points of the general theology of kingdom, and this clarity may be in part responsible for the further elaboration of the special theology of the two governments.

In the first place, Luther in De servo arbitrio achieves an extreme and unconditional statement of God's active omnipotence. "This we assert and contend, that God, when He acts this side of the grace of the spirit, works all things, even in the impious, for He alone who created all things, by Himself moves all things, guides them, and propels them by the omnipotence of His motion. . . . Then, when He acts with the grace of the spirit in them, whom He justifies, that is, in His Kingdom, He guides and moves them similarly with His omnipotence, and they, as they are the new creature, follow and cooperate or rather, as Paul says, they suffer His action (aguntur)." [176] Thus Luther has separated out the concept of an absolute kingdom of God over everything all

---

[174] See pp. 162 f. above.

[175] For a general survey, see P. Althaus, Luthers Haltung im Bauernkrieg (Benno Schwabe & Co. Verlag, Basel, 1953?).

[176] De servo arbitrio XVIII,753,28.

the time, what he will sometimes call God's "invisible kingdom." [177] This is an aspect of the God of majesty, and it does not immediately concern the Christian who lives under the two governments which we have already noticed as God's spiritual government and His world-government. But Luther can now more easily move to a clearer statement of these two governments of God, since he is after the De servo arbitrio able to separate them from this other concept of God's "invisible kingdom."

In the second place, the De servo arbitrio includes a precise statement of the absolute contrast between the kingdoms of God and of Satan. We need not here inquire into the relation of Satan's kingdom to God's absolute omnipotence. Luther's purpose in the contrast of these two kingdoms is rather to express in this terminology the absolute contrast between Christian justice as against a justice of works which claims salvation in its own right. "Whatever is flesh, the same is impious and under the wrath of God, foreign to His kingdom. And if it is foreign to the kingdom and spirit of God, it follows necessarily that it is under the kingdom and spirit of Satan, for there is no middle kingdom between the kingdoms of God and of Satan, which fight together perpetually. This shows that the highest virtues in the heathen, the best things in the philosophers, appear honourable and may be said to be honourable before the world, but before God they are in truth flesh, and they serve the kingdom of Satan." [178]

Such a theology of the kingdom of Satan does not directly solve the problem of the two governments, but like the theology of God's invisible kingdom, it puts into better perspective the problem to be solved. God's invisible kingdom is seen to be a characteristic of the God of majesty, and it is thus not involved in the two governments. Similarly the kingdom of Satan is seen to be for the theory of kingdom what the theological use of the law is for the theory of law, and again this aspect of kingdom is not involved in the two governments. When these extraneous prob-

---

[177] Sermon (1537), XLV,280,2: "quia duplicia regimina dei: 1. ist das Christlich. Das geht uns an. Ibi seipsum revelavit in praesepio, ut potest a nobis comprehendi. Das regimen Christiani intelligunt. Das ander regiment dei nobis invisibile, quomodo omnia creavit, regit mundum, quomodo zughet, das der so lebt, thut. Ibi deus tantum novit." Compare also XLV,252,27. On this problem, see Törnvall, Geistliches (note 144, above), pp. 43 f.

[178] De servo arbitrio, XVIII,743,31 f. Compare 627,24 f.; 635,7; 782,21 f.

lems have been excluded, Luther is now better able to see that in broad outline God's spiritual government is comparable to passive justice in the heavenly realm while His world-government is comparable to civil justice and the civil use of the law in the world.

Luther adumbrates such a solution in the De servo arbitrio in the terminology of kingdom, but he does not relate it specifically to government. He distinguishes between two kingdoms in which man exists, one in which God controls him absolutely and the other in which He leaves man free. "Let us understand that man is divided under two kingdoms. In the one he is moved by his own choice and decision, apart from the precepts and commands of God, that is to say, in the things which are beneath him. Here he reigns and is a lord. . . . But by the other kingdom he is not left in the hand of his counsel, but he is borne and led by the choice and council of God, apart from the commands of another, so that just as in his kingdom, he is borne by his choice, so, in the kingdom of God, he is borne by the precepts of another without his choice." [179] And in a similar context later in the work, Luther remarks: "We are not disputing of nature but of grace, nor are we asking what (*quales*) we are on earth but what we are in heaven before God. We know that man has been established as lord over the things which are below him, with respect to which he has his right and his free choice. . . ." [180]

It is difficult to be sure just what are the implications of this distinction between the two kingdoms in which man finds himself, but it is clear that Luther is working toward a more general contrast than that originally involved in the doctrine of the two governments. In the Sermons of 1521-22 and in the Von weltlicher Obrigkeit of 1523, Luther when he is not contrasting the kingdoms of God and of Satan works mainly with the contrast between God's spiritual rule on the one hand and on the other the worldly sword of secular government. Now in De servo arbitrio he contrasts God's spiritual rule with a whole other kingdom comparable to polity or the world, and we shall see the

[179] Ibid., XVIII,672,7.
[180] Ibid., XVIII,781,6.

same move toward greater generality in his further discussion of the two governments.

In Ob Kriegsleute auch in seligem Stande sein können (1526) Luther goes on to clear up a number of the points left unsettled in Von weltlicher Obrigkeit. In the simple description of the two governments, he starts from the same point as in Von weltlicher Obrigkeit. "God has established two kinds of government among men, one which is spiritual through the word without the sword, by which men should become pious and just . . . and another worldly government through the sword, so that those who do not wish to become pious through the word for eternal life, should nevertheless be forced through the worldly government to be just for the world." [181]

In 1526, however, Luther is better able to relate this description to his fundamental theology. In the first place he drops the emphasis of Von weltlicher Obrigkeit on the division of mankind into two exclusive groups. In the second place he brings the doctrine of the two governments into direct connection with his basic doctrine of the two justices.

On the first point, Luther makes a distinction between the office (*Amt*) and the person exercising it, or between a work and the doer of it.[182] The office may be good, and yet the person holding it may be wicked. Thus the distinction between those in God's kingdom as against those in Satan's does not affect the goodness of the offices which they exercise or to which they are subject, for the offices are God's ordinance for the world.

More fundamentally, Luther can now explain that the two governments are not to be defined simply in terms of the two groups, the Christians and the non-Christians. The Christians, to use Luther's later terminology, bear two "persons"; while as Christian persons they are free of worldly government, as persons in the world they are subject to it along with all non-Christians. "Indeed the Christians do not engage in strife nor do they have worldly magistracy among them. Their government is a spiritual government, and according to the spirit they are subject to no one but Christ. But they are nevertheless with body and goods

[181] Ob Kriegsleute auch in seligem Stande sein können, XIX,629,17.
[182] Ibid., XIX,624,18.

subject to the worldly magistracy and owe it obedience. Hence
if they are called to arms (*zum streyt*) by the worldly magistracy,
then they should and must fight (*streyten*) out of obedience, not
as Christians but as members and subjects, obedient persons
according to the body and temporal good." [183] And later in the
work, Luther is even more precise, "A Christian is a person for
himself alone; he believes for himself and for no one else. A
prince is not a person for himself, but for the sake of others that
he may serve them, that he may protect and defend them. It
would of course be good if he were also a Christian and believed
in God, and then he would be highly blessed. But being a
Christian is not princely. . . ." [184]

Luther in Ob Kriegsleute also clarifies the relation of the two
governments to the two basic kinds of justice, passive and civil.
He explains that when he discusses the rightness of the soldier's
office, he is not speaking of the justice which makes men pious
before God, for such justice comes only through faith. "But
I speak here of external justice, which is found in offices and
works." [185] He goes on to relate God's spiritual government to
the justice of faith and God's worldly government to the justice
of works. "Thus God Himself is the founder, lord, master,
supporter, and rewarder of both these justices, both spiritual
justice and bodily justice. There is no human power within them,
but what is purely and simply divine (*eytel Göttlich ding*)." [186]
What Luther does here is in the first place to generalize the concept of God's worldly government; it can now comprehend the
whole area of polity and of civil justice, not merely the one special
aspect of coërcive rule. In the second place, he now tends to
give a more positive value to world-government; it is not simply
a way of checking the wicked but rather a divine ordinance for
the world.

Luther reaches his final precisions on the two governments in
his Sermons on Matthew V–VII (1530–32), in an argument
which we have already noticed in part.[187] In his own Preface

___

[183] Ibid., XIX,629,2.
[184] Ibid., XIX,648,19.
[185] Ibid., XIX,625,1.
[186] Ibid., XIX,629, 30 f.
[187] See pp.68 f., Chapter II above.

Luther maintains that the distinction between the two governments is basic to a Christian understanding of the Sermon on the Mount, and he notes that here as elsewhere the devil tries constantly to "mix" the realms which the Christian must always keep distinct. Sometimes the devil attempts this from the side of the Law, as with the sophists who would extend legal demands into the realm of Gospel forgiveness; sometimes he attempts it from the side of the Gospel, as with the enthusiasts who would extend passive, Christian justice into the legal realm of the world.[188]

In the course of the Sermons on Matthew V-VII Luther is more precise than earlier on the close connection of the world-government of God with reason. Thus he urges, for example, that the laws of divorce and marriage be left to the jurists and the worldly government. "The estate of marriage (*der Ehestand*) is a worldly, outward thing, just as wife, child, house, court, and what ever else belongs to magistracy to rule (*zur öberkeit regiment*). As such it is entirely subject to reason, Genesis I,28. Accordingly one should allow to stand whatever the magistracy and men of wisdom conclude and order about it on the basis of right and reason." [189]

Luther is also more precise in the Sermons on the relation of the individual Christian to the two governments, and he here works out in detail what he had suggested in Ob Kriegsleute. He starts from the question, whether or not a Christian can go to law or defend himself. Luther replies that he cannot; "A Christian is such a person or man, that he has nothing to do with such worldly things (*welt wesen*) or with the law of the world. He is himself in such a kingdom or government, where nothing happens except as we pray, 'Forgive us our trespasses as we forgive those who trespass against us'." [190] But there is another question, whether or not "A Christian can also be a worldly man and carry on the office or work of government and law, so that the two persons or offices devolve on one individual, who will then at the same time be a Christian and a prince, judge, lord, servant, or

[188] Sermons on Matthew V–VII (1530–32), XXXII,301,3.
[189] Ibid., XXXII,376,38 f.
[190] Ibid., XXXII,389,37 f.

maid, which are called pure world-persons (*welt personen*), for they belong to the worldly government. And we reply that he can." [191]

Luther goes on, in passages which we have already noted,[192] to explain how all Christians must exist in two realms and are thus subject both to God's spiritual government and also to His world-government. "Every Christian must be some sort of world-person, since he is at least in body and goods subject to the emperor. But for his own person in his Christian life, he is all alone under Christ . . ." [193] "A prince can surely be a Christian, but as a Christian he cannot rule. . . . The person is surely a Christian, but the office of prince has nothing to do with his Christianity (*Christentum*)." [194]

Luther can again make the same point in terms of estates. A man's Christian estate (*Christen stand*) lies simply between him and God, but at the same time he is in another estate and office in the world, according as he is, for example, a prince. In the world the Christians should give unto Caesar what is Caesar's, but as Christians "we are placed in another higher existence (*wesen*), which is a divine eternal kingdom, where one needs none of the things that belong to the world, but every one of us is for himself in Christ a lord both over the devil and over the whole world." [195]

Luther has thus developed a doctrine of the two governments adequate to his general theology. He can now explain that just as a Christian has two realms of existence, so he is subject to two governments of God. In the realm of heaven and of Christian justice, God rules alone; this is His spiritual government. In the realm of the world and civil justice, He rules through reason and polity; this is His world-government.

---

[191] Ibid., XXXII,390,8.
[192] See pp.68 f., Chapter II, above.
[193] Sermons on Matthew V–VII, XXXII,390,19.
[194] Ibid., XXXII,440,9.
[195] Ibid., XXXII,389,17. Luther can also state the contrast between these two governments as between God's governments of the right hand and of the left; e.g., Sermon (1532), XXXVI,385,7: "(Das weltlich Regiment) . . . ist wol auch unsers herr Gotts reich, sed ist ein zeitlich gesetze und regiment, aber er wil gleichwol haben, das man es hallt, und ist das Reich mit der lincken hand. Sed sein rechts Reich ist, ubi ipse regnat, da er nicht parentes, magistratus, lictores darff hinsetzen, sed ipse ists selber" (= Hauspostille (1544), LII,26,21.).

The spiritual government of God is closely connected with the concept of the church but not identical with it. Under the aspect of heaven, the spiritual church coincides with God's spiritual government, but the temporal organization of the church on earth is a part of God's world-government of reason.[196]

As elsewhere, so in government Luther does not develop a systematic terminology. He has worked out a general contrast between God's world-government and His spiritual government, but both terms can still be used in their traditional narrower sense where "world government" refers to the earthly sword of the ruler and "spiritual government" to the clergy.[197] By and large, the terminology of world-government and spiritual government serves primarily for the most general contrast between God's two ways of rule, and it therefore becomes less useful for the solution of the special problems of ecclesiastical and secular organization. To some extent Luther can solve these problems with the concepts of estates and callings,[198] but these have no direct relation to the problem of rule. Perhaps for this reason Luther at a relatively late date developed his doctrine of the three "holy rules" or "hierarchies," a doctrine which may be regarded as a special aspect either of the theory of world-government or of the theory of estates and callings.

4. *The Three Hierarchies.*

The three hierarchies [199] of the church, the household, and the polity first appear in Luther's thought toward the end of the 1520's, and they are closely connected with his new general statement of his theology. As we have seen, the doctrine of the three

---

[196] See pp. 148 f., above.

[197] E.g., Dass man Kinder zur Schule halten solle (1530), XXX,2 pp. 555,2 f. where Luther contrasts *das weltliche regiment* with *das predig ampt*; or Sermon (1529), XXIX,598, 2 f.; or note 137, above.

Luther can also describe the two main "hierarchies" as "regiments"; see below p. 175.

[198] See pp. 153 f., above.

[199] On the doctrine of hierarchies, the article by F. Lezius is still the most complete collection of citations, "Gleichheit und Ungleichheit. Aphorismen zur Theologie und Staatsanschauung Luthers," Greifswalder Studien (Hermann Cremer Festschrift), Gütersloh, 1895, pp. 285–326. See also K. Köhler, "Die altprotestantische Lehre von den drei kirchlichen Ständen," Zeitschrift für Kirchenrecht, 21, N.F. 6 (1886), 99–150, 193–231; Kattenbusch, op. cit. (note 2, above), pp. 314–47.

hierarchies may be regarded as a special aspect either of the theory of God's two governments or of the theory of estates and callings, and it reflects the same intent as these theories. Against the traditional depression of marriage and secular rule in contrast to the exaltation of the monastic life and the clerical estate, Luther maintains that there are three "holy rules." The housefather and the prince exercise an office which is equally God-ordained and holy with that of the clergy, and accordingly the office and estate of the clergy is as such no higher than that of the two other hierarchies.

The traditional basis for Luther's doctrine of the three hierarchies may be seen in the three estates of his Sermon von dem Sakrament der Taufe (1519), noted above.[200] There Luther presents a roughly traditional theory of estates, in which the clergy as the spiritual estate, occupy the most prominent place. As we have seen, Luther in his theory of estates modified this traditional view by making all the worldly estates and callings equal in contrast to the primary and unique "Christian estate" of heaven. Similarly we have seen that Luther eventually rejected any human "spiritual government" in the strict sense, for only God can exercise such rule.[201]

Against this new background, Luther first states a new theory of the hierarchies (though he does not yet use the term) in the Vom Abendmahl Christi Bekenntnis (1528). In the "confession" which comprises the third part of the work, Luther condemns various errors, among which he includes the foundation of religious orders as ways to salvation, for there is no such way but the justice of Christ. In contrast to these false, human orders, Luther lists the three true orders. "The holy orders and right foundations of God are these three: the priestly office (*ampt*), the married estate, and the world magistracy." [202] In his further description Luther emphasizes the holiness of all three orders, for all are founded in God's word.[203] Above all three orders is the "common order of Christian love" which applies to all men at all times.

[200] See p. 154, above.
[201] See pp. 161 f., above.
[202] Vom Abendmahl Christi Bekenntnis, XXVI,504,30.
[203] Ibid., XXVI,504,31 f.

Luther makes it perfectly plain that none of these orders leads to blessedness, which we attain only by faith. Blessedness and holiness are two very different things; the first comes through Christ alone, but the second comes through faith in Christ and through this holy orders.

Luther restates esssentially the same doctrine in Der grosse Katechismus (1529) in a terminology of the three "fathers." As in his earlier writings, he starts from the fourth commandment,[204] and he finds as before that this includes honor not only to parents but also to the worldly magistracy and to our spiritual fathers. But in contrast to his early writings and in agreement with Vom Abendmahl Christi Bekenntnis, Luther now asserts the equivalence of the three "fathers" as holy ordinances.[205] Luther in Der grosse Katechismus can also speak of the three "governments" (*Hausregiment; weltliches Regiment; geistliches Regiment*); here he is of course using world-government and spiritual government in their limited meaning and not to refer to the general contrast between the two governments of God.[206]

In 1539 Luther works out a systematic doctrine of three hierarchies in the Zirkulardisputation über Matthew XIX,21. The theses for the disputation appeared under the title: Septuaginta Propositiones disputandae de tribus hierarchijs, Ecclesiastica, Politica, Oeconomica, et quod Papa sub nulla istarum sit, sed omnium publicus hostis.[207] Thesis § 52 declares: "God ordained three hierarchies against the devil, that is the houeshold, the polity, and the church (*oeconomiam, politiam, et Ecclesiam*)." [208] As Luther's doctrine of the three hierarchies often involves a limited sense of spiritual and worldly government, so it here involves a limited sense of polity and of church. Thus "polity" here refers simply to the secular magistracy, and it does not bear the general sense of polity as synonymous for the realm of the world and of reason. Similarly the "church" here refers simply

---

[204] See pp.160 f., above.

[205] Der grosse Katechismus, XXX,1, pp. 147,22 f. and 152,27.

[206] Ibid., XXX,1 pp.152,37; 156,25.

[207] Disputations (1537), XXXIX,2, p.35. Luther's terminology is less fixed in the translation; the Latin *Hierarchia* can appear as *Ertzgewalt* or *Regiment*, p.48,21.

[208] Ibid., XXXIX,2, p. 42,3.

to the clergy and its office (Luther sometimes substitutes "priest-hood" for "church" in the triple classification),[209] and it is not a synonym for the communion of saints.

Luther restates his doctrine of the three hierarchies in Von den Konziliis und Kirchen (1539), in the Enarratio capitis noni Esaiae (1546), and frequently in the Genesis Commentary (1535-45);[210] it does not appear that these other statements add to the ideas we have already noted.

When we attempt to draw the implications of Luther's doctrine of the three hierarchies, we face many of the same difficulties as in the case of church and polity. Luther shows no desire for systematization as such; he does not discuss at all what seem to be some of the logical possibilities involved in his statement; and certain questions which almost force themselves on us evidently do not occur to him.

The immediate purpose of the doctrine of the hierarchies is clear. In the light of his distinction between two realms of Christian existence, Luther is revising traditional ideas of society, and he concludes that none of the three hierarchies is a "spiritual rule" in the old sense but that all of them, even "secular rule," are holy. Within the Christian society, then, Luther is classifying all three hierarchies as "worldly." As we have seen earlier, the preacher as such is a world-person, not a Christian person.[211] It is of course true that from another standpoint the preacher is incomparably more important than the house-father or the prince, but this is only because of what God does through the preacher; it does not affect the position or rule of the preacher himself.

One cannot, to my knowledge, find in Luther the extension of the three hierarchies to a non-Christian society, and we must therefore be cautious in relating the hierarchies to the non-Christian categories of reason and polity. The crux is of course the hierarchy of the church or the priesthood. Luther recognizes a pagan polity and a pagan economy; in each case they are ordi-

[209] E.g. Genesis Commentary (1535–45), XLIII,524,22: "Hae igitur sunt tres hierarchiae, quas saepe inculcamus, videlicet oeconomia, Politia, et Sacerdotium, sive Domus, Civitas, et Ecclesia."

[210] See Von den Konziliis und Kirchen L,652,18 f.; Enarratio capitis noni Esaiae XL,3 pp. 646,35 ff.; and for the references in the Genesis Commentary, see R. Seeberg, op. cit. (note 25, above), IV,1, p.329, note 2.

[211] See p. 156 above, with note 135.

nances of God against the devil, who constantly tries to pervert them. In contrast, for the hierarchy of the church, God establishes only the Christian form, though Luther admits that the devil imitates Him by building a chapel wherever God builds a church.[212] Luther does not know of any non-Christian church or priesthood as an ordinance of God against the devil.

This aspect of Luther's theory of the three hierarchies is significant for his whole theology of society. From one standpoint his main achievement was the development of a new theology of the "world" and of "reason" by which to analyze society here on earth in contrast to the "heaven" of passive and Christian justice, and we have seen this world in the doctrines of civil justice, the civil use of the law, polity, the estates and callings, and of God's world-government. But in every case, Luther develops a theology of the world only for Christians in a Christian society; he affirms a Christian secularization and not a secularization without qualification. Indeed, from Luther's standpoint, we never find any true secularization apart from Christianity, for only Christianity teaches us not to "mix" the two realms, which the natural man cannot even distinguish. Apart from Christianity, what ought to be the world or reason or polity will always falsely claim to be more than the world, to be in some way a means of salvation, or a stage on the way to heaven, or a "church."

Hence we must recognize how wide a gap separates Luther from later forms of secularism and that from the standpoint of these later forms we can raise questions which for Luther are irrelevant. In the light of a modern secular history, for example, one might ask whether other civilizations do not have their "signs" as well as Christianity, or whether contrariwise Christianity itself is not one of the "masks" of God. Similarly one might ask whether the three hierarchies are not found in all societies and whether in consequence the Christian church is not simply one special form of a universal institution. But for Luther the tremendous reality of Christianity as the one true way of salvation makes it impossible for such questions ever to appear. It may be that there are historical connections between Luther and the modern forms of secularism which are non-Christian or even

[212] TR, §5010, VI,612,11.

anti-Christian; it may be that we have kept Luther's world where God is hidden and lost his heaven where God is revealed. It is nevertheless certain that Luther's own secularism is one which can exist only in Christianity and because of Christianity, that the three hierarchies in the Christian society are "worldly" only because the members of that society are already justified in Christ in heaven.

APPENDIX

The Writings of Johannes Heckel on Luther's Social Thought

Among recent writings on the social thought of Luther, those of Johannes Heckel are the most ambitious and the ones which most challenge received opinions. It is not possible here to give them their due critical evaluation, but his main contributions may be listed, together with some of the critical discussions of Heckel's position and a few brief comments from the standpoint of the present essay.

Heckel's most important work is the "Lex charitatis . . . " (note 2, Chapter I, above), which deals with virtually all of Luther's ideas on society from the standpoint of law. For summary statements of his position, see his "Naturrecht und christliche Verantwortung im öffentlichen Leben nach der Lehre Martin Luthers," in: Zur politischen Predigt, hgg. vom evang.-luth. Dekanat München (München, 1952), 35–56, and his review in Zeitschrift für Rechtsgeschichte, kan. Abt. 71 (1954), 313–20. Two long articles deal with the genesis of Luther's thought: "Recht und Gesetz. . ." (note 10, Chapter I, above), and "Initia iuris ecclesiastici. . ." (note 2, Chapter IV, above). See also "Widerstand gegen die Obrigkeit. Pflicht und Recht zum Widerstand bei Martin Luther," Zeitwende 25 (1954), 156–8; "Luthers Lehre von den zwei Regimenten. Fragen und Antworten zu der Schrift von Gunnar Hillerdal," Zeitschrift für evangelisches Kirchenrecht, 4 (1955), 253–65.

For some representative discussion of Heckel's position, notably in the "Lex charitatis. . . ," see the review by E. Schott, Theologische Literaturzeitung, 79 (1954), 692–94; E. Wolf, "Der christliche Glaube und das Recht. Zu J. Heckel, Lex charitatis," Zeitschrift für evangelisches Kirchenrecht, 4 (1955), 225–53; Franz Lau, "Leges charitatis. Drei Fragen an Johannes Heckel," Kerygma und Dogma, 2 (1956), 76–89; P. Althaus, "Die beiden Regimente bei Luther. Bemerkungen zu Johannes Heckel 'Lex charitatis'," Theologische Literaturzeitung, 81 (1956), 129–36.

In commenting on Heckel's studies, one must first of all pay tribute to their great learning; all of his works reveal the widest reading in Luther and in the secondary sources, and they are frequently illuminating in points of detail. Nevertheless I do not believe that Heckel has grasped the essential structure of Luther's social thought nor the direction of his development. This criticism could only be justified through a detailed analysis of Heckel's arguments and evidence, and here one cannot do more than to notice the main points at issue. In the first place, Heckel's analysis of Luther, notably in the "Lex charitatis. . . ," is not stated in the language or terminology of Luther, and Heckel himself recognizes this (ibid., p.57, note 373, or p. 71, note 499). Doubtless any study of Luther must to some extent "systematize" Luther's terminology, but in Heckel's case this is carried so far that one finally ends up with a system for which there is no justification in Luther and which nevertheless controls the meaning of Luther's statements. Thus, for example, in the "Lex charitatis. . ." Heckel sets up such categories of law as: 1. das göttliche Naturgesetz; 2. das positive göttliche Recht; 3. das materielle weltliche Naturrecht; 4. das institutionelle menschliche Naturrecht (e.g., ibid., pp. 4–5). In the second place, and more important, Heckel's systematization does not do justice to the position of the mature Luther. Notably it blurs the distinction between the two realms of Christian existence or, more generally, between the Law and the Gospel. Hence Heckel imposes on the texts of Luther's mature period an alien "mixture"; where Luther's intent is to separate Christ and the Law as far as possible, Heckel's intent is rather to bring them together. And when the texts of Luther assert his basic dualism, Heckel endeavors to explain them away (e.g., his denial that anyone is a citizen in two realms, ibid., pp. 134 f., or his contention that the two governments of God apply only to two different groups of men, the Christians and the godless, pp. 31 ff.). It may be noted, however, that Heckel's account, if false for the Luther of the 1530's, is much more adequate for the Luther of 1513–18 (see, e.g., his contention that the central point in Luther's doctrine of law is the *lex spiritualis*, ibid., p.21).

INDEX OF CITATIONS

All references to Luther's writings are listed in the order of the Weimar edition (Schriften, Briefwechsel, Tischreden, Deutsche Bibel). The few passages not found in the Weimar edition are listed at the end in the order: Erlangen edition, Theologische Studien und Kritiken, and Unbekannte Fragmente aus Luthers zweiter Psalmenvorlesung. References which include some discussion of a particular passage, as against mere citation, are printed in heavy type. For a concordance with other editions and for further bibliographical information, see Kurt Aland, Hilfsbuch zum Lutherstudium (Gütersloh, 1957?); the number of each work in Aland's alphabetical listing has been added in parentheses following the title.

Ein Sermon von dem hochwürdigen Sakrament des heiligen wahren Leichnams Christi und von den Brüderschaften. 1519. (Aland #655) II,742–58.

Dictata super Psalterium. 1513–16. (Aland #593) III,11–652; IV,1–462. See also XXXI, 464–80 and Theologische Studien und Kritiken 90 (1917) 521–26.

Annotationes Quincuplici Fabri Stapulensis Psalterio manu ascriptae. 1513 f. (Aland #627)
IV,466–526.

Praelectio in librum Judicum. 1516 f. (Aland #353) IV,529–86.

VI,292,9	131 n.52	VI,296,30	132 n.58
VI,292,15	131 n.52	VI,296,39 f.	**132 n.59**
VI,292,37	132 n.53	VI,300,26	133 n.61
VI,293,4	132 n.54	VI,301,3	133 n.60
VI,293,37	132 n.55	VI,318,27	134 n.64
VI,295,25	132 n.56	VI,321,31 f.	134 n.66
VI,296,17	**132 n.57**		

Ein Sermon von dem Neuen Testament, das ist von der heiligen Messe. 1520. (Aland #502) VI,353–78.

| VI,370,25 | **155 n.131** | |

An den christlichen Adel deutscher Nation von des christlichen Standes Besserung. 1520. (Aland #7) VI,404–69.

General	136–40; 155–56	VI,408,18	**156 n.135**
VI,404,13	137 n.75	VI,408,26	**138 n.78**
VI,407,13	155 n.133	VI,409,17	**139 n.79**
VI,408,3	156 n.134	VI,410,3	**139 n.80**

De captivitate Babylonica ecclesiae praeludium. 1520. (Aland #120) VI,497–573.

| VI,564,11 | 161 n.151 | |

Von der Freiheit eines Christenmenschen. 1520. (Aland #227) VII,20–38.

| VII,25,34 | 82 n.29 | |

Epistola Lutheriana ad Leonem X. summum pontificem. Tractatus de libertate christiana. 1520. (Aland #413) VII,42–73.

| VII,54,18 | 87 n.43 | |

Ein nützlicher Sermon D. M. Luthers gepredigt an der heiligen Dreikönige Tag von dem Reiche Christi und Herodes. 1521. (Aland #634) VII,238–45. See IX,501–03, below.

| VII,240,31 | **161 n.152** | VII,242,13 | 162 n.153 |

Enarrationes epistolarum et evangeliorum quas postillas vocant. 1521. (Aland #572, Nr. 9) VII,463–537.

| VII,508,31 f. | 99 n.87 | |

Das Magnificat verdeutschet und ausgelegt. 1521. (Aland #444) VII,544–604.

| General | 49 | VII,578,22 | 161 n.151 |
| VII,550,23 | **48 n.16** | | |

Auf das überchristlich, übergeistlich und überkünstlich Buch Bock Emsers zu Leipzig Antwort. 1521. (Aland #190) VII,621–88.

| VII,636,8 f. | 132 n.55 | VII,683,9 | 135 n.69 |

Ad librum eximii magistri nostri Mag. Ambrosii Catharini, defensoris Silv. Prieratis acerrimi, responsio M. Lutheri. 1521. (Aland #122) VII,705–78.

| General | 117; 134–37. | VII,709,31 | 135 n.68 |
| VII,709,20 | 135 n.67 | VII,710,1 | 135 n.69 |

Enarratio capitis noni Esaiae, collecta per M. Joh. Frederum. 1546. (Aland #206) XL,3 597–682.

XL,3 607,22	145 n.98	XL,3 646,29	146 n.102
XL,3 608,11	145 n.98	XL,3 646,35 f.	176 n.210
XL,3 612,31 f.	145 n.99		

Genesis-Vorlesung. 1544–54. (Aland #517) XLII,1–673; XLIII,1–695; XLIV,1–825.

General	xiii n.8	XLIII,537,12	43 n.3
XLIII,524,22	176 n.209	XLIV,485,25 f.	43 n.4

Sermon. 4 November, 1537. (Aland #577, Pr. 1672) XLV,250–55.

XLV,252,27	167 n.177

Sermon. 21 November, 1537. (Aland #577, Pr. 1675) XLV,265–97.

XLV,280,2	167 n.177

Die schmalkaldischen Artikel. 1538. (Aland #672) L,192–254.

L,213,1 f.	134 n.63

Von den Konziliis und Kirchen. 1539. (Aland #382) L,509–653.

General	148–50.	L,642,32	**150 n.115**
L,552,21	**149 n.109**	L,643,6	150 n.115
L,559,33	149 n.111	L,649,7	**150 n.116**
L,579,28 f.	**149 n.110**	L,649,34	50 n.117
L,580,13	149 n.111	L,649,34 f.	149 n.111
L,624,15	150 n.113	L,651,12	150 n.117
L,624,26 f.	150 n.114	L,652,18 f.	176 n.210

Der 101 Psalm durch D. M. Luther ausgelegt. 1534–35. (Aland #614) LI,200–64.

LI,211,36	109 n.129	LI,214,14	109 n.130
LI,212,14 f.	109 n.128	LI,214,35 f.	109 n.127

Wider Hans Worst. 1541. (Aland #777) LI,469–572.

General	148	LI,479,4 f.	150 n.115

Hauspostille D. M. Luthers. 1544. (Aland #272) LII,1–839.

LII,26,21	172 n.195

Vorrede Luthers zum ersten Bande der Gesamtausgabe seiner lateinischen Schriften. 1545. (Aland #753) LIV,179–87.

General	xii n.3; 42–44.	LIV,186,6	43 n.4
LIV,183,25	**43 n.3**	LIV,186,16	**61 n.50**
LIV,185,17 f.	81 n.25	LIV,186,25	xi n.1

Vorlesung über den Römerbrief. 1515–16. (Aland #646) LVI,3–528 and LVII,1 5–127; 131–232.

General	20–40 passim; 41 n.1; 116.	LVI,23,8	34 n.145
		LVI,36,11	24 n.109
LVI,3,13 f.	32 n.138	LVI,72,10	35 n.147; 106 n.110.

Erlanger Edition (1st. ed. Erlangen, 1826–57). Disputatio Phil. Melanchthonis cum D. M. Luthero. 1536–37. (Aland #492a) Erlanger LVIII,347–54.

Theologische Studien und Kritiken 90(1917)521–6 = Dictata super Psalterium. 1513–16. (Aland #593.) See Weimar edition III,11 ff. above.

Unbekannte Fragmente aus Luthers zweiter Psalmenvorlesung. 1518. (Arbeiten zur Kirchengeschichte, Heft 27. Berlin, 1940.) See Aland #594.